VICTIMS

VICTIMS

Textual Strategies
in Recent American Fiction

PAUL BRUSS

Lewisburg: Bucknell University Press
London and Toronto: Associated University Presses

Associated University Presses, Inc.
4 Cornwall Drive
East Brunswick, N.J. 08816

Associated University Presses Ltd
69 Fleet Street
London EC4Y 1EU, England

Associated University Presses
Toronto M5E 1A7, Canada

Library of Congress Cataloging in Publication Data

Bruss, Paul, 1943–
    Victims, textual strategies in recent American
fiction.

    Bibliography.
    Includes index.
    1. American fiction—20th century—History and
criticism. 2. Fiction—Technique. 3. Nabokov,
Vladimir Vladimirovich, 1899–1977—Criticism and
interpretation. 4. Barthelme, Donald—Criticism
and interpretation. 5. Kosinski, Jerzy N.,
1933–   —Criticism and interpretation.
I. Title.
PS379.B76   813'.5'091   80-67319
ISBN 0-8387-5006-0

Printed in the United States of America

Contents

for Kath

Preface

This book is about texts. More specifically, it explores the strategies whereby three very different writers create fiction against the grain of their profound sensitivity to the insufficiency of all human texts. American fiction in the past has generally reflected a strong realist tradition in which the text was presumed to contain the essence of human experience, but in recent years there has emerged a host of young writers who, having recognized the virtual impossibility of achieving any final textual authority, have committed themselves to a fiction that offers little definitive theme or character analysis and that, consequently, depends for its energy upon the sophistication with which the authors themselves explore the deeper processes of perception and language. Such authors, represented in this book by Nabokov (he actually belongs to the previous generation), Barthelme, and Kosinski, may on occasion continue to employ certain realist techniques (such as climactic narrative structure), but finally they all ally themselves with the idealist tradition of Proust, Kafka, Joyce, Borges, and Beckett—the tradition in which structure opens itself up to the possibility of dissolution and thus to the need for a new configuration that frustrates at once both the desire for content and the desire for form. What underlies my choice of the particular examples in this book is that in the face of the recent crisis in fictional theory Nabokov tends to emphasize the dilemmas of the author, Barthelme the problems of the text itself, and Kosinski the dilemmas of the reader-perceiver. The fiction of these three authors is very different, but because each of them employs what I shall later call a strategy of murder in order to surmount the insufficiency that attends all their text-making, they represent—together—certain crucial tendencies in recent American fiction that might, in fact, become the measure of fiction in the future.

Acknowledgments

This book had its origins in the Art Department at Brown University, where I held a National Endowment for the Humanities Fellowship in Residence (1975–76) for research into the relationships between recent developments in fiction and those in painting and sculpture. During that year at Brown several of my colleagues (William Jordy, Steve Shipps, Nancy Jay, Kim Smith, Tom Schlotterback, and Silvio Gaggi) substantially influenced my thinking about the research project, and together they contributed heavily to what eventually became the first draft of this study. In addition, Eastern Michigan University granted me a sabbatical leave during 1978–79 so that I could complete the project. During that time Donald Lawniczak, Milton Foster, Ivan Schreiber, and Mary Lee MacDonald served as sounding boards (and on occasion as readers) for the book that finally emerged. Let me record my thanks to these friends and colleagues (and to the NEH and EMU) for their assistance and support.

I also wish to thank the following publishers for having given me permission to quote from published works:

From *The Dead Father* by Donald Barthelme. Copyright © 1975 by Donald Barthelme. Reprinted by permission of Farrar, Straus and Giroux, Inc., and Routledge & Kegan Paul Ltd.

From *Snow White* by Donald Barthelme. Copyright © 1967 by Donald Barthelme. Reprinted by permission of Atheneum Publishers and Jonathan Cape Ltd.

From *Steps* by Jerzy Kosinski. Copyright © 1968 by Jerzy Kosinski. Reprinted by permission of Random House.

From *Pale Fire* by Vladimir Nabokov. Copyright © 1962 by Vladimir Nabokov. Reprinted by permission of G. P. Putnam's Sons.

VICTIMS

1

Introduction: The Artist as Victim

The supreme influence upon the art of the twentieth century is essentially epistemological. That this is the case is not surprising if one considers the technological innovations of the last century, for the more man has faced the necessity of coming to terms with the social conditions underlying the development of the vast urban and industrial centers of Western civilization, the more he has had to acknowledge the increasing complexity within the pattern of sense perceptions even in his everyday life. It is as if, the viability of isolated rural living having gradually faded away, Western man in the last century has suffered the loss of that luxurious illusion of personal control over his own affairs and has, instead, become the victim of the very complexity that has defined his recent achievements over matter. Because he is no longer confident about the character of what he perceives, the man of the technological age—and especially the artist—has had to make significant modifications in his conceptions of the three major areas of artistic activity: the nature of the artist himself, the nature of his medium, and the nature of his audience. These modifications are obviously crucial to any thorough discussion of trends in contemporary fiction, and thus in this introductory chapter I want to examine the three developments that have, since 1860, transformed the nature of Western art: (1) the artist's assumption of impersonality, (2) the artist's desertion of content, and (3) the artist's shifting of responsibility for his work to his audience.

One of the best means of establishing a large perspective of what has happened to the contemporary novelist is to examine, if only briefly, what has occurred in the fields of painting and music during the past century. Painters before 1800, wedded to the principles of perspective, had little difficulty positing the reality or the significance of the subject matter within their work. What was on the canvas was generally regarded as a true representation of what the painters had perceived, and usually that representation supported a fairly public notion of an idea or human activity that men agreed deserved artistic treatment. In the latter half of the nineteenth century, however, and largely as a result of an explosion of photographic activity in the middle of that century,[1] such positing became very problematic and eventually led to a radical reconsideration of what constituted the art of painting. In the 1860s, for example, Manet led the Impressionists in a movement that rejected the traditional emphasis upon subject matter and that, in doing so, forced the world of art to adopt new standards of objectivity and even of impersonality in painting. Having recognized that they could not compete with the precision and the detail available to the photographer who attended to the recording of significant subject matter, the Impressionists turned their art into a consideration of the process of perception itself. Whether it was the shifting quality of light, or the relationship between the various grounds in any given field, or the peculiarity of form in a particular moment in time, these artists made sure that it was the process of perception, rather than a subject matter, that now counted heavily in their work. The result of this new emphasis was nothing less than a new conception of the artist himself, for at the very time that he might have seemed—with his rapid and spontaneous handling of pigment—to be concentrating upon the subjective character of his own perceptions, he was actually viewing himself as the objective and thus impersonal receiver (or vehicle) of those perceptions. It was as if he were himself a camera—a camera with a very special, highly personalized lens, but still a camera that could claim to be even more objective and impersonal than the camera of the photographer. While the photographer focused his camera on subject matter replete with public significance, the Impressionist increasingly divorced himself from the excesses of representation and attended only to the process of perception itself.

The immediate result of this new impersonality and objectivity in painting was the explosion of the traditional categories of subject matter. Interested primarily in the process of perception, the artist could now paint virtually any object that claimed, for whatever reason, his attention. The artist of Manet's still somewhat traditional bent might have wished that the great subjects were yet available to him (consider, here, Manet's desperation over, perhaps, the last of the great history paintings, *L'Execution de l'Empereur Maximilien*), but, having discovered that the complex and baffling character of the perception process itself now frustrated any lingering desire to develop the conventional canvas of the public artist, he, too, feverishly devoted himself to the objective examination of whatever was at hand. By the turn of the century, therefore, when, say, Cezanne had completed his *Mont St. Victoire* series, Manet's commitment to the new character of the artist as the objective vehicle of perception had gained considerable currency. For once it was clear that the Postimpressionists had continued the Impressionists' retreat from grand subject matter in favor of exploring the subtleties inherent in the perception even of everyday objects, the development of new methods for realizing the nature of perception as a process had accelerated manyfold. It was not until 1910, however, with the institution of what is now termed analytic cubism, that the new direction in painting probably received its greatest impetus. In a certain sense Picasso's new technique merely extended the late nineteenth-century artist's concern with light and with shape, but what is interesting about his new technique is the fact that, while never entirely escaping the uncomfortable tension between subject and object (between the perceiver and the perceived) that had surfaced in the Postimpressionists' work, Picasso emphasized in a series of dramatic moves the primacy of the perceiver over the perceived. Regardless of which of the portraits from 1910 is examined,[2] it is clear that for him the matter of technique had surpassed all other considerations in the making of art. Objects (faces) might still be visible in the unforgettable canvases of that year, sometimes strikingly so, yet there is no question that it was the exploration of technique itself that served as the primary impulse for the work as a whole. With analytic cubism (as well as with the work of Kandinsky) painting began its final divorce from a public subject matter. Thereafter it focused almost entirely upon itself and became an art that explored its own character.

While Picasso was extending the Impressionists' desertion of content, Duchamp was experimenting with the possibility of transforming the nature of the medium altogether. In certain respects Picasso, with his laconic productions in ceramic and tin, might have prepared the way for Duchamp, but finally it was Duchamp's introduction of a long series of Readymades (such as *Bicycle Wheel, Bottlerack, Fountain*) that signaled what Picasso's emphatic concern with subject as object had already entailed. Duchamp's gestures or "moves" (he was a master chess player) generally reflected the assumption that it was not the painting itself but the transaction in the artist's mind that was crucial to the artwork. In fact, because he had also come to believe that no representation could realize the particular qualities of the original transaction in the artist's mind, Duchamp even began to question whether it was at all necessary for the artist to demonstrate his ability by rendering with his own hands and in his own special techniques. For him, therefore, the act of perception that generated a new configuration of sensibility but that required little or no skill in traditional techniques emerged as the logical culmination of the artist's adoption of the stance of impersonality and his retreat from a subject matter laced with significance. As with Picasso's cubist paintings, Duchamp's objects were still visible (in a gesture that foreshadowed more recent artists' attention to the "art" of their careers, he even created a portable museum for miniatures of his work), but from Duchamp's perspective their visibility was to serve only as a goad for the viewer to attempt a recovery of that act of perception (the artistic transaction) which had originally been the artist's. In his view there was nothing intrinsically grand in the artifact. The artifact merely represented the occasion for the viewer to become actively involved in the artistic process that had first engrossed the artist himself. With Duchamp the viewer's importance to the artwork obviously increased.

By 1920, then, Picasso and Duchamp had virtually cut off any remaining possibility that the artist could yet serve as a public commentator by focusing upon a significant subject matter. It is true that both of them would eventually—e.g., in *Guernica* and *Etant Donnés*—return to subject matter and even to illusionism, but generally their work terminated the long tradition in which the artist had served as the public perceiver and interpreter (as, say, in the work of Jacques-Louis David). Thus, while there would still occur, in the fifties and sixties, several more flings of subjectivity as in movements such as Abstract Expressionism and Pop Art, it was clear that art must finally arrive at that minimalization which, already apparent in Duchamp's work, would require as much from the viewer as from the artist himself. Even in Abstract Expressionism, with the artists' avoidance of a concrete subject matter, the subjectivity that seemed to dominate their work was limited to the painter's expressive handling of pigment. Or in Pop Art, with the artists' playing down of any overt message-sending that might open their work to topical analysis, the apparent subjectivity was limited to the use of common sign systems (e.g., advertisements, comic strips, everyday objects, etc.). It was with Minimal Art, however, that the full culmination of all the art activity in the past hundred years finally occurred. Already in the fifties, with the work of Robert Rauschenberg, it was clear that the new relationship that existed in Duchamp's work between the artist and his audience had achieved a new level. Rauschenberg's *White Paintings*, which depended for their surface texture upon the play of shadows that the viewer himself could manipulate (by shifting his vantage point), or his *Erased deKooning*, which forced the viewer to address the question of what constituted the artifact, challenged audiences to establish a new view of their relationship to art. What this relationship is was even more apparent in the work of the minimal sculptor Robert Morris.

When Robert Morris first installed his primary structures in the early sixties, the viewer immediately found himself in a predicament because the structures, made of plywood and painted in a flat off-white or black, presented themselves merely as prosaic geometrical shapes. Their "meaning" was disturbingly absent. Eventually, with the related work of other minimalists such as Carl Andre, Dan Flavin, and Donald Judd in mind, the viewer might become conscious of these shapes as interruptions in his field of perception—interruptions that served to condition the space in which they were installed and into which the viewer himself had now intruded—but such consciousness presented a dilemma because it tended to turn the viewer into an artist in his own right. Instead of relying upon Morris for meaningful signs of intention, the viewer had—as with Rauschenberg's *White Paintings*—to reconstitute the work somewhat in his own image by attending to the subtleties of the perceptual field in which both he and the structure were situated. In a profound sense, consequently, the art experience in this situation became a function of the viewer's own perceptual capabilities. Morris himself described the phenomenon in terms of the viewer's ability to formulate a gestalt.[3] In fact, by the time Morris turned to his felt pieces, which allowed the audience to redistribute an artwork as it saw fit, he had made sure that the viewer who responded to the work had also entered into a compact with the artist for reconstituting the artwork.

From the rise of Impressionism to the recent art of the minimalists, then, the artist's determined pursuit of impersonality and objectivity has resulted in what may originally have seemed a shocking disregard for traditional content and meaning but what was essentially only a new responsibility for the viewer—who must himself now fill up much of the vacuum created by the absence of content. The experience of the painter and the sculptor in the last century also has its parallels in the fields of music and literature. Consider, for example, the response of late-nineteenth-century musicians to the heavy burden of romanticism that had lingered on in that cult of suffering which had found a sanctuary in the philosophy of Wagner. While the important advances in music probably surfaced about a generation later, pressure was already building throughout the 1880s for a new freedom that could match up with the Impressionists' rejection of the Academy. With the contributions of such musicians as Debussy, Mahler, and Bruckner, all three of whom increasingly separated themselves from strict adherence to the well-defined forms and the heroic contents of the academicians, it became clear that the musician, too, was seeking a new contact with the problematic nature even of his everyday perceptions. It was only in 1910, however, with the appearance of Schoenberg, Stravinsky, Berg,

Webern, and Ives, that the field of music finally revealed such a ferment of varied activity that there could be no doubt that it had caught up with the remarkable developments in painting. By then the old taboos concerning form and organization, taboos that had steadily impoverished the tonality and the rhythm of Western music since the high crest of polyphony in the sixteenth century, had shown their essentially arbitrary character. Just as perspectivism had impoverished painting, so the emphasis upon sonata form had severely limited both the range of technique and the character of content in music. Once a whole generation of composers, therefore, having adopted the more objective stance of a musician such as Debussy (who knew there was nothing inherently sacred about the sonata form), initiated an extensive theoretical reconsideration of their medium, the whole tradition of the previous four centuries came crashing down in astonishing disarray.

Consider, here, the new attitudes toward sound that were emerging about the time of analytic cubism. While Mussorgsky and Reger may have already taken the initial steps toward a "musical prose" late in the previous century, it was Schoenberg who, in 1906, took the crucial step toward the new objectivity in sound—a step away from content—and blurred the difference between consonance and dissonance. In fact, because he allowed chords that previously had been used only as transitional harmonies to stand alone and even to complete phrases and sections, he almost by himself established the now widely accepted but then very radical principle that all combinations of notes were equal. In a certain sense, to draw a parallel with Picasso's suspension of foreground and background, it was as if Schoenberg were eliminating the distinction between the various grounds of his medium. Some musicians at the time, such as the Italian futurist Russolo, who was heavily influenced by the experimental poetry of Marinetti, went even further in the reaction against the traditional restrictions of tonality. By 1913 he was not only calling for a methodical investigation of noises but was also inventing noise machines for realizing striking new possibilities of sound. Audiences, if the occasional riots are any indication, were not very receptive to such advances. George Antheil's *Ballet mécanique* (1924), possibly the most "infamous" of the noise pieces, for example, brought about a violent audience reaction in April 1927 during its first Carnegie Hall performance. The intensity of this controversy over noise remained so strong that even in his famous 1937 lecture "The Future of Music: Credo," John Cage found himself arguing as if the introduction of noise had just begun: "Whereas, in the past, the point of disagreement has been between dissonance and consonance, it will be, in the immediate future, between noise and so-called musical sounds."[4]

Schoenberg's position in 1910 might never have approached the extreme stance of Russolo and Antheil, but his commitment to pantonality (the inclusion of all tonalities) and then his determination to discipline the suddenly wide-open field created the circumstances in which the reconsideration of music moved forward.

If Picasso and Duchamp inaugurated a new freedom in painting and art, Schoenberg did the same for music—and like the two painters, he was the first to realize the dangers of the new freedom. Already in 1912, with the infusion of traditional musical forms (which led to a kind of neoclassicism) into the atonal language of such works as *Pierrot Lunaire*, Schoenberg revealed his anxiety concerning the new freedom. The use of traditional forms, however, was a compromise that failed to please him. What he wanted was a means of building up musical structures from one unifying idea, and in 1921, while working with the piano, he was finally able to apply consistently a twelve-tone technique that satisfied his needs. By using the twelve tones of the chromatic scale in a determinate and unchanging order, yet with the flexibility of the mirror forms (the retrograde, inversion, and retrograde inversion) and transposition still available, he managed to develop forty-eight permutations of the original series at his disposal. In effect, to be sure, as is now clear, Schoenberg's reliance upon these new conditions proved to be stricter than the adherence to the old rules of tonality. Such a method of constructing music might have helped him rescue music from the tempting dangers of the freedom it had so recently gained, but at the same time—and ironically much in the fashion of the traditionalists who continued to rely upon the tempered scale—the use of this method meant that Schoenberg, even at his most experimental moment, still resolved the octave into twelve parts. He himself justified such resolution on the grounds that some structure was necessary, but to many composers this resolution was equally as arbitrary as the tempered scale—and again reflected Schoenberg's neoclassical bent. The new impersonality and objectivity in Schoenberg's music obviously had its limits.

Just as Picasso's and Duchamp's work forced all artists to become more conscious of the nature and the limits of their medium, however, so Schoenberg's work encouraged other composers not only to reconsider for themselves the traditional forms and techniques of music but also to explore further the problems of composing within the newly opened field of their medium. Schoenberg was at the leading edge of the experimentation, and thus his example served for a long time as the measure of what was possible in the new music. Eventually, however, many composers separated themselves from his conservatism. Already at the time that Schoenberg was working out his twelve-tone technique, in fact,

Alois Hába introduced a composition for string quartet in the quarter-tone system and two years later, in 1923, founded a class in quarter-tone composition at the Prague Conservatoire. His system, which developed twenty-four divisions in the octave and thus required abandonment or total revision of traditional instrumentation and notation, initially served little more than a theoretical purpose. Today, however, with a great many composers (such as Macero, Hamilton, Lybbert, and Johnston) exploring its possibilities, his theory has become wide practice. As an approach to the open field, furthermore, microtonal music (the term includes all the fractional possibilities, not merely quarter-tones) fully exposes the timidity that characterized Schoenberg's determined pursuit of form in 1921. Ben Johnston's assessment in "How to Cook an Albatross" is very much to the point: "In our laziness, when we changed over to the twelve-tone system, we just took the pitches of the previous music as though we were moving into a furnished apartment and had no time to even take the pictures off the wall."[5] In Johnston's view Schoenberg's solution in the early twenties was hardly radical enough. Like the minimalists and the conceptualists of the sixties and seventies, who found themselves impatient with Picasso and Duchamp, recent composers insist upon the emptiness of the apartment. For only in the emptiness is there the opportunity to escape the content of the past and to explore the musical processes of the present.

Like art, then, music is today much less about something than it is a process that expands and sensitizes the listener's awareness of the field of his hearing. Johnston, in a note to an April 1974 concert at the University of Wisconsin–Milwaukee by the Fine Arts Quartet, makes this fact especially clear:

> Over the whole of the historical period of instrumental music, Western music has based itself upon an acoustical lie. In our time this lie—that the normal musical ear hears twelve equal intervals within the span of an octave—has led to the impoverishment of pitch usage in our music. In our frustration at the complex means it takes to wrest yet a few more permutations from a closed system, we have attempted the abandonment of all systems, forgetting that we need never have closed our system.[6]

The field, once about to open but then closed by Schoenberg, is now again open, and with this renewed openness the relationship between the composer and his audience, as opposed to that between the composer and his text, has become steadily more important.

Consider, for example, what happened in the summer of 1952, when John Cage, David Tudor, Robert Rauschenberg, and Merce Cunningham joined up in the first multimedia "happenings" at Black Mountain College. While the principals had chosen the lectures, the records and the projections, the dances and the paintings, all of which were to be used in the presentations, the actual sequence of the performance was not fixed. The sequence, in fact, was to emerge as part of the interaction between the performers and the audience—on the grounds, at least from Cage's viewpoint, that it had become necessary to accept equally all sensory experiences occurring in and around a performance situation, regardless of their origin. Essentially what Cage wanted was to enlarge, not antagonize, the audience's field of communication and participation. A better example of this intention, perhaps, is Robert Ashley, who in his *Public Opinion Descends upon the Demonstrators* (1961) created a situation in which a member of the audience, by acting or reacting in a specific manner such as speaking, gesturing, looking about, or leaving, evoked prerecorded sounds produced by a single performer on electronic playback equipment. There the audience begins to become equally responsible for the work. Another example is Barton McLean, who in his *Identity* series of environmental music (a specific work for a specific situation) extended the notion of the audience exercising significant control over sound. As McLean himself has noted, the *Identity* series invited the listener to participate in "highly meaningful choices":

> the hearer, in exercising creative choices of his own which shape the smaller details of the work, enters into the actual creative experience. . . . No musical training is necessary for this interaction, since it is set up so that all choices made by the hearer on this smaller structural level are equally valid. . . . For those who have more time and intuitive ability, it is possible to grow with the work and, upon repeated hearings, to exercise intelligent choices on gradually higher and higher planes.[7]

In McLean's music the activity of the audience generates a wide range of sounds. When the audience discovers the various control devices (e.g., microphones and photoelectric cells), it has the opportunity for creating its own particular textures.

What all this new emphasis upon the audience's response comes down to is the increasing minimalization of music. While there have been attempts to make a minimum of materials the basis for a musical texture of almost unbelievable richness, it is the audience's new importance that characterizes the main stream of this minimal music. Contrast McLean's work with Luciano Berio's, for example. In Berio's *Thema: Omaggio a Joyce* (1958) a recognizable human voice slowly turns, by means of tape manipulation, into a fantastic array of sounds. Or in his *Visage* (1961) a voice speaks only the word *parole* (Italian for "words") but through vocal manipulation creates an emotional range that is nearly incredible. Unlike McLean's work, Berio's compositions still reflect a conventional commitment to the act of intention: the composer continues to dominate his music. McLean tries to avoid such domination—and yet, while he succeeds up to a point, it is probably John Cage and La Monte Young who have best separated themselves from music's traditional control. With his *4'33"*, first performed in 1952 at Woodstock, New York, Cage virtually turned the audience, specifically its sounds, into the work. Like Rauschenberg's *White Paintings*, which despite their apparent blankness became by way of the play of light, shadow, and reflection a surprisingly varied texture of visual activity, Cage's piece turned into such a significant texture of sound that the composer was eventually moved to argue that this giving up of music "leads to the world of nature, where, gradually or suddenly, one sees that humanity and nature, not separate, are in this world together; that nothing was lost when everything was given away. In fact, everything is gained."[8] Young's *Composition 1960 #3*, in turn, simply announced its duration and allowed the audience to do whatever they wished for the remainder of the composition. In *Composition 1960 #6* the performers, taking the approach a step further, turned the table on the audience by staring and reacting as if the audience were the performers. In such works as these, of course, it was clear that man, having long ago retired from the center of the universe, could no longer attempt those intricately artificial, sometimes gymnastic, representations of life characteristic of traditional art. The contemporary artist had moved from the customary pedestal of high art, and now he has almost become indistinct from his audience. As Cage has suggested, "Now he's no more extraordinary than we are."[9] In minimal art the artist and the audience become one.

What happened in art and music during the past century occurred in literature as well. In the novel (the focus of this book), for example, nineteenth-century writers such as Flaubert and Maupassant began to move fiction away from its customary thematic orientation and in the process to deflect their readers' attention from the matters of society to the matters of perception. Whereas novelists such as Balzac and Thackeray had been primarily conscious of weaving together a narrative texture that incorporated aspects of their own moral imagination, Flaubert committed himself to the presentation of character and event without explicit analysis of motive and intention. In fact, by avoiding any extensive moral statement that might reflect his own attitudes, he provided his characters with a new freedom to be themselves. In a sense, therefore, it was as if the author now unleashed in his characters, somewhat spontaneously, a complex of contradictory impulses and feelings that belied easy categorization. Flaubert, to be sure, despite having largely equated the act of narrative with the act of perception, continued to influence the shape and thus the moral content of his narrative by choosing which events and which characters to portray, and in the end—as with his portrayal of Madame Bovary—it is even possible to talk about the nature and character of Flaubert's own moral imagination. What writers such as Flaubert and Maupassant created in their work, nevertheless, was a new aesthetic distance that enabled them, much like the Impressionist painters, to become more conscious of the processes whereby they developed the textures of their narrative. Flaubert once remarked to George Sand:

> Quant à mes ⟨⟨manques de conviction⟩⟩, hélas! les convictions m'étouffent. J'éclate de colère et d'indignations rentrées. Mais dans l'idéal que j'ai de l'art, je crois qu'on ne doit rien montrer des siennes, et que l'artiste ne doit pas plus apparaître dans son oeuvre que Dieu dans la nature. L'homme n'est rien, l'oeuvre tout![10]

Flaubert's emphasis here upon the author's godlike impersonality is so strong that it may initially seem to have little relationship to the Impressionists' rather spontaneous techniques, but if one remembers that the Impressionists' new interest in the character of light and shape—or the late-nineteenth-century composer's exploration of chromaticism—was a response to the subjective excesses inherent in romanticism (Wagner's music serving as the prime example), then that impersonality can serve as an important concept unifying all the artists of the period. In fact, without this impersonality, which to a large degree reflected current developments in science, and which certainly supported the artists' commitment to exploring the processes of perception itself, there is little doubt that these artists would never have managed the extensive modifications of their media that were apparent by the turn of the century.

Like other artists, Flaubert had lost the confidence of subjective vision that underlay all the romantic posturing of the nineteenth century. In an era of new scientific objectivity, with the inescapable limitations within all viewpoints suddenly apparent, he believed that he had little choice but to assume an impersonality that would allow him the opportunity for observing and thus identifying the character and the range of his own responses to the circumstances of his life and his fiction. In a very paradoxical fashion, however, the stance of impersonality became the basis for a new yet different subjectivity—this time a subjectivity not focused upon content but upon technique. For just as the Impressionists increasingly shifted their attention to the more objective considerations of technique yet made their techniques very individual, so Flaubert, having retreated to the status of the disciplined observer who allowed the texture of his creations to unfold as they would, still laced his seemingly detached narrative with an irony that was unmistakably his. To the extent that he injected a strong dose of terse irony into his narrative, in fact, he might be accused of having clung to the content-oriented style of most nineteenth-century writers, because in the end, at least in the absence of explicit moral commentary, his irony served the function of establishing the peculiarity of his own vision of experience. Despite—and perhaps even because of—his significant use of irony, Flaubert became an important foundation upon which the modern novel built its character—a fact that is especially evident in the work of such modernists as Conrad and Ford Madox Ford.

That Flaubert was an important influence upon these modernists is surely apparent in Ford's admission that he and Conrad had read Flaubert "daily together over a space of years."[11] As an artist committed throughout his career to the exploration of new techniques, Conrad deeply appreciated Flaubert's impersonality, yet when he himself modeled his narrative upon Flaubert's method—usually that of an omniscient author who conducted intimate character analysis and even interior monologue—he found it impossible to separate himself from the significance of the events he was writing about. For Conrad, many of the events at the heart of his early fiction possessed considerable personal significance, and thus his presumably objective narrators (as in *The Nigger of the "Narcissus"*) sometimes got caught up in explicit subjective rhetoric over such themes as the demoralizing effects of isolation, the emptiness of idealism, and the profundity of fear. Conrad, in short, could not sustain the irony of Flaubert's third-person technique. Eventually, taking a cue from Maupassant, whose use of indirect narration allowed for more flexibility of narrative voice (such as a balancing of sympathy and irony), Conrad rejected Flaubert's direct approach and developed an indirect scheme that around 1900 culminated in the achievements of *Heart of Darkness* and *Lord Jim*. What is striking about Conrad's adjustment in perspective is the fact that, much like the Impressionists, Conrad ultimately decided upon a technique that instead of concerning itself only with matters of content emphasized the importance of the process of perception to any narrative act. In a genuine sense Marlow's self-conscious act of narrative in Conrad's fiction around 1900 was an answer to the Impressionists' demand for a new objectivity in art—an objectivity that could only be rooted in a sensitive and shrewd understanding of the attitudes and assumptions influencing any act of perception or narration. Marlow provided Conrad with a new technique, but it was Maupassant who had prepared the way.

Ford once characterized Maupassant's method as "the introduction of a character in a word or two, a word or two for atmosphere, a few paragraphs for story, and then, click! a sharp sentence that flashes the illumination of the idea over the whole."[12] Despite the tight dramatic structure, the compact narration and description, the skillful characterization, however, over half of Maupassant's three hundred stories primarily depended on the fact that they began with the setting up of a stage for the narrative act: the narrator told his tale to a group of strangers, to a judge, to old friends sitting around a table. By including some listeners in the story, Maupassant effectively made the narrative act a rather self-conscious gesture: now the narrator not only had to explore matters of conventional content, but he also had to attend both to his own and to his listeners' attitudes and responses toward that content. What was so appealing about this narrative situation, at least for writers impressed with the new objectivity in art, was that the arbitrary but time-honored distinction between the various grounds of the story, such as background and foreground, virtually disappeared. By the time Conrad extended the technique in *Heart of Darkness* and *Lord Jim*, in fact, there had even emerged some question about the identity of the principal characters in each novel: was the major character Marlow (the subject) or was it Kurtz and Jim (the objects)? Indeed, because it was impossible (as with Picasso's great work from 1910) to discuss Kurtz's and Jim's cases without analyzing the techniques whereby Marlow had assembled his portraits of the two men, it finally had to be said of both novels—and of Conrad's art in general—that technique counted more heavily than content. That is why, of course, Conrad remains such an important impressionist writer.

There were obviously many other impressionist writers. Ford Madox Ford himself wrote *The Good Soldier*—a work that expanded upon the technique of indirect narration by exploring the possibility of unreliable narration and thus a work that seemed designed to exacerbate the reader's frustration over texts written in the impressionist mode. Perhaps a better illustration, however, of the increased tension between the author and his reader—and thus of the building importance of the reader as respondent and even artist in his own right—is Faulkner's *The Sound and the Fury*, a novel that virtually destroyed the reader's customary reliance upon the text for a statement of content and vision. Faulkner divided his novel into four sections, and in the first three the Compson brothers (Benjy, Quentin, and Jason) provided the narrative voices. All three of them presented views of the Compson experience, both past and present, but because their views reflected their own individual biases, it was left to the reader to establish an overall coherence for the text. That this would be difficult was surely implicit in the handling of Benjy's section, for there, with a fragile narrative pattern rooted in an idiot's association of strong sensory perceptions, the reader quickly discovered that his own active participation in the text was crucial to any ultimate definition of its character. Furthermore, if the narrative acts of the Compsons reflected certain ingrained biases, the reader had to reckon with the same problem in his own reconstituting of the narrative. Because the perspective in the novel's fourth section was that of a third-person narrator, the reader might for a time hope to rely upon its presumed objectivity for a statement of the novel's vision, but finally that hope, too, proved to be problematic. The third-person narrator clearly possessed the air of authority, and since his apparent objectivity contrasted rather sharply with the obvious subjectivity of the three brothers' unreliable narration, the reader initially had good reason to accept as definitive that narrator's assessment of the events on Easter Sunday. In the end, nevertheless, because that narrator stuck to the present and avoided the reverie and recall that complicated the brothers' acts of narrative, little final assessment emerged. The fourth section, even though it seemed to move toward that moment of vision which supported, say, the earlier texts of Conrad, provided the reader with almost no additional foundation for establishing a comprehensive reading of the novel. The ritual of Easter Sunday, with all of its emphasis upon salvation and hope, might have served as an impressive contrast to the hell of the Compsons, but whether that ritual had become a viable alternative in Faulkner's own imagination remained highly debatable. Lacking a definitive statement in the novel itself, the reader was forced back upon himself: as an artist, he now had to reconstitute the text for himself.

Like Flaubert, Maupassant, Conrad, Ford, and a host of other major novelists whom I have slighted in this brief discussion (Proust! Joyce!), Faulkner helped prepare the way for the writers I am focusing upon in this book. By referring in this chapter to some of the major developments in the art of the last hundred years, and by concentrating especially upon the artist's assumption of impersonality, his desertion of content, and his shifting of responsibility for his work to his audience over that hundred years, I have tried to provide a broad perspective whereby the differing achievements of Nabokov, Barthelme, and Kosinski develop a greater clarity. All three of these writers, even Nabokov, who is recently dead, belong to the present, and as shrewd artists each of them is thoroughly aware of the incredible transformations that have altered the tradition of fiction over the past hundred years. In a general sense, the work of all three men reflects the authorial impersonality and the desertion of content in favor of reader involvement that have defined the tradition following Flaubert. At the same time, however, given this very general similarity, and then given the fact that all three of them find themselves victimized by the textual insufficiency that attaches to the modernist awareness of the intricacies of perception and language, it is at least interesting to note that Nabokov solves the problem of generating texts by developing complex narrative structures; Barthelme, by playing the various languages available in contemporary texts against each other; and Kosinski, by aggressively challenging his readers to become more aware of the processes of perception and language in their own lives. A hundred years of avant-garde art have passed, but with these writers, artists who belong to an age in which texts have become notorious for their lack of convincing stature, the problems of narrative perspective, of the text and its contents, and of the audience and its responsibilities remain. In the fiction of Nabokov, Barthelme, and Kosinski, therefore, readers today have an unusual opportunity for updating themselves on the dilemmas that first emerged in the art of a century ago—and that yet, because there is none, have achieved no solution.

One final matter. Much of the discussion in succeeding chapters depends upon a basic distinction, largely formulated by Nabokov (but also applicable to the fiction of Barthelme and Kosinski), between text and texture. That such a distinction is necessary is probably most apparent in the fact that all three of these writers regard the term *text* as a contradiction of what is possible. From their view no text in recent times enjoys the epistemological and ontological sufficiency that had previously attached to literary texts in the realist mode, and thus the primary objective that organizes their fictions seems to focus upon the playful exploration of a complex texture of experience that does not in any final way purport to contain human experience but that does, by virtue of the authors' own increasing sophistication from novel to novel, capture aspects of the bewildering worlds these novelists have themselves known as inhabitants of the twentieth century. For them, text represents a closed field that, once narrowed and defined by such writers as the realists, has in recent years emerged as a hoax—as an arbitrary imposition of order and value that in fact enjoys no validity except as agreed upon by the writer and his audience. Texture, on the other hand, is that open field which, recently entered by a host of young writers, challenges the writer to match his wits against what is unknowable and thus what is, finally, beyond words. Instead, then, of developing texts that possess an ultimate authority, the writers discussed in this book tend to regard their novels as exercises open to unlimited variation and play. In other words, instead of dominating a text (i.e., making that text conform to preconceived notions of what human experience is or is not), these writers not only suspend themselves in the quandary that underlies their recognition of life's fundamental inexplicability but turn that quandary into a gamelike situation in which they can manufacture new associations and relationships that speak to the complex and contradictory world of the present, if not to the more confined world of the past.

Throughout this book, especially given such adroit gamers as Quilty and Shade in Nabokov, or a series of clever narrators in Barthelme, or the masterful Tarden and Levanter in Kosinski, gaming serves as the crucial ground of human experience. That fact needs stressing at the outset, for unless readers accept from the beginning the necessity of gaming in the fiction of these three writers, there is little chance that they—the readers—will fully appreciate how extensive the transformation in recent narrative assumptions has been. Texts, once closed by the realists, are now again wide open; and again open, they require a new sophistication on the part of their readers, who instead of responding to the more traditional process of narrative editorializing (as in Roland Barthes's *readerly* texts) now find themselves fully suspended in a text of plural signification (Barthes's *writerly* texts).[13] The game is everything, and in light of this fact the reader must accept a new responsibility for his reading of the text.

Part I
NABOKOV

2

Nabokov's Texts: Authors vs. Editors

Nabokov's English fiction is generally characterized by the bewildering complexity of its narrative strategies. Given the careful attention of the modernists to the matter of viewpoint, of course, it is not surprising that Nabokov should have explored the curious nexus between the two primary sources of all texts, memory and the imagination, or that he should have made the nexus between memory and the imagination the touchstone for all his narratives—whether fictional or autobiographical (*Speak, Memory* enjoys at least a quasi-fictional status). Indeed, in light of the fluid character of all human impressions, both in the past and in the present, Nabokov seems to have recognized that the various texts of his own experience could not enjoy the sufficiency that once attached to the narratives, say, of the realists at the end of the previous century. In other words, having realized that no text in the present adequately contains the full character of any human experience, Nabokov invested his efforts as a writer into the difficult task of recovering for his readers the peculiar, fluid status of all texts, both literary and nonliterary. In order to clarify some of the issues involved in Nabokov's careful narrative strategies (as well as to prepare for my discussions of *Lolita*, *Pale Fire*, and *Ada* in succeeding chapters), I want in this chapter to examine briefly an earlier novel, *Pnin*, in which the problem of textual insufficiency possesses a distinctly extraliterary significance, and then to contrast that extraliterary situation with the explicitly literary manifestation of the same problem in Nabokov's last two novels, *Transparent Things* and *Look at the Harlequins!* Such an approach will at least have the advantage of demonstrating the range of Nabokov's interest in the problem of texts and, more specifically, in the distinctions between text and texture and between an authorial and an editorial relationship to texts—distinctions that have considerable importance to any sensitive appreciation of Nabokov's achievement. Such an analysis will also serve to underscore why Nabokov places so much emphasis upon textual discontinuity or upon the technique of doubling in all of his English novels.

Whereas *Lolita, Pale Fire,* and *Ada* all possess deliberately evasive artists who finally do achieve full command over their complicated and bewildering materials,[1] *Pnin* possesses a narrator who, despite his assertions of control in the final chapter, actually loses much of his authority over the text. While early critics of the novel have generally dismissed this narrator as unimportant,[2] recent critics have pounced upon the narrator's intrusions into Pnin's life as evidence of his cruelty toward Pnin,[3] of his violation of Pnin's privacy and honor,[4] and thus of his essential unreliability as a recorder of Pnin's experience.[5] Even more important than this new emphasis upon the narrator's manipulations of Pnin, however, is the larger theoretical question, which both Paul Grams and William Carroll have addressed, of whether fictional biography constitutes "an unethical operation"[6] or whether an "inventor" has the right to create stories.[7] Grams has concluded that fictional biography is indeed unethical because it represents an invasion of the biographee's privacy. Carroll, on the other hand, has concluded that because "all of us, everything, is 'authored' in one sense or another," there is no stopping an artist who wishes to fabricate a story about someone else. Both arguments are intriguing, and though the debate between the two positions may never be resolved, it has at least had the effect of encouraging readers of *Pnin* to attend carefully to the subtleties of narrative strategy that permeate the novel.

For *Pnin* as a whole, the argument that the narrator violates Pnin's experience by containing it within his own narrative conceptions addresses only half of Nabokov's strategy. The other half concerns the matter of Pnin's own perception of the character of his experience—a matter that is itself very complicated. For most critics Timofey Pnin seems to represent a character who, by establishing significant contact with the immediacy of the present, maintains a life of genuine vitality and thus deserves the warm appreciation of a narrator.[8] Pnin, however, despite his strong contact with the present, also possesses what amounts to a rich strain of sentimentality. Consider, for example, his repeated recovery of intense scenes from the past, especially in moments of recurring chest pain. Whether it is again experiencing a childhood illness, or seeing old friends and his parents, or responding to his old loves, or merely rambling through some former woods, Pnin always seems on the verge of renewing significant contact with numerous aspects of his past—a fact that surely qualifies his perception of what transpires in the present. At first glance these moments of vivid memory may strike the reader as an indication that Pnin has merely succumbed to a gross sense of sentimentality and has thus rather blithely, perhaps in a fashion similar to that of the narrator, absorbed himself only in the deliberate recovery of the precise character of his past experience (when, presumably, he was far happier). Pnin's brand of sentimentality, nevertheless, is more complicated than that.

Toward the middle of the novel, while remarking about his wearing of a "Greek Catholic cross on a golden chainlet," Pnin tells his friend Chateau, "I wear it merely from sentimental reasons. And the sentiment is becoming burdensome. After all, there is too much of the physical about this attempt to keep a particle of one's childhood in contact with one's breastbone" (P, 128).[9] Such a comment clearly suggests, I think, that Pnin is not the easy victim of sentiment that he may appear to be. While his experience in the present is rich in associations with the past, his interweaving—within his own mind—of past and present by way of particular qualities associated with the two time periods is finally evidence, not of his determination to recover or establish the precise character of the past as a defense against the present, but of his sensitivity to the manner in which the resonance of the past lingers into the present, thus complicating the acts of the present. Contrast, here, Pnin's sentimentality with that of Humbert Humbert. Whereas Humbert wastes away the last months of his life as an "editor" pursuing a memoir that he hopes will fully contain his hopeless relationship with Lolita and that will thus explain his present circumstances (his arrest), Pnin never gets caught up in the pursuit of a definitive web of coherence that unites all his experience, past and present. As an exile who has frequently had to shift about, he in fact does not in any final sense comprehend what has happened to him in the past (or, for that matter, what is now happening to him in the present), and thus, while a sentimental Humbert determinedly forces his experience into a one-dimensional textual configuration that in the end exhausts him, the vital if confused Pnin even at the end of his respective novel continues to allow his world to develop largely as it will.

What attracts the narrator (and Nabokov himself) to a narrative focused upon Pnin's life at Waindell, then, is the rich, if somewhat bewildering and unpredictable, texture of Pnin's imaginative experience. At one point in the novel, while recounting Victor's childhood, the narrator makes the statement that "genius is non-conformity" (P, 89). Such a formulation is probably a bit reductive, but given Pnin's haphazard manner of adjusting to his American context even years after his arrival, there is a profound sense in which this definition can serve as a fundamental key to appreciating his achievement. Exiled, and then forever unable to submerge himself in the prevailing social patterns of the West, Pnin has had no choice but to create an unusual texture of personal experience. In another significant comment, this time very early in the novel, the narrator elaborates the point and identifies the necessity of discreteness, which is finally the basis for all nonconformity, as crucial to human existence:

> One of the main characteristics of life is discreteness. Unless a film of flesh envelops us, we die. Man exists only insofar as he is separated from his surroundings. The cranium is a space-traveler's helmet. Stay inside or you perish. Death is divestment, death is communion. It may be wonderful to mix with the landscape, but to do so is the end of the tender ego. (*P*, 20)

Here, of course, the matter of discreteness is applied to physical considerations, and yet what is true for the body is also true for the mind. Through language, particularly through an appreciation of the specific character that attaches to his personal language acts, a man such as Pnin gains the discreteness of mind that is so necessary to vital, creative human experience. Pnin may not possess the style of language that will provide him with significant stature in the professional community, but by indulging himself freely in the playful, yet sometimes messy and contradictory, interweaving of his several languages—Russian, French, and English, as well as those languages of experience associated with the past and the present—he separates himself from his surroundings and thus gains for himself an unusually rich sense of awareness and intensity. Whereas so many of Nabokov's characters (e.g., Humbert Humbert, Charles Kinbote, the younger Van Veen) determinedly pursue texts of experience organized around one specific objective and in the process actually turn mad, Pnin's style is to suspend himself constantly in the confusion that envelops him and thus to turn the fundamental complexity of his experience into its own rich reward. If for a moment he, too, should during the course of the novel desire the security of tenure and the stability of inhabiting his own home, finally he continues—when circumstances prevent the award of tenure—that life of nonconformity which lies at the heart of all his past experience. Rather than accepting a comfortable situation at Waindell, in a capacity directed by the narrator (whom he despises), he summons his courage, flees Waindell, and thus again opens his life to new events.

Before Pnin flees, however, the conflict between himself and the narrator breaks out into the open. Toward the end of chapter 6, when

Hagen encourages Pnin to work for the narrator in the English department, Pnin categorically refuses such an arrangement: "I know him [the narrator] thirty years or more. We are friends, but there is one thing perfectly certain. I will never work under him" (*P*, 170). Despite the similarities of their background and exile, Pnin knows that he shall never again have anything serious to do with the narrator. The reason for this stubborn resistance centers, as I have already implied, upon the struggle between Pnin and the narrator for possession of the text of Pnin's life. Pnin may not be aware of the narrator's development of a novel entitled *Pnin*, but he is conscious of how the narrator perceives, even interprets, the events of his—Pnin's—life and how, consequently, the narrator is committing an act of textual cannibalism that differs only in degree from what Charles Kinbote will do to John Shade's poem in *Pale Fire*. The fact of the matter is that if Pnin is to maintain his own, somewhat fragile, messy, unpredictable suspension in the rich texture of his affairs, he must keep his distance from any man, friend or narrator, who would contain his vitality, whether at Waindell or before, within a one-dimensional, i.e., fixed, text. To be sure, once the narrator has rather painstakingly detailed his credentials in chapter 7, it is possible to argue that his narrative merely recovers what is his own view of Pnin's experience, and thus that the narrative reflects only his own selective acts of the imagination. Much the same, in fact, might also be said of Jack Cockerell's imitations of Pnin, which appear several times in the text, and which in the last chapter—when the narrator must listen to an evening's worth of them—actually begin to rival the narrative creations of the narrator himself. What must be recognized here, however, is that Pnin himself has never managed to establish a secure narrative for his rich and varied past. This failure probably serves as the basis for his maintaining the courage to face up to the confusing textures of the present, and thus when the narrator and Jack Cockerell, in the process of pursuing their interest in Pnin's foibles and idiosyncrasies, attempt to fix the nature of Pnin's experience, they become a serious threat to Pnin's existence—even before *Pnin* has emerged as a fictive text. Essentially the fixing of their respective texts is tantamount to the closing of a life that Pnin himself has deliberately left open, and in the last chapter, when the narrator recounts two very strained moments of confrontation between Pnin and himself, the reader can determine the effect of this closing upon Pnin.

In the first instance, which already takes place at a Paris cafe in the early 1920s, the narrator tries to remind Pnin of certain earlier meetings, but Pnin denies all the references that the narrator cites. As the narrator recalls, "[Pnin] said he vaguely recalled my grandaunt but had never met me. He said that his marks in algebra had always been poor and that, anyway, his father never displayed him to patients. . . . He repeated that we had never seen each other before" (*P*, 180). What is so interesting about this encounter, it seems to me, is that Pnin not only contradicts the narrator's reminiscences but also seems determined to deny any previous relationship at all to the narrator. The narrator concludes in this instance that Pnin is merely reluctant "to recognize his own past" (*P*, 180), but in the context of the whole novel, in which there is abundant evidence to the contrary, there can be little doubt that Pnin's conduct has an altogether different motivation. Several years later, again on a trip to Paris, Pnin once more interrupts the narrator's reminiscing with the accusation, "Now, don't believe a word he says. . . . He makes up everything. He once invented that we were schoolmates in Russia and cribbed at examinations. He is a dreadful inventor" (*P*, 185). The outburst astounds the narrator, but in the sense that the attack originates in Pnin's determination to retain the rich, if obscure, resonance of the past that he has enjoyed over the years while playing with the various languages at his disposal, there is some justification for Pnin's conduct. Pnin has no intention of becoming a fixed text in the repertoire of a glib inventor such as the narrator or, even worse perhaps, Jack Cockerell. In a certain sense, it is true, Pnin's determination may signal a failure on the part of his own imagination. By trying to preserve the peculiar, somewhat haphazard character of his own sense of past experience, he effectively prevents the narrator's assessments of that experience from adding another dimension to the languages of his existence. The experience that is the source of the narrator's and Cockerell's tales, nevertheless, is Pnin's, and to the extent that he must consequently be accorded a primacy of ownership over its fluid textures, his reactions demand respect. After all, it is Pnin—not the narrator, not Cockerell, perhaps not even Nabokov—who has given his experience such an unusual shape.

There is one pattern of detail in the novel that helps explain, I think, this conflict between Pnin and the narrator. Throughout the novel, as a number of critics have noted,[10] there appear at least seven references to squirrels—from those of Pnin's boyhood (*P*, 23, 177) to those he encounters while pursuing his duties at Waindell (*P*, 24, 58, 73). Two of the references are especially noteworthy. The first is part of the narrative in which Pnin establishes his correspondence with Victor and thereby assumes the role of Victor's father. After mailing his first letter, Pnin also sends along "a picture postcard representing the Gray Squirrel" (*P*, 88) and presumably informs Victor of the fact that " 'squirrel' came from a Greek word which meant 'shadow-tail' " (*P*, 88). The second

reference is part of the narrative of Pnin's party. At one point, responding to Margaret Thayer's mention of the Cinderella story, Pnin remarks
that Cinderella's shoes were not made of glass but "of Russian squirrel
fur—*vair*, in French." He explains:

> It was . . . an obvious case of the survival of the fittest among words,
> *verre* being more evocative than *vair* which, he submitted, came not
> from *varius*, variegated, but from *veveritsa*, Slavic for a certain
> beautiful, pale, winter-squirrel fur, having a bluish, or better say
> *sizïly*, columbine, shade—from *columba*, Latin for "pigeon." (*P*, 158)

Together, these two references are nothing short of remarkable, for while
Pnin in the first instance merely recites etymological fact, in the second,
perhaps under the influence of the punch, he seems to indulge himself in
an etymological hunch that reinforces the character of his genius.[11]
What is at stake here, it seems to me, is that Pnin, on the eve before his
meeting concerning the buying of his house, feels himself free to play
with whatever associations come to mind and which, together, create a
striking resonance of mind.

Even more important than revealing Pnin's confident play within the
world of his own associations, however, the two passages seem to address
that crucial relationship between the protagonist and his creator which
underlies all of Nabokov's English fiction. Throughout his life, as Pnin
once remarks to his friend Chateau, Pnin has been conscious of living
with "a shadow behind his heart" (*P*, 126), and while he has consulted
doctors about its presence, no X-ray has ever explained the problem. In
the sense, nevertheless, that Pnin has had to contend with such men as
the narrator and Jack Cockerell as shadows for control over the actual
shaping of his life, the emphasis upon the squirrel and then Pnin's
enthusiastic creation of what appears to be his own etymological text
reinforce the notion that Pnin is determined to maintain the sanctity of
his own experience. Pnin's fundamental problem is obviously a matter,
not of squirrels, but of containing the shadow-tail, i.e., the narrator
figure who would cannibalize his—Pnin's—life. Although no one ever
fully escapes the presence of such shadows—to the extent that Pnin
provides Victor with advice he himself becomes Victor's shadow—Pnin's
awareness of the shadow at least enables him to struggle with any
would-be narrator over the manner in which the text of his experience is
laid down. Put bluntly, the situation in the novel is this: the narrator,
although an acquaintance of Pnin from the past, has over the years fixed
an interpretation on Pnin's life that is based largely upon hearsay
evidence and that, consequently, hardly recovers the full character of
Pnin's being. He may not yet have written the text of *Pnin*, but he has

already fixed much of its eventual content. In the presence of this preliminary fixing a sensitive Pnin, in turn, at least if he is to retain the vitality and the originality of mind that are his distinction, must prevent that interpretation from crystallizing his own perceptions of experience. In the last sequence of the novel, therefore, when the narrator does manage momentarily to get Pnin on the phone, Pnin again thwarts the narrator by denying that he is yet in Waindell. The next morning the narrator gets a glimpse of Pnin in his car, but in that instance, too, with a sudden burst of speed up the hill,[12] Pnin escapes this now more than embryonic textual domination by a man who seems to have spent a lifetime pursuing him. The narrative does not indicate whether Pnin here escapes the narrator's presence forever, but it is clear that Pnin, although well armed for future narrative intrusions, can never entirely escape the critical challenge to his own well-being: after all, the narrator, despite Pnin's resistance, commits the ultimate act of textual cannibalism by writing and publishing the narrative of *Pnin*.

Pnin himself never gains the ground of final authority or absolute control over the textures of his experience. Those textures defy full comprehension. For a time he appears to approach the fixed text of a settled life at Waindell, of tenure and a home, but at the end of the novel he remains as isolated and as vulnerable to the vagaries of chance as he was on his lecture trip to Cremona. That fact having now been demonstrated, it is at this point that the narrative strategy of *Pnin* becomes most clear. Pnin cannot narrate his own life because the rich character of his experience frustrates any attempt at containment. Because he has never possessed a definitive, coherent text for himself, in fact, he will probably be doomed forever to playing out a very fluid web of associations and relationships that heightens his imaginative experience but that also leaves him vulnerable in view of its essential instability. The narrator, for example, in the process of appropriating Pnin's life for himself, has given Pnin's life a shape that Pnin himself could not muster. That fact points to the fundamental paradox of human experience (and of art) in Nabokov's fiction: the character who plays with the rich textures of his experience has difficulty establishing a concrete text for his existence. On the other hand, the character who does establish a text for himself is suspect—whether he is the narrator of *Pnin* or, in the other great English novels, Humbert Humbert, Charles Kinbote, and the younger Van Veen. In Nabokov the lack of a secure text leads to vitality and originality.

If *Pnin* demonstrates the difficulty of fixing the character of one's personal text, *Transparent Things* clarifies the problem by elaborating upon the distinction between the editorial and the authorial handling of text. In a certain sense, with his immersion in the rich textures of imaginative life, Pnin already represents what underlies the authorial relationship to text. By the same token, with his determination to fix the nature of Pnin's genius, the narrator of *Pnin* reveals the editorial relationship to text. It is in Nabokov's late fiction, however, and in *Transparent Things* in particular, that this distinction receives its most thorough analysis.

That the establishing of text remains a significant problem in Nabokov's last novels is evident in the characterization of Mr. R. in *Transparent Things*. As an accomplished writer, Mr. R. has possessed throughout his life that expansive and fluid perspective which is in touch with the essential arbitrariness of human experience. When it comes to writing his own fiction, however, Mr. R. has created a world of stature and significance that belies this fundamental arbitrariness. The narrator of *Transparent Things* provides a shrewd insight into the contradiction of Mr. R.'s position when he recounts how Mr. R.'s editor, Hugh Person, tries to cajole him into modifications of the characters and the title of his latest novel, *Tralatitions*. Mr. R. determinedly refuses on the ground that any alteration would radically disfigure the character of his conception for the work. Indeed, when reminded of the libel suits the book would probably encounter in its present form, Mr. R. merely suggests that he had "paid for [his art] once in solitude and remorse, and now was ready to pay in hard cash any fool whom his story might hurt" (*TT*, 74).[13] Obviously confident and self-assured, Mr. R. has generated over the years a profound respect for his own handling of experience and thus, without hesitation, thinks nothing of committing himself completely to the development of his own peculiar text. With such an insistent claim to the realization of his own text, however, he seems to transgress the one law common to all of Nabokov's fiction—that there exists no text of authority whereby human experience can finally be measured and judged.

The irony that attaches to Mr. R.'s stance applies even more specifically to his editor. *Transparent Things* focuses upon Hugh Person, a character whom Mr. R. himself regards as "one of the nicest persons I knew" (*TT*, 83), but a character who by failing to explore the textures of his own imagination finally becomes conscious of having squandered his life "in a sick dream" (*TT*, 96). Hugh does possess some genius, but because he lacks originality, or because he does not act upon his genius by challenging and extending it, he ends up throwing his life away—first as a secretary to Atman (a fraudulent symbolist), then as an entrepreneur in stationery (who markets the Person fountain pen), and finally as an editor for a publishing firm (where he eventually takes charge of Mr. R.'s texts). At one point in the novel, shortly after meeting Armande, he even confides in his diary that "I am an all-round genius" (*TT*, 28), but by then it is evident that something has gone wrong with his life. Lacking that confidence which is crucial to the success of the artist in any field and which certainly underlies Mr. R.'s distinguished career as a writer, Hugh at that point finds himself not only separated from a life of achievement but also at a serious disadvantage when dealing with other people. His relationship with Armande is a good case in point.

Hugh is fearful of approaching Armande, and from the beginning he allows her to define the character of their relationship, particularly in matters of sex. Such allowance is disastrous. Armande fancies herself a realist, one who reads "hard realistic stuff" (*TT*, 26) and who thus expects Hugh to be likewise "serious, and plain, and believable" (*TT*, 26). Moreover, by depending upon ideas derived from other people, she has moved completely out of touch with the imaginative character of being that is the source, throughout Nabokov's fiction, of emotional vitality. In her presence, therefore, Hugh himself never has the opportunity to develop that same primary source of energy. Not surprisingly, having deferred to her perspective, he eventually discovers in himself a profound core of hate: "I hate Witt. . . . I hate life. I hate myself" (*TT*, 55). By marrying Armande, Hugh has fully separated himself from any lingering sense of responsibility for exploring his own world of perceptions, and finally, having given up the one marginally original game that has continued into his adult life (that of the tennis played while he lulls himself to sleep), he becomes the complete victim of his own folly. Throughout the marriage, instead of examining his own perceptions, Hugh engages only in what amounts to an editorial examination of Armande's unpredictable behavior. By regarding the strange aspects of her conduct "as absurd clues in a clever puzzle" (*TT*, 63), he tries to establish the emotional equivalent of an authoritative text for her life. Despite his repeated analyses of her behavior, however, he never locates reasonable explanations. His efforts lead to nothing.

Hugh's editorial relationship to Armande's life is obviously inferior to Mr. R.'s authorial relationship to the texts he creates, but both characters, by committing themselves to the establishment of their respective texts, seem to violate that fundamental textlessness which is at the heart of Nabokov's fiction. In Nabokov's work all "reality" is a text in need of editing. If, however, the process of editing assumes that there is an ultimate "reality" that is discoverable by careful scrutiny of the available evidence, then that process must emerge as self-defeating and dangerous to its originator. One of the dictionary definitions of *text* is "an ultimate source of information or authority." This definition alludes to the sort of text for which many of Nabokov's characters search—Armande in her admiration for "hard realistic stuff," Hugh in his editorial search for the "reality" of Armande's life. But there is another kind of text, the Nabokovian literary text, which imitates the shifting nature of reality and becomes an authoritative source by virtue of showing that there are no authoritative sources. In his last two novels and throughout his career Nabokov parodies the first kind of text in order to establish the second kind, the text that creates "reality" by dramatizing the many ways in which "reality" eludes human perception.

At the very beginning of the novel the narrator provides a telling comment concerning the delicacy that must attend any relationship to a text. Recognizing that the past is particularly seductive because the future enjoys "no such reality . . . as the pictured past and the perceived present possess" (TT, 1), the narrator suggests that most people, in the process of perceiving an object (person, place, or thing), "involuntarily sink . . . into the history [the text] of that object." For the narrator, consequently, any sustaining of the imagination requires, above all, a facing up to this dangerous skewing of perception toward the past. As he suggests, "Novices must learn to skim over matter if they want matter to stay at the exact level of the moment" (TT, 1). Jonathan Raban, in disparaging such skimming, has cited both Lolita and Armande as good examples of skimmers.[14] In actuality, however, Lolita and Armande represent the opposite tendency, for both of them have submerged themselves in the attitudes and conceptions that have over the years created the social fabric of their respective milieus. The narrator makes their position clear: "A thin veneer of immediate reality is spread over natural and artificial matter, and whoever wishes to remain in the now, with the now, on the now, should please not break its tension film" (TT, 1). Lolita and Armande simply do not take such care. They are both so dominated by prevailing attitudes that they repeatedly break through the tension film at the surface. If, in Nabokov's world, genius and originality depend upon maintaining sufficient distance between oneself and the texts of the past so that imaginative responses to the present remain viable, then Lolita and Armande represent colossal failures.

The narrator's emphasis upon skimming over matter shows Nabokov's determination to clarify in this novel his uses of the past. While critics have sometimes applauded his characters' retreat into the past, Nabokov himself recognizes that all texts, even those of the past, are multifaceted, very complex, and frequently contradictory. When his most original characters mine the resources of the past, therefore, they are not so much retreating into it as attempting to create a web that can contain it in all its complexity. Whether I cite Pnin or Shade or the elder Van Veen, it should be clear that none of these characters inhabits a stable past from which he can extract a single, authoritative text. Instead, each of them, with each succeeding moment of the present, finds himself in the predicament of having to create a new web for the past that takes into account all the adjustments in attitude and insight that have emerged in the present. Van Veen's extensive modulation of his past and present relationship with Ada is probably the best example of this process, but Pnin's juxtaposition of Russia and America also serves nicely. In Nabokov's fiction static texts, the texts that presume to possess a final authority, are dangerous commodities because they no longer engage their originators in the modifications that are crucial to sustained vitality and creativity. In *Transparent Things*, which begins and ends with Hugh's return (at the age of forty) to the Ascot Hotel, where he expects to recover "a moment of contact with [Armande's] essential image in exactly remembered surroundings" (*TT*, 95), the danger becomes fully apparent. For when Hugh commits himself to the recovery of an exact configuration of the past, he divorces himself from the necessity of making his present act of perception a condition of that past. The consequence is that he cuts himself off from the processes of perception and virtually commits aesthetic suicide. In these terms, of course, the difference between Hugh and Mr. R. finally emerges. Both men may commit themselves to their texts, but while Hugh's commitment reflects an editorial relationship in which the text dominates him, Mr. R.'s commitment reflects an authorial relationship in which the text, even when located in the past, remains a function of his acts of perception in the present. In the letter he writes as he is dying, Mr. R. declares:

> I used to believe that dying persons saw the vanity of things, the futility of fame, passion, art, and so forth . . . but now I feel just the contrary: my most trivial sentiments and those of all men have acquired gigantic proportions. . . . The more I shrivel, the bigger I grow. . . . If I could explain this . . . in one big book, that book would become no doubt a new bible and its author the founder of a new creed. Fortunately for my self-esteem that book will not be written—not merely because a dying man cannot write books but because that particular one would never express in one flash what can only be understood *immediately*. (*TT*, 84)

Mr. R. scrupulously establishes the texts of his various books, but he is not, finally, dominated by their versions of the truth. On the contrary, he dies with a sense of his insufficiency as an artist and of his previous failure to express the "totality" of things.

It is striking that the narrator of *Transparent Things* seems to fall himself into the very textual trap he forswears. Repeatedly, as when he recounts the history of the pencil located in the desk in Hugh's room at the Ascot or the history of the room in which Hugh takes his first prostitute, the narrator seems to indulge in the kind of textual reconstruction of the past with which he associates Hugh. Finally, though, Hugh is engaged in an editorial (or sentimental) pilgrimage, in the "enforced re-creation of irrecoverable trivia" (*TT*, 94), whereas the narrator plays with the texts of the past in the fashion of Mr. R. The narrator is not directly involved in the history of the pencil or of the room and thus does not seek to establish the exact configuration of the past. Knowing, in fact, that such an attempt is impossible, he moves well beyond Hugh's stance and allows himself the luxury and the imaginative stimulation of playing with the open textures inherent in all texts, even those of the past. Whereas Hugh has victimized himself by committing himself to the pursuit of exact texts, the narrator constantly expands his play with the multidimensional texts before him and takes genuine delight in ferreting out each new facet or "flavor" (*TT*, 36). In a somewhat paradoxical sense, then, the source of this narrator's genius is that he suspends himself in as "textless" a reconsideration of his experience as possible. Such suspension, much like Pnin's, allows him to bring the texts of experience into genuine contact with his present mode of being. More than that, however, once in this new contact with each other, the play between the texts of the past and of the present can create those wonderful, sometimes completely unanticipated textures with which readers have come to associate Nabokov's fiction. At the same time, this narrator has avoided the pursuit of an avant-garde text, which in his mind "means little more than conforming to some daring philistine fashion" (*TT*, 34). Having created for himself a spaciousness of mind that separates him from conformity to the sentiments of the past, he has also recognized the dangers of succumbing to the prevailing fashions of the present. He is—as much as any narrator can be in Nabokov's fiction—his own man.

The narrator of *Transparent Things* reinforces the creative character of his relationship to the text by developing the contrast between Mr. R. and Hugh Person and then indicating his own similarity to Mr. R. The doubling of his own situation in these two men is of crucial importance to his narrative, but when contrasted to the use the narrator of *Look at the Harlequins!* makes of doubling, its role in *Transparent Things* seems fledgling at best. There is a good reason for this. Once Nabokov has clarified his use of the past—explained that it is predicated upon a creative rather than an editorial relationship to the texts of the past—he can free his narrator to seek out facets in the texts of the past that still lie unrealized. One of the best—and now very familiar—means of realizing such facets is the technique of doubling. By its very nature doubling separates the narrator from the obligation of realism or, more properly, from the requirement of textual exactitude. Not surprisingly, therefore, in *Look at the Harlequins!*—which is a retrospective on a whole career—doubling serves as the structural principle for the novel. Not only does Vadim N.'s career play off that of Nabokov himself,[15] it also plays off the lives of other characters who represent what Vadim N. might have become had he not pursued a career as an author. The novel, consequently, enjoys a very ambiguous status. Whereas the reader might be tempted to regard Vadim N. as a loose disguise for Nabokov himself (and the considerations of Vadim N. as Nabokov's own), it eventually becomes apparent, if only because Vadim N. is such an adroit gamer, that he must be given his due as a character in his own right. By giving him his due, moreover, the reader will perceive Vadim N. as the full realization of that creative relationship to text which supports the narrator's genius in *Transparent Things*.

Vadim N. frequently employs the double as a means of measuring a particular aspect of his experience. Near the beginning of the novel, for example, while recounting the history of his " 'numerical nimbus' syndrome" (*LH*, 15),[16] Vadim alludes to a "Mr. V.S." with whom the doctor treating his syndrome has associated him. A little later, he alludes to Lieutenant Starov, who has taken the job in the White Cross that Vadim himself has turned down. Then it turns out that it is this man—a "White Russian, Wladimir Blagidze, *alias* Starov" (*LH*, 69–70)—who guns Iris down. And finally, much later in the novel (and in this instance within a parenthetical remark), Vadim considers whether "Count Starov [presumably the lieutenant's father] . . . was my real father" (*LH*, 227). By the time the reader has accumulated all these references, he should have begun to suspect that the lieutenant—with the frustrations of a boring job that lead him, perhaps, to the act of murder—represents what Vadim believes he himself might have become, had he not concerned himself with the very difficult but enlivening creation of texts. While the lieutenant—in the manner of Hugh Person—has wedded himself to a well-defined, rather restrictive career, Vadim has plumbed the depths of the imagination and has created for himself a texture of experience far beyond the lieutenant's ability to conceive.

Professor Notebooke and his wife are also doubles for Vadim N. Professor Notebooke, while described as "meek myopic old" (*LH*, 131), is at least a skilled translator whose sister is rather suggestively named

Phoneme (*LH*, 159). He, too, much like Vadim, has interested himself in the deployment of texts. Unlike Vadim, however, who is chiefly concerned with exploring and fostering his own texture of experience, Notebooke seems interested only in the extension of other writers' texts. In this context, therefore, the distinction already cited between Mr. R. and Hugh Person again surfaces with some intensity. As a translator who attends to the subtle dimensions of language, Notebooke does not have as narrow a relationship to text as Hugh Person, but it is clear, especially given Vadim's rather summary presentation of Notebooke's abilities, that he does not enjoy the spacious fields of imaginative play that belong to Vadim himself. Notebooke simply represents that academic dryness of mind which would have been Vadim's had he not devoted himself to the evocation and the extension of his own being. The contrast between Vadim and Notebooke, while rather boldly hinted at in the latter's name, is probably most evident in the fact that it is Notebooke's wife who suggests that Vadim purchase a "Junior Manicure Set" (*LH*, 163) for Bel and encourages him to hire "an experienced, preferably German, governess to look after [Bel] day and night" (*LH*, 173). The wife represents the text of propriety—a text from which Vadim, by virtue of the rather idiosyncratic character of his life as an artist, has increasingly separated himself. Because the hiring of a governess would interfere with his relationship with Bel, Vadim ignores the views of the Notebookes.

A third—and perhaps the best—example of Vadim's use of doubling occurs late in the novel, when Vadim repeatedly alludes to the man who shadows him on his trip to Leningrad. Vadim believes that he has known the man in Paris in the early thirties, and he suspects throughout the trip that the man is Russian at least by birth. When the mystery man turns out to be Oleg Orlov, all his earlier suspicions prove to be well founded. Some forty years ago, Oleg had "joined the small number of *litterateurs* who decided to sell the bleak liberty of expatriation for the rosy mess of Soviet pottage," but during his long association with the Soviets he has achieved little more than a "medley of publicity pieces, commercial translations, vicious denunciations" (*LH*, 217). In the novel, therefore, he serves as a sharp contrast to Vadim himself. Once he has identified himself, Oleg may attack Vadim's "obscene novelette about little Lola or Lotte," as if he—Oleg—were morally superior to Vadim and his work, but in the end the reader recognizes that it is Vadim who is superior—especially when Vadim deals Oleg a blow "with the back of my left fist . . . of quite presentable power" (*LH*, 218). Vadim's reference to Oleg in the narrative certainly indicates that Vadim himself has realized that his decision to surrender to the difficulties of life as an émigré rather than to settle for "the rosy mess of Soviet [or, for that matter, American] pottage" has become the basis for a life of genuine moral distinction.

All three of these doubles, while hardly exhaustive of the technique, clearly point to the lack of textual stability within Vadim's own tenuous grasp on existence. Because of the possible combinations of level and attitude available to him, there has emerged during his lifetime an almost continuous modulation of text that is once more evident in this—his final—narrative. Such continuous modulation of imaginative consciousness has in the past served to goad Vadim through a succession of marriages and relationships—from Iris to Annette to Louise, with some additional attention to Dolly and even to Bel—and now, in the very face of his desire to assess his life, to give it a final shape by establishing the character of his relationship with "You," he discovers that this process of modulation is as relentless as ever. In the past the complexity of Vadim's marital (and extramarital) experience has only served to corroborate his difficulty in accepting any one text as the final basis for his existence. The first two sentences, which focus on a doubling situation, say it as well as any other passage in the novel: "I met the first of my three or four successive wives in somewhat odd circumstances, the development of which resembled a clumsy conspiracy, with nonsensical details and a main plotter who not only knew nothing of its real object but insisted on making inept moves that seemed to preclude the slightest possibility of success. Yet out of those very mistakes he unwittingly wove a web, in which a set of reciprocal blunders on my part caused me to get involved and fulfill the destiny that was the only aid of the plot" (*LH*, 3).

While somewhat enigmatic, and perhaps even deliberately ambiguous, this passage seems to extend the distinction between text and texture that underlies John Shade's artistry and probably serves as the principal key to Nabokov's fiction. First, in the terms of *Look at the Harlequins!*, it helps to explain why Vadim's relationship with "You" will remain tenuous even in this narrative of retrospective self-definition. For Vadim the web of this present relationship is simply not yet complete and, in the world of textual insufficiency, never will be complete. Second, and more generally, the passage alludes to a "main plotter," who, as opposed to Vadim himself, initiates certain actions that resemble "a clumsy conspiracy" that even the plotter himself did not know existed. Despite all their complex posturing in full view of each other, apparently neither Vadim nor the "main plotter" possesses an authoritative text of experience to which he is committed. For both of them existence is problematic and elliptical. Third, because Vadim lacks a preconceived text that can organize his experience, he actually has no choice but to give over the ground of his being to that plotter who makes decisions at least in the sense that he initiates action. On the surface, such a transfer of authority may seem a desertion of moral responsibility, but finally it is this stance which ensures the continued vitality of Vadim's existence. Having avoided the rigorous observance of a specific text, Vadim, much like the narrator of *Transparent Things*, is free to suspend himself in the imaginative possibilities that have emerged, over the course of several decades, in the strange dialogue between the plotter's "inept moves" and Vadim's own "blunders." On the surface, again, this suspension may not seem very promising, but to the extent that it separates Vadim from that sterile observance of a preconceived text which characterizes Hugh Person's existence, the suspension guarantees Vadim a life rich in realization and understanding. His life will never be predictable, but in light of his preference for imagination rather than text, there is little doubt that his life will be intense.

This relationship between Vadim and the main plotter possesses a double-edged character. Given the presence of the main plotter, Vadim must remain conscious—even to the very end of his life—that there is no means of achieving absolute control over the field of his experience. He may over the years have become an accomplished writer, with many texts written under his name, but despite the long accumulation of success he remains prey to the notion that his life is "the non-identical twin, a parody, an inferior variant of another man's life, somewhere on this or another earth" (*LH*, 89). While this notion obviously alludes to the shadow of Nabokov himself stalking his narrator, the notion also re-covers, it seems to me, that profound sense of self-doubt which must accompany the artist's suspension of himself in the textures, rather than the texts, of human experience. Try as he may to establish the character of his own art, every true artist is in the end conscious only of the insufficiency of his achievement. Vadim is himself such an artist, and thus it is not surprising that he remarks late in the novel, "The hideous suspicion that even *Ardis*, my most private book, soaked in reality, saturated with sun flecks, might be an unconscious imitation of another's unearthly art, *that* suspicion might come later" (*LH*, 234), but come it must. In this instance, too, what the urbane Vadim finally recognizes is that he will never possess a text that fully recovers the character of his deepest (his most private) imaginative experience and that must, there-fore, be associated only with his name. The artist craves identity, specifically the identity that emerges in his best art, but in view of the ultimate insufficiency of all texts he is—as Vadim here realizes—forever disappointed. Late in the novel, following a stroke, Vadim actually loses all sense of his own identity. At that point Nabokov's shadow almost completely overwhelms him: "Poor Vivian, poor Vadim Vadimovich, was but a figment of somebody's—not even my own—imagination" (*LH*, 249). When he suggests on the same page that "in rapid Russian speech . . . 'Vladimir Vladimirovich' becomes colloquially similar to 'Vadim Vadimych,' " there may exist no further reason for maintaining the distinction between this narrator and Nabokov himself. Even then, nevertheless, the reader must realize that Vadim's difficulty is not so much with Nabokov (although that is a significant problem) as it is with the limited character of texts in general. Vadim, like any determined artist, wants the authority of text that is finally available to no man. When he loses his bearings, his sense of identity, it is because the struggle for what is impossible has finally overwhelmed him.

The Vadim who has heeded the advice of his grandaunt to "look at the harlequins" (*LH*, 8) and who has chosen for himself the "essential, hysterical, genuine [muse]" rather than "her apprentice, her palette girl and stand-in, a little logician" (*LH*, 44), is an artist who has reached for the heights. Aware, in fact, of a fundamental inability to "cope with the abstraction of direction in space," he has turned the peculiarities of his own perception into the foundation for a very idiosyncratic art: "My battle with factual, respectable life . . . consisted of sudden delusions, sudden reshufflings—kaleidoscopic, stained-glass reshufflings!—of fragmented space" (*LH*, 85). Reshuffling is, of course, the key term. Just as Joan Clements in *Pnin* characterizes the texts of a particular novelist as the attempt "to express the fantastic recurrence of certain situations" (*P*, 159), so Vadim has allied himself with that openness of text which allows for continuous modulation of one's experience, past or present. Indeed, lacking the concrete text that organizes, say, Hugh Person's life, he has actually found that he must rely upon the process of reshuffling in order to retain his sanity. As he himself acknowledges, "only the writing of fiction, the endless re-creation of my fluid self could keep me more or less sane" (*LH*, 97). An even better self-assessment, however, probably appears a few pages later when he remarks that his "average age has been thirteen" all his life (*LH*, 103). Vadim has become the artist adroit at turning his dreamlike reshufflings into the textures of art and has thereby discovered Nabokov's fountain of youth.

In general, then, Nabokov's English fiction depends for its intensity upon the sophistication with which Nabokov explores the problem of text, both literary and nonliterary. Whether one examines the earlier *Pnin* or attends to the character of the last two novels, the one denominator common to the fiction is Nabokov's careful and sensitive separation of the open field of texture from the closed field of text—or, in other terms, of the authorial relationship to text from the editorial. Nabokov's fiction is always a matter of subtle nuance and attitude and thus a cagey contest between author and reader, but if its complexity is regarded as a function of the textual difficulties that confront all men, not merely the mature writer who has become sensitive to the slightest textual quibble, then that fiction can also serve as a basis for sustaining the reader's own vitality. Nabokov, of course, would have it no other way. Above everything else, he would teach his admirers how to read—and, furthermore, how to handle their own texts.

3

Lolita: The Pursuit of Text

Not surprisingly, given the fact that both of them were written around the same time that Nabokov was writing *Pnin,* both *Lolita* and *Pale Fire* explore, but in much greater detail, the problem of textual ownership that surfaces in the last chapter of *Pnin.*[1] In *Pnin* this problem is never really resolved, for at the end of that novel the narrator is simply left in Waindell, preparing for his future position within the English department, while Pnin himself leaves town in pursuit of whatever "miracle" lies ahead. The conflict that has emerged between the two principals in the distant past, therefore, particularly when Pnin accuses the narrator of gratuitous inventions in his account of Pnin's life, never reaches that climactic moment common to most of Nabokov's late fiction—the moment in which one of the two parties involved assumes control of the narrative precisely on the grounds that he is determined to function as the maker of that text. To be sure, once Pnin leaves Waindell, the narrator probably feels comfortable enough in his possession of at least his account of Pnin's existence. After all, he spends the last chapter detailing the nature of his credentials as the originator of that account. In the end, nevertheless, if only because Pnin simply flees the scene, the narrator possesses his version of Pnin's existence largely by default. While Pnin has years ago challenged the narrator's authority to interpret the character of his—Pnin's—experience, finally he fails to press his case against this narrator-inventor-author whom he feels has made such a travesty of his experience. In *Lolita* and *Pale Fire* Nabokov rectifies this failure, for in both these novels the character whose experience the narrator has created actually reverses Pnin's retreat and turns the tables on the narrator himself. The consequence is that both novels become radical explorations of that problem of textual ownership which so many readers of *Pnin* have glossed over.

In general, of course, readers of *Lolita,* unaware of Nabokov's deep interest in the problem of textual ownership, have regarded Humbert

Humbert as the dominant, if somewhat bizarre, force in the text of the novel. Obviously there is good reason for such a response, especially in light of the fact that in this century there has occurred the complete collapse of stable psychological and philosophical models with which one can confidently organize one's experience. There is always in Nabokov's English novels a sense in which narrators and characters have difficulty enclosing the fields of their experience, and to the extent that Humbert's strange narrative seems to originate in the confusions of his feelings, his madness may appear as all too typical for an age of epistemological uncertainty. There is, moreover, the assessment of Humbert himself, who, after he has been arrested and has begun his most serious effort to sift the past, recognizes that there is no means for stabilizing the textual character of his past conduct. In the very process of analyzing the deeds and the intentions of the past, in fact, he discovers that he must surrender himself to "a sort of retrospective imagination which feeds the analytic faculty with boundless alternatives and which causes each visualized route to fork and re-fork without end in the maddeningly complex prospect of my past" (*L,* 15).[2] Even in retrospect Humbert cannot categorize the nature of his experience with Lolita. When he first happens upon her, he appears to have gained a vision of uncommon rapture, one that completely organizes his experience, but by the end of his relationship with her it is clear that this vision, too, has succumbed to the textless confusion that seems the mark of the twentieth century. In this chapter, nevertheless, I want to explore another possibility—that Humbert's confusion is not so much a function of twentieth-century epistemological difficulties (although they play a part) as it is a failure to maintain the authorial relationship to the text of his experience that he has initiated long before he meets up with Lolita. This failure, as shall become evident, is in turn bound up with Humbert's relationship with Quilty.

At the beginning of his relationship with Lolita, Humbert seems to be fully aware of the realm where all his best experience takes place. When he is enjoying his first, "innocent" climax while Lolita is sitting in his lap, for example, he certainly feels a physical reaction, but as he continues to babble away with words unleashed from any strict context ("barmen, alarmin', my charmin', my carmen, ahmen, ahahamen"), he knows that he is enjoying the prolonged glow of release within the province of the imagination—where he has "safely solipsized" (*L,* 62) Lolita. In a genuine sense Lolita is not involved in the situation at all. As Humbert himself realizes a few moments into the aftermath, what he had enjoyed was not Lolita herself, but his own creation of her: "another fanciful Lolita—perhaps, more real than Lolita; overlapping, encasing her; floating between me and her, and having no will, no consciousness—indeed, no life of her own" (*L*, 64). This Humbert is the man, it must be remembered, who regales Charlotte and Lolita with his stories about an expedition into arctic Canada, upon which he had served as the "recorder of psychic reactions." When it came time to submit his records for the expedition, he concocted "a perfectly spurious and very racy report" (*L*, 36) that was subsequently even published. Then, while recovering from a "bout with insanity" following the expedition, he initiated a complex game with his psychiatrists (he invented dreams and fake "primal scenes") that provided him with endless enjoyment. This Humbert is accustomed to imaginative play. Even in Lolita's absence at Camp Q. he does not find it at all difficult to keep his image of her beauty very much alive. To be sure, when he picks her up from the camp following Charlotte's death, he will be struck by the impression that Lolita's face is not as pretty as the mental image he has nourished for the month of their separation, but that fact only reinforces what he already knows—that it is the imagination that provides him with his greatest delight. Like the resourceful author, Humbert inhabits the fields of imaginative play, and thus when he begins his journey with Lolita to the Briceland hotel, it is hardly surprising that he then regards himself as having achieved that "ineffable" existence which he himself had "willed into being" (*L*, 115). The key phrase here is "willed into being," for it implies that Humbert recognizes his own responsibility for his acts of creation. He is shrewd enough, at least when contrasted to a drudge like Charlotte, to realize that there are finally "only words to play with" (*L*, 34), and with the freedom of mind that generally attends such a realization he manages to avoid that "wrought-iron world of criss-cross cause and effect" (*L*, 23) which, in less original minds, tends to suppress the vitality commonly associated with Nabokov's privileged characters.

What seems to underlie Humbert's vitality of imagination, then, is his awareness of the processes whereby words create their ephemeral and finally insufficient webs of significance amid the rapid succession of everyday events.[3] Humbert does not inhabit a "real" world, i.e., a world in which "reality" has achieved a stable and reliable character, and without such a world he is forever reduced to having to manufacture and sustain an identity for every moment of being. It is for this reason, I think, that as the "author" of his own experience he finds himself so attracted to the idea or the state of immaturity, which clearly parallels his strong sense of personal immaturity and tentativeness in a world that resists final realizations. Late in the novel, shortly before receiving Lolita's letter from Coalmont, and while thinking about peeping at nymphets through his window, Humbert even recognizes that his interest in the state of immaturity "lies not so much in the limpidity of pure young forbidden fairy child beauty as in the security of a situation where infinite perfections fill the gap between the little given and the great promised—the great rosegray never-to-be-had" (*L,* 266). This passage is particularly interesting because of its contradiction in terms. In the process of celebrating the idea of immaturity, Humbert identifies the "gap between the little given and the great promised" as the source of perfection. In actuality, however, because the process of immaturity is relentless, there is no stable moment of true perfection. Each stage of immaturity merely emerges from the previous and blurs into the succeeding; and thus, while each of these moments might be regarded as a perfection in itself, the process whereby the succeeding moment helps complete what was insufficient a moment before tends to resist any genuine sense of perfection. If Humbert is interested, as I think he is, in the process of immaturity on account of its dynamic, always-changing character, then one must question his determined pursuit of a perfection where it is theoretically impossible.[4]

The contradiction in Humbert's position fully emerges in his pursuit of girls who are yet in the stage of pubescence. While he at times seems to recognize that the perfection of a final, stable (and thus mature) form of beauty is impossible, at other times he also seems to think that the perfection within the subtle changes that attend the metamorphosis associated with pubescence, a perfection that is paradoxically fluid and unstable, is yet available to an imagination such as his own. With only words to play with, and with nothing real, i.e., stable, to pin those words on, Humbert may have a point—he can create whatever perfections he desires. In the sense, however, that Humbert cannot dominate and control the processes of nature, which never grant the moment of perfection or of complete realization, he opens himself to the profound disappointment of finally recognizing that he cannot even achieve the limited perfections of immaturity. With his heavy investment in the life of the imagination, Humbert the author unquestionably escapes the boundaries that limit the more pedestrian lives about him.[5] For a long time he thrives upon the pursuit of pubescence and thus, much like the narrator of *Look at the Harlequins!,* he might even be said to have an average age of thirteen throughout his adult life. Finally, nevertheless, the pursuit of perfection in pubescence, because it involves a fundamental contradiction, and because it requires a crucial modification in his authorial stance, will bring him to his knees.

Throughout his English fiction Nabokov generally associates immaturity with fancy, with the vitality of change—and maturity with logic, with stability and a consciousness of boundaries that limit and even squelch the flights of imagination. Not surprisingly, therefore, it is when Humbert is himself only a "faunlet" (L, 19) that his lifelong interest in the perfections of pubescence begins. While his elders at that stage of his development worry about the propriety of two youngsters of the opposite sex being alone together, the young Humbert savors the delight that underlies his attraction to the pubescent Annabel. At that point, to be sure, he may not yet be entirely at home in the wide fields of imaginative play, but if in the aftermath of that brief relationship with Annabel he has already begun to reckon with the fact that he shall never possess a girl to the extent that he has desired Annabel, then there may be some warrant for arguing that Humbert has already achieved a rather sophisticated understanding of his relationships with others. The extent to which Humbert perceives the problem of possession in his experience with Annabel is, however, not entirely clear. What is certain is that at some point, perhaps after a succession of relationships (even marriage), Humbert's interest in girls takes a radical shift: instead of pursuing the girl herself (a pursuit that is impossible), he focuses his attention only on the image of the girl, particularly upon those subtle transformations which occur in "the gap between the little given and the great promised." For Humbert it is the pubescence in young girls that finally awakens and captures his deepest flights of fancy—not the girl herself. When Humbert recites his definition of pubescence, with a precision that calls attention to itself, the character of this interest, I think, fully emerges: "Between the age limits of nine and fourteen there occur maidens who, to certain bewitched travelers . . . reveal their true nature which is not human, but nymphic (that is, demoniac)" (L, 18). Such a definition suggests that, given the impossibility of possessing the perfection of beauty, a shrewd Humbert has simply elected to concentrate his attention upon that stage in young girls' lives in which they know the most physical (and emotional) change. By focusing upon that stage he shall at least maintain some contact, in his own life, with that relentless pattern of change which prevents any text of experience from gaining the illusion of sufficiency and security, but which at the same time introduces into that text an intensity that is its own perfection. In his view, presumably, such contact will at least maintain his own vitality of mind.

The big question of Humbert's experience, then, is whether he can maintain the act of play that is predicated upon, even required by, this interest in a pubescence that he shall never be able to dominate or control. What is crucial, here, is his attitude—whether or not he can, like the artist, suspend himself almost continuously in an unraveling of experience that possesses no content or objective other than observing the stages of pubescence. A little beyond the midpoint of the novel Humbert admonishes his readers in a manner that fully addresses this crucial matter of attitude: "I now warn the reader not to mock me and my mental daze. It is easy for him and me to decipher *now* a past destiny; but a destiny in the making is, believe me, not one of those honest mystery stories where all you have to do is keep an eye on the clues" (*L*, 212–13). While the context of this passage is generally focused upon recovering Humbert's attitude following his imprisonment for the murder of Quilty, the passage itself captures the plotless character of Humbert's life before the murder. In fact, with its emphasis upon a "destiny in the making," not made, the passage strongly parallels John Shade's view of the artist's need for suspension in *Pale Fire*. Shade, near the end of his poem, cites texture (or "combinational delight") rather than text as the goal of his art. In his view there is no final text available to any man, and thus for him text emerges only as the artist plays with the texture— especially the everyday texture—of his experience. Whether it is Shade's emphasis upon texture or Humbert's upon immaturity, the important consideration is the artist's appreciation of *process*. As long as Humbert recognizes the inadequate character of all the texts of experi- ence and, with his imagination unleashed, playfully suspends himself in his delight over the stages of pubescence, he enjoys that stature of artistry which lies at the heart of Nabokov's fiction. Despite his some- times genuine sophistication of attitude, however, each time Humbert comes into contact with pubescence, he almost immediately violates the artist's stance and tries to possess the girl.[6] With Lolita, largely because he has become her guardian, this attempt becomes especially evident, and again the contradiction, which I earlier defined as Humbert's search for perfection in a process that knows no perfection, defines his experi- ence. Humbert cannot possess a girl in pubescence, but he does a good job of trying—first in Briceland and then many times thereafter. At one point he will even confess to a desire to turn Lolita inside out and to press his "voracious lips to her young matrix, her unknown heart, her nacreous liver, the sea-grapes of her lungs, her comely twin kidneys" (*L*, 167). Such a passage demonstrates how fully Humbert is involved in the contradiction between suspension of himself and domination of the other, and finally the effects of this contradiction, as might be expected, are quite horrible.

The principal consequence is that Humbert must increasingly give up the imaginative ground that is the source of his genius. Like her mother before her, Lolita is an absolutely conventional girl who has picked up the majority of her attitudes from movie magazines and schoolmates and who has, therefore, accepted the social context of her experience as quite "real." She is so conventional, in fact, that from the beginning of their life together following the stay in Briceland Humbert hardly seems to enjoy much chance of bringing her to a new ground of perception and understanding. Already when he tries to maintain the arbitrary quality that defines the unpredictable crisscrossing of their first American journey, for example, he soon discovers that Lolita requires a sense of destination that goes against the principle of suspension in life's uncertainties. In order to keep Lolita happy on this journey Humbert actually finds that he must provide each day with "a shaping and sustaining purpose" (L, 153), and while he can exercise some ingenuity in developing such a provision, eventually such a necessity must accelerate that contamination of Humbert's spirit which may have already begun with his marriage to Lolita's mother. Indeed, the more that Humbert tries to meet Lolita on her terms the more the reader should anticipate the failure of that process of suspension which is Humbert the author's principal genius. By the time Humbert moves to Beardsley, of course, such suspension is clearly a matter of the past.

In Beardsley all of Humbert's fears concerning discovery and reprisal during the first American trip result in his deliberate pursuit of propriety. There, in fact, he completely commits himself to the development for himself of "a label, a background, and a simulacrum" (L, 177) that might secure him against the suspicions of others. Even though he continues to feel contempt for the mindlessness of a conventional Miss Pratt, he himself reviews each concluded day by checking the conduct of that day against what is expected of him. Despite his intentions, consequently, the time that he spends in Beardsley buries whatever lingering spirit he yet possesses. Instead of renewing the fields of his imaginative play in Beardsley or instead, perhaps, of pursuing even more striking fields, he gets increasingly bogged down in trying to establish the credibility of his pose as a father—and finally his sources of vitality simply dry up. At the very moment that Humbert, much in the fashion of the editor rather than the author, draws up for Lolita "a list under 'absolutely forbidden' and another under 'reluctantly allowed' " (L, 188), there can be no more doubt that he has completely violated the nature of his original interest and suspension in the processes of pubescence. The Humbert who is bent upon establishing propriety for himself and Lolita, a propriety that severely delimits (and ultimately destroys) the character of their relationship, may not degenerate into the conventionality of a Miss Pratt, but he has fully profaned the perspective that had originally separated him from the drudges of human experience. In the terms established in *Transparent Things*, he is now the editor rather than the author of his experience.

Ironically, at the very time that Humbert is losing ground to social considerations, Lolita's sophistication concerning the nature of her experience increases. Although there have appeared previous suggestions (Lolita's unexplained absences in Beardsley) of such a reversal, the situation that fully dramatizes its occurrence is Lolita's participation in Quilty's play, *The Enchanted Hunters.* In the role of Diana, Lolita falls under the spell of a vagabond poet (Quilty himself) and in the process gains her first significant opportunity for release from the web of Humbert's influence. With someone to pursue, who is at the same time interested in her, she immediately becomes more cagey and resourceful, certainly more determined to rule her own fate. Significantly, when Humbert the editor tries to pinpoint the authorship of the play, Lolita twice manages to disguise Quilty as a woman. Then, on the second American trip, it is she—not Humbert—who maps out a sequence of arrivals that matches up with Quilty's own cross-country tour. This new authority becomes even more evident when Lolita turns ill in Kasbeam. While she is removed to the hospital, Humbert himself suffers from the same fever in his hotel room—and, ominously, from hallucinations that he is losing control over her. Humbert has reason to be delirious, for on July 4, Independence Day, Lolita does effect her escape. For the Humbert who has increasingly concerned himself with propriety, with the editorial fixing of a relationship with Lolita, it is obviously a terrible blow. In a profound sense, one that underlies the whole conception of the novel, however, he gets exactly what he deserves. The Humbert who originally had been in touch with pubescence but who then tried to possess that pubescence even though he recognized the impossibility of such a pursuit has begged to be disappointed and outraged. The reader here dare not commiserate with him. He is a failed "author."

That is not to say that Lolita comes off better than Humbert. Although she removes herself to Quilty's arms and thus escapes Humbert's domination, she, too, finally fails to secure for herself that privileged position of artistry which Humbert himself had enjoyed early in the novel.[7] When Quilty wears down her freshness and enthusiasm with his strange sexual conduct, she merely finds herself in possession of a broken heart, and at that point, somewhat disillusioned, she even concludes that the world is "just one gag after another." And instead of gaining the marvelous ground of imagination that belongs to Nabokov's originals, who—like Pnin—turn disasters into riches, she rather quickly succumbs to the conventional habits of marriage and pregnancy. In light of her failure to achieve new ground, or at least ground that displays more originality, the crucial question in the latter part of the novel again centers on Humbert himself: does he recover the relationship to pubescence that had been his before he concentrated his attention upon Lolita? He does not. Already during the second American trip, which Lolita has orchestrated, Humbert the editor has shown strong signs of the disintegration that is to overtake him. Where he on the first trip only worried about propriety, on the second he becomes fully paranoid about the loss of the pubescent Lolita—a loss that he should know is inevitable but that he foolishly intends to prevent anyway, whatever the cost. When he becomes conscious of the protean presence of an Aztec Red convertible driven by a pursuer named Trapp, of course, his paranoia turns to hysteria. At one point a desperate Humbert tries to break the new pattern of fate that seems to have emerged by spending another gratuitous night at a motel named Chestnut Court, but for him there is no longer any easy relief. The relationship that he, the editor, has tried so hard to fix is rapidly dissolving, and finally, overwhelmed by the continued uncertainty about what is happening to him, he begins—not surprisingly—to rely for comfort on the gun that suddenly appears in his pocket. No longer suspended in the unraveling of pubescence, of imaginative vitality, this Humbert is only the shell of his former self. Hallucinations, the mania of persecution, paranoia—all build up to that moment when, confronted with the fact of Lolita's escape, Humbert despairs over the knowledge that Lolita is "so tantalizingly, so miserably unattainable and beloved on the very eve of a new era, when my alembics told me she should stop being a nymphet" (L, 241). The Humbert who was the artist knew how to play within the limits of pubescence. This Humbert, hysterical and bewildered over a loss that was inevitable, is neither artist nor gamer. He is, like Hugh Person, the editor who must be disappointed.

The fact that Humbert is now an editor is evident, thereafter, in his long trek in search of clues whereby he might locate Lolita and her presumed captor. What is so disturbing about such a trek is his failure to recognize not only that the nymphet whom he desires no longer exists, but also that such a pursuit again involves him in the stabilizing of a text that is inimical to his genius as an imaginative being. In his search for Lolita, to be sure, Humbert may seem to create a new texture of at least twenty different clues, but in this instance, because the objective of the search is so well defined from the outset, the texture achieves an ironic character and finally serves only to underscore the fact that Humbert has entirely separated himself from the original sources of his vitality. No longer suspended in the unraveling of experience, Humbert now tries to force the circumstances of his life to fit the configuration he desires. With his desperate search for Lolita, therefore, Humbert demonstrates only that he has lost all authority as an artist. At the point, in fact, that he suggests that Trapp has "succeeded in thoroughly enmeshing me and my thrashing anguish in his demoniacal game" (*L*, 251), it is clear that he shall never recover himself. Now the victim, the man who has begun to feel that he is "losing contact with reality" (*L*, 257), he has edged toward that madness in which the artist has lost the confidence in his own language and creations. As part of a poem Humbert eventually composes the following, rather telling lines: "I talk in a daze, I walk in a maze, / I cannot get out, said the starling" (*L*, 257). The Humbert who has earlier responded with enthusiasm to the verbal foundation that underlies all imaginative experience now has no sense at all of the glory—albeit the ephemeral glory—of words. Reduced to seeking plot and content in the circumstances of Lolita's disappearance, he no longer plays with the unpredictable textures of his experience. Instead, suspicious that others might know more about his circumstances than he himself does, he even considers whether the services of a hypnotist, who can weave a new pattern from Humbert's memories, might help him to discover the now long-lost Lolita. Humbert the artist, the man who had created his own imaginative worlds, has completely disappeared.

Ironically, however, after receiving the letter from Dolly Schiller, Humbert does discover the name of the man in the Aztec Red convertible and thus does believe that he has finally come to terms with his experience. Remembering the episode at Hourglass Lake in which Jean Farlow recounted a damaging story about Clare Quilty, Humbert even has the feeling that a number of strands from the past are weaving together: "Quietly the fusion took place, and everything fell into order, into the pattern of branches that I have woven throughout this memoir" (*L*, 274). And yet, even though Humbert still regards himself as the weaver here, in reality it is now Quilty's text that matters more. Humbert has committed himself, following Lolita's disappearance, to "logical recognition," to patterns that are consistent and comprehensible, but in the process he turns himself from the marvelous artificer into the victim of another man's text.[8] In a certain sense, as shall be more evident in a moment, Humbert may have always been the victim of Quilty's text, but to the extent that Quilty—as the ultimate source (besides Nabokov himself) of the narrative—has allowed Humbert an almost complete freedom to fashion the character of his own experience, Humbert must be accorded the stature of being an artist in his own right. Clearly Humbert is not to be easily reduced to the mere status of serving as a character in another man's fiction, but when he concludes that he is finally on the track of a text that has heretofore been hazy, and especially when he clutches the pistol that he now terms his "chum," he plays out a role—that of murderer—devoid of all subtlety and imagination and thus a role that originates in considerations external to himself.

It is at this point, I think, that the essential textual situation of *Lolita* becomes clear. Once Humbert commits himself to revenge and thus loses the play of mind that had been his, the reader faces the necessity of identifying the real source of the text—the source that can appreciate the subtle character of Humbert's failure with Lolita and of his subsequent madness. That source is Clare Quilty.[9] Through most of the novel Quilty may seem a rather marginal character. At the end he may appear, as many critics have argued, as the one character who is "clearly guilty." There is, however, another side to this Quilty, the side that is engaged in "clearly quilting." Late in the narrative, for example, Lolita informs Humbert that Quilty was a genius who saw "through everything and everybody" (*L*, 277). Then, when confronted with Humbert's gun, Quilty himself claims an uncommon stature of mind and of artistry; "My dear sir, . . . stop trifling with life and death. I am a playwright. I have written tragedies, comedies, fantasies. . . . I'm the author of fifty-two successful scenarios. I know all the ropes. Let me handle this" (*L*, 300). What is important about such comments is that they grant Quilty the supremacy over the text which, at least initially, the reader has assigned to Humbert. That Quilty is the source of the text becomes even more clear, however, when Humbert, having finally dispatched Quilty after a succession of shots (each of which seemed momentarily to give him more life), reaches the remarkable conclusion: "This, I said to myself, was the end of the ingenious play staged for me by Quilty" (*L*, 307). If earlier Humbert had worried about being trapped in the games of G. Trapp, now there is no question that he is bound up in the texts of Clare Quilty. Finally, then, at least in the light of this discussion, the principal question of this novel must revolve around Quilty's relationship to the narrative.

Given the fact that Quilty is a collaborator of Vivian Darkbloom (an anagram of Nabokov's name), the reader might be tempted to associate Quilty with Nabokov himself. There is, however, no getting around Lolita's appraisal that while Quilty is "a great guy in many respects," he is also "all drink and drugs" and "a complete freak in sex matters" (*L*, 278). Lolita never defines the nature of Quilty's sexual escapades, other than to refer to them as "weird, filthy, fancy," but given the pitch of her disgust the reader can conclude, I think, that Quilty verges upon being one of the jaded who, having seen "through everything and everybody," no longer possesses a conventional (and usually sentimental) structure of values whereby he can maintain a comfortable relationship with the community. I have no intention of turning Quilty into Nabokov (or vice versa), but in terms of imaginative experience there is a profound sense in which both Quilty and Nabokov inhabit the same ground: both of them generally exist outside the pale of social coherence, and content themselves with playing out the games that have captured their fancy. When Quilty responds to Humbert's threats by alluding to the urbane wisdom of experience that the two of them presumably hold in common, the comment might easily be taken to include Nabokov himself: "This pistol-packing farce is becoming a frightful nuisance. We are men of the world, in everything—sex, free verse, marksmanship. If you bear me a grudge, I am ready to make unusual amends" (*L*, 303). Like Nabokov in all his fiction, Quilty is very adroit at playing with the various textures of human experience, especially in moments of crisis. For him human experience even sets up as a test of one's ability to play—whether one can suspend oneself in the confusion and uncertainty common to virtually every context of human activity. In this novel the best example of Quilty's own play resides in the very situation that prompts the creation of this text ultimately called *Lolita*.

Here the crucial matter of play as form requires some consideration. Late in the novel, when Humbert refers to the ingenious play staged by Quilty, the reader enjoys at least a glimpse of the possibility that the whole of the narrative in *Lolita* constitutes a "play" developed by a master playwright. When Quilty is at the Briceland hotel, apparently seeking material or inspiration for a new play, something—perhaps the appearance of a middle-aged man with his daughter—triggers his imagination, and at that point, remembering a girl aged ten whom he has pulled onto his lap, he creates—if only in his own mind—an unbelievably rich and suggestive scenario of the relationship between Humbert and Lolita that serves as a superior, i.e., more developed, version of the play that Lolita herself rehearses while at Beardsley. In these terms, it is true, Humbert becomes little more than an extension of Quilty's imagination. In light of the peculiar, dreamlike logic that permeates this novel (and all of Nabokov's fiction), however, such an appraisal of Humbert's status is hardly extraordinary. Indeed, just as Lolita herself is largely an extension of Humbert's imagination (at least early in the novel), so there is a profound sense in which Humbert must be seen as an extension of Quilty's imaginative play. In fact, because Humbert's narrative of pubescence depends for its vitality upon Humbert's continuous act of suspension, the reader might even conclude that the vitality of *Lolita* as a novel finally depends upon Quilty's ability to surrender to those processes which he has unleashed by instituting the text in Briceland. In the end, of course, Quilty enjoys much more success in this matter of suspension than does Humbert. Whereas Humbert late in the novel becomes increasingly editorial and tries to establish a coherent account of his relationship with Lolita (after his arrest for the murder of Quilty he even devotes himself to the writing of a detailed memoir), Quilty is able to delight in the play and the illogic that attaches to the vitality of his ruminations. Like the plot of the play he writes, which hinges upon a girl hypnotizing a number of lost hunters and then falling herself "under the spell of a vagabond poet" (L, 202), Quilty allows himself to fall under the spell, the imaginative power, of his own words. In Beardsley and beyond Humbert has tried to dominate words in order to fix the character of his experience and ends up living in the past. Quilty, however, manages to maintain the act of suspension to the end and thus remains in the present. Indeed, one measure of Quilty's success is the fact that he does not, unlike Humbert, completely overwhelm the narrative with his own appearance. Another measure is the fact that it is he, not Humbert, who dies at the end of the novel.

In a certain sense the relationship between Quilty and Humbert merely reflects the course of any imaginative undertaking. For a long time the Quilty who is intrigued by the girl who has sat on his lap or who has acted in his play can invest heavily in his "realizations" of a surrogate Humbert. Just as Humbert knows the pleasure of deep imaginative play and intensity during his association with a girl in the early months of pubescence, so Quilty knows the initial joy of realizing a new text. As Quilty extends his realization of the relationship between Lolita and his surrogate, however, Quilty's act of projection loses some of its force. In other words, the projection of himself into Humbert achieves a character of its own that suddenly seems to exclude its original maker—Quilty himself. At that point, not surprisingly, the struggle for the possession of the text turns into a somewhat sordid exploitation of the original object of Quilty's desire, Lolita herself. The Humbert who becomes increasingly more desperate over Lolita's repeated resistance to his attentions eventually reduces her to the most shameful depravities as he strives, by manipulation, to keep her at the original stage of pubescence. Then Quilty, who has in turn become impatient with Humbert's domination of Lolita, decides to intrude more definitively into the narrative and to seduce Lolita for himself. In these circumstances Lolita herself seems to enjoy no real hope of achieving for herself that life of imaginative intensity which is at the heart of Nabokov's English fiction. Because she has been exploited rather than encouraged, she cannot face up to the unstable and ephemeral quality of imaginative experience and thus elects to get married and to embrace the well-defined boundaries of life with Richard Schiller. What happens to

Humbert and to Quilty following her departure, however, is far more interesting.

I am, of course, alluding to that curious moment of reckoning, of confrontation, between Humbert and Quilty at the end of the novel. If it is true that Humbert is merely the projection of Quilty, such a moment may smack of the incredible, but in the sense that the texts of the past linger into the present, Humbert does possess some ground for confronting this Quilty who has given him everything yet, in the end, nothing at all. For Quilty, it must be realized, the text has already played itself out with Lolita's escape first from Humbert and then from himself. As a writer of fifty-two scenarios (and thus accustomed to the inevitability of texts having been played out), Quilty hardly remarks at the situation. For him the experience with Lolita merely constitutes another failed dream—another insufficient attempt to realize a desire beyond human grasp. Humbert, however, less familiar with the managing of personal scenarios (despite his background in literature), cannot accept so easily the demise of a cherished text. Because he has, regardless of previous disappointments, established his relationship with Lolita as the primary text of his experience, his pursuit of the object of all his attentions remains strong long after Quilty has already played out the original text. In fact, once his loss of Lolita becomes irrevocable even in his own eyes, Humbert commits himself to a plan of revenge that is tantamount to the creature (character) rebelling against the creator (author). He may not yet be aware of the fact that Quilty has initiated the whole game, not merely the moment of Lolita's disaffection, but he is the character who is demanding that his text be given its due—even after its author has largely dismissed it. That creature and creator, Humbert and Quilty, are so involved with each other becomes very clear, I think, rather early in the scene of their confrontation. At the point when Quilty momentarily dislodges Humbert's gun, the two men become entangled in a rather telling manner. Humbert will later narrate, "I felt suffocated as he rolled over me. I rolled over him. We rolled over me. They rolled over him. We rolled over us" (*L*, 301). Here the usual distinction between creature and creator loses all substance, and in light of this loss the confrontation between the two men must be regarded as a struggle for possession of what little remains of the text.

What is interesting about the end is that the creator allows the creature to possess the text. For a time Quilty does seem to thwart Humbert's intentions, first by dislodging the gun, then by displaying tremendous bursts of energy despite having been shot, and finally by appearing one more time on the landing after it would appear that he cannot possess any more life. Humbert does, however, manage to force upon Quilty the text of revenge that he, the creature, has brought with him. Indeed, when Humbert compels him to read the sentence of doom that he—Humbert—has written for him, Quilty loses any vestige of privileged authority that may yet linger in the scene. By reading the sentence, Quilty virtually allows Humbert to reverse their roles and to manufacture a textual situation in which Quilty himself appears merely as a character. What is happening here, however, is that Quilty—who, like Nabokov, is always the artist—is simply acknowledging that, once the original text (which has its analogue in *The Enchanted Hunters*) has played itself out, he can no longer dominate its characters. Instead of playing the text out further and thus trying to maintain control indefinitely, he lets the text stand—in a version that hardly contains all that he had hoped to realize, but still a version that shall now haunt him for the rest of his days. It is in this sense of haunting, perhaps, that Humbert now gains the upper hand and kills—for the rest of Quilty's life—his creator. The realized text becomes a boundary, a condition, maybe even a crime against its originator's future. Quilty probably does not die, as the text implies, but he also does not escape the past. His creatures will stalk him to the end.[10]

Humbert's domination of Quilty toward the end of *Lolita* does not argue, of course, that he becomes another Quilty, an artist in his own right. Because Humbert does not—at the end—possess the degree of imaginative play that is the source of Quilty's genius, such a development is impossible. He may gain his revenge, and while writing his memoirs he may even speak in terms of "the melancholy and very local palliative of articulate art" (*L*, 258) or "the refuge of art" (*L*, 281), but finally, instead of always moving ahead to new texts and visions (as does Quilty), he allows himself to become trapped in the old text of his relationship with Lolita. He lacks the courage to be a true artist. Humbert appears to have the last word in the novel, but it is Quilty who is the supreme artist capable of extending Nabokov's world of texture and artifice.

4

Pale Fire: The Reader's Possession of the Text

If *Lolita* contrasts the two very different arts of Clare Quilty and Humbert Humbert, *Pale Fire* expands upon the contrast by focusing upon the divergent texts of John Shade and Charles Kinbote. In *Lolita* Nabokov had generally addressed the problem, indeed the impossibility, of sustaining the imagination within the boundaries of one concrete text. In that novel, however, because Humbert's determined pursuit of text completely overwhelms Quilty's more artistic creation of texts, most readers never recognize the terrible irony that attaches to Humbert's fixing of his relationship with Lolita and that finally turns Quilty's strange creations into the achievement of supreme art. With *Pale Fire* and Nabokov's more careful balancing of texts between Shade and Kinbote, this failure among readers largely disappears. In light of the fact, nevertheless, that the contrast between the editorial identification of text and the authorial play with texture, which had surfaced in the different arts of Humbert and Quilty, now becomes the fundamental key to approaching the wonderful achievement of *Pale Fire*, the reader must anticipate the advent of new irony—in this case, an irony that is actually focused upon the reader himself.

Whereas Quilty had largely hidden himself in his text, in an effort to allow Humbert as much freedom to engage in the process of text-making as possible, John Shade the poet takes great care to present both himself and the character of his experience in his poem of 999 lines. What is immediately striking about this fact is that such blatant self-presentation goes against the grain of Nabokov's usual narrative strategies—the strategies in which he creates such a complicated web of narrative relationships that the question of textual ownership serves from beginning to end as the major problem of the narrative. In the sense that Kinbote's commentary sabotages Shade's poem and thus enormously complicates the reading of the novel, *Pale Fire* as a whole may still possess such a strategy. In the poem itself, however, Shade not only seems to take genuine delight in rehearsing his life as boy and man, husband and father, poet and critic, but he also displays no hesitation or uncertainty about his possession of the text. Because his ownership—like Humbert's—is so obvious, in fact, one must, especially in light of the irony that surrounds Humbert's fixing of text, become somewhat skeptical about the character of Shade's verse. Clearly its rather straightforward, chronological autobiography shows little awareness of the more experimental tendencies in the poetry of recent decades. Shade is an accomplished artist, but Charles Kinbote's defense of his artistry is hardly enough to establish his genius. What is needed, here, is an appreciation of the ironic cast of Shade's art.

By presenting his poem in rhymed Popian couplets Shade seems to indicate from the outset how little he is involved in the formal experimentation of contemporary poetry. More than that, by turning his poem into a rather blatant thematic discussion of major concerns from his past, he captures that seriocomic quality of Pope which most readers connect with a literature of traditional content orientation. Cantos 2 and 3, for example, as examinations of his daughter's bitter life before suicide and of his subsequent quest into the nature of the afterlife, present the kind of topical analysis that, largely reflective in character, tends toward the containment of a vision of experience. If this poem is at all representative of his art, therefore, Shade has completely divorced himself from the recent tendency to interrupt the text, to fracture and defeat its content—in general, to open up the structure of the text in an effort to reflect, not a vision of experience, but the difficulties of formulating a perspective of substance. The text that calls into question the very process of assembling a text (the self-reflexive text in much recent criticism) has emerged as a dominant tendency in twentieth-century art and literature, but John Shade seems to have scrupulously avoided its influence. What is apparent in Shade's technique and content, nevertheless, is not the point. There is more to this poet than this superficial reliance upon traditional models of verse.

In canto 2 Shade does for a moment face up to the problems underlying the creation of vision when he acknowledges that *"Life is a message scribbled in the dark"* by some anonymous hand (11. 235–36)[1] or that man's problem "isn't that we dream too wild a dream" but that "we do not make [that dream] seem / Sufficiently unlikely" (11. 227–29). In the sense that Shade is here profoundly aware of the arbitrariness of imagination that lies at the heart of any text of experience, he does reveal some of that cast of mind which generally characterizes the narrative handling within all of Nabokov's English novels. It is only at the end of canto 3, however, when Shade, having discussed his tenure as a lecturer at the I.P.H., subjects the confirmation of his vision of a fountain[2] in the hereafter to the irony of a misprint—it is only then that the reader enjoys a full look at the real genius of this artist who has initially seemed so superficial. The woman who has been reported to have seen in the moment of "death" a fountain has actually seen a mountain, and in light of this discrepancy, now brought up short against the notion that his pursuit of a "content" (or vision) of the hereafter has turned into a ludicrous preoccupation, Shade engages himself in a reconsideration of his relationship to his texts. In a manner that recalls Quilty's handling of text in *Lolita,* Shade now suggests:

> But all at once it dawned on me that *this*
> Was the real point, the contrapuntal theme;
> Just this: not text, but texture; not the dream
> But topsy-turvical coincidence,
> Not flimsy nonsense, but a web of sense.
> Yes! It sufficed that I in life could find
> Some kind of link-and-bobolink, some kind
> Of correlated pattern in the game,
> Plexed artistry, and something of the same
> Pleasure in it as they who played it found.
>
> (Ll. 806-15)

Such a passage, as a number of critics have already commented, goes a long way toward establishing Shade's credentials as the equal of Nabokov's other clever narrators. Because the passage reveals such a strong commitment to an art of texture rather than of text, it has virtually become the *locus classicus* within the novels themselves for a statement about the general character of Nabokov's art. The matter of Shade's stature as an artist within his own poem to the side for a moment, however, there are also many passages in Kinbote's commentary that reinforce this notion of Shade's genius.

As Kinbote on several occasions points out, Shade is a poet who has definite ideas about what literature should be and what form literary instruction should take. Kinbote quotes, for example, one of the variant readings to Shade's poem in which the poet argues that the salvation of poetry and, by implication, of all literature and art lies in the poet's actual divorcing of himself from the dull presentation of topic and theme and his recovery of fancy:

> England where poets flew the highest, now
> Wants them to plod and Pegasus to plough;
> Now the prosemongers of the Grubby Group,

> The Message Man, the owlish Nincompoop
> And all the Social Novels of our age
> Leave but a pinch of coal dust on the page.
>
> (*PF*, 270)

Despite his own use of Popian techniques with their heavy reliance upon matters of content, Shade is here clearly determined to separate the present practice of poetry from limited rules of content and meaning. By the same token, when he gives his advice concerning the teaching, say, of Shakespeare, he encourages teachers to "dismiss ideas, and social background, and train the freshman to shiver, to get drunk on the poetry of *Hamlet* or *Lear*, to read with his spine and not with his skull" (*PF*, 155). As a teacher himself, he despises students who read with an eye "for symbols" or who when writing about poetry and poets use such terms as "simple" and "sincere" in a laudatory sense (*PF*, 156). The Shade who in his own poetry is committed to imaginative texture rather than to literal text may not turn himself into a messiah in the classroom, but he obviously resents the tendency to reduce instruction to a matter of content.

Beyond the references to Shade's literary attitudes, Kinbote also alludes frequently to Shade's rambles in nature. According to Kinbote's notes, in fact, there are at least nine sunset rambles in June and two in July. On these walks, much to the dismay of a Kinbote interested in establishing the literal text of Zembla, Shade "never tired of illustrating . . . the extraordinary blend of Canadian Zone and Austral Zone. . . . At our altitude of about 1,500 feet northern species of birds, insects and plants commingled with southern representatives" (*PF*, 169). While Kinbote is at best conscious only of such rudimentary distinctions as that between moths and butterflies—and even then with little precision—it is evident on these walks that Shade has garnered, with the help of a rather eccentric farmer named Paul Hentzner, an impressive array of knowledge about his surroundings. Much in the manner of his parents, who were expert ornithologists, he has thoroughly involved himself in the idiosyncrasies of plant and animal life indigenous to the area and thus finds himself comfortable in his surroundings in a way that is unavailable to most men. In addition to making him more at home in the wide universe, this interest in nature seems to prevent Shade from becoming trapped within a narrow pursuit of content. Just as he responds to the magnificent texture of nature, so he insists, in the writing of an autobiographical poem, on playing with the curious texture of his experiences rather than defining their precise significance. Shade's imaginative world, rooted in his many interests, is capacious, and in view of its breadth and range the reader must anticipate that Shade's poem will ultimately justify his genius.

Back to the poem itself, then, the reader who has become aware of Shade's profound contact with the various textures of his experience has even more reason to expect the poem to justify its maker's artistic stature. Shade is indeed in touch with the crucial problems of twentieth-century literature, for already at the beginning of the very first canto he establishes the problem of perception as the touchstone for his foray into the circumstances of Hazel's death and his reaction to it. When he opens the poem with a presentation of his room reflected in the window glass overlooking a scene of snow—a "crystal land" (1. 12)—the reader confronts immediately an ambiguous situation (the glass both as transparent mediator and as reflector) that must call into question the nature of perception itself. In that situation Shade even considers the possibility of "retaking the falling snow": in the process of taking another "picture" of the scene a new configuration might emerge. As if all these hints of perceptual instability were not enough, he then wonders why his present perception of his front porch from Lake Road does not match up with his remembered perception years ago. Much like his Aunt Maud, who was "a poet and a painter with a taste/For realistic objects interlaced/With grotesque growths and images of doom" (11. 87–89), Shade here emerges as a poet whose appreciation for the status of objects and things is tempered by his awareness of the limits of perception.[3] Indeed, while "the regular vulgarian . . . [may see] the Milky Way/Only when making water" (11. 125–27), Shade, the poet in intimate contact with nature, recognizes that he is "most artistically caged" (1. 114) between an "infinite foretime" and an "infinite aftertime," both of which qualify his sense of the present and actually prevent him from regarding that present as real. Caged as a man, he becomes the poet who deals in games.

Such a strong appreciation for the problems of perception ultimately has the effect of involving this poet in a very self-conscious development of his text. In canto 4, for example, which generally considers in mock-heroic fashion the possibility of "Man's life as commentary to abstruse/Unfinished poem" (11. 939–40), Shade discusses his own methods of composition and in the process turns the canto into a very sophisticated analysis of the problem of textual creation. In addition to identifying such circumstantial preferences as writing in the morning and at midsummer, he characterizes in fairly specific terms how, at least for him, the act of writing takes place. In a delightful, mock-heroic sequence he weaves the process of his shaving in the bath with his determination to "speak" as a poet. Consider, for instance, these lines:

> Now I shall speak of evil and despair
> As none has spoken. Five, six, seven, eight,
> Nine strokes are not enough. Ten. I palpate
> Through strawberry-and-cream the gory mess
> And find unchanged that patch of prickliness.
>
> (Ll. 902–6)

The crucial aspect of these lines is not their content but their tone. In the process of developing an equation between the haphazardness with which he shaves and that with which he "speaks," Shade tends to play down any need he might feel for achieving the finality of a brilliant pronouncement whereby he can presume to "own" a given text. Even when he again asserts, in l. 915, that "Now I shall speak . . .", as if he were about to dominate the text with his profundity, he immediately suspends his intention with a comment on the poet's delight in the "sudden image" that manages to make his "hairs all stand on end" as if "held up by Our Cream." Finally, near the end of his poem, he does deliver on his intention to "speak":

> Now I shall speak of evil as none has
> Spoken before. I loathe such things as jazz;
> The white-hosed moron torturing a black
> Bull, rayed with red; abstractist bric-a-brac;
> Primitivist folk-masks; progressive schools;
> Music in supermarkets; swimming pools;
> Brutes, bores, class-conscious Philistines, Freud, Marx,
> Fake thinkers, puffed-up poets, frauds and sharks.
>
> (Ll. 923–30)

In a peculiar sense, here, the poet does "speak" of evil and he does create a text of content, but by trying to list everything that belongs to his conception of this strange category, especially in only seven lines without subtle commentary, he virtually provides no text or analysis of evil at all. For this poet, the problems of perception destroy all reliable ground from which he might deliver a compelling commentary, and thus in his view the game of composition, the play with texture, becomes everything.

It is true that in the face of this lack of a firm ground for delivering a definitive commentary about evil Shade may merely have felt himself reduced, like many another recent artist, to the necessity of turning shaving or some other physical activity into the foundation of his art. At the same time, however, conscious of at least "two methods of composing"—one that "goes on solely in the poet's mind,/ A testing of *performing* words, while he/Is soaping a third time one leg" and the other that, "much more decorous," occurs when "He's in his study writing with a pen" (ll. 841–46, emphasis added)—the Shade of *Pale Fire* is aware of having invested his energies principally in the first of the two methods. Shade thrives on the method of word performance. In fact, it is only while shaving and dressing, while engaging in the daily activities of human existence, that he is able to humor those verbal and syntactical connections and permutations that delight his imagination: "Dressing in all the rooms, I rhyme and roam/Throughout the house with, in my fist, a comb/Or a shoehorn, which turns into the spoon/I eat my egg with" (ll. 941–44). For Shade this method of composition does not represent a reduction in poetic spirit. Such a method may tend to separate him from traditional theories of literary composition, which require that the literary text possess the privileged status of superior vision and thematic significance, but because he recognizes that no man today can contain within a text the fullness of his words and deeds, he has learned to indulge himself fully in the aesthetics of playing with and extending the peculiar qualities of his own vitality from day to day. Instead, then, of limiting his art to a matter of whether or not his texts enjoy the privileged stature of traditional literature, he accepts himself as poet on the shrewdly conceived ground that his perceptions and the transformation of those perceptions into linguistic statements that presume to be art are at least realizations of his personal games, which have become steadily more sophisticated over the years. Toward the end of the poem, in fact, when he establishes his poetry as the source of all his own understanding, he makes the game of "combinational delight," which provides the bridge between his imagination and the world about him, the basis for all his genuinely vital experience:

> I feel I understand
> Existence, or at least a minute part
> Of my existence, only through my art,
> In terms of combinational delight;
> And if my private universe scans right,
> So does the verse of galaxies divine
> Which I suspect is an iambic line.

(Ll. 970–76)

Like the passage at the end of the first canto, in which Shade alludes to the moment in boyhood when he has felt himself "distributed through space and time" (ll. 148–56) as if he were the basis of the very universe itself, this passage turns the poet himself, by virtue of his sensitivity to the processes of perception and language, into the foundation for any apprehension of the universe.[4] As his own foundation, to be sure, the poet must rely completely upon the games that he himself has constituted over the years, but in the face of this limitation he can at least content himself with the realization that a poetry based upon such games generates its own intensities—a fact that should distinguish his poetry from that of the pedestrian "realists" of the present.

If Shade is committed to his own games, however, why does he employ in his poem a fairly conventional prosody and, even more importantly, a conventional narrative structure? Whereas Nabokov's other narrators, when deprived of privileged ground from which to speak their minds, generally resort to complicated, artificial strategies in order to establish their narratives, Shade seems in *Pale Fire* to be in ready possession of a full and direct statement about both his life and the character of his art. The disparity between Shade's shrewd analysis of poetic theory in the fourth canto and his own use in the poem of rather conventional techniques almost points to his questionable stature as a poet. And yet, even though his poem approaches the character of a privileged text replete with meaning and significance, Shade himself knows that the text of *Pale Fire* merely represents his collection of that text which has emerged, over the course of his long life, in his spectacular play with texture.[5] Whereas other Nabokovian narrators such as Clare Quilty and the young Van Veen in *Ada* have had to explore the very difficult problems of establishing a text that presumes to be art, Shade releases his autobiographical poem as the text that has accumulated, in retrospect, as the realization of texture. It is true that the act of consciousness in the present does alter the character of the past, but in this novel and in the poem proper John Shade is allowed the luxury of a fairly stable sense of his past experience. The poem, as a result, becomes a delightful Nabokovian exercise in contradiction: despite the theoretical impossibility of achieving a text, particularly the text of a simple, conventional character and structure, this poet who has invested so heavily in "texturing" ends up, over the course of many years, with a certain configuration of experience that he even manages—much to the reader's surprise and delight—to contain in a traditional prosodical structure. The poem is what the reader might least expect of a Nabokovian artist, but in the sense that the poem as text is finally nothing other than "realized texture," it represents a wonderful play in Nabokovian irony.

Shade's work, nevertheless, is not merely the poem of 999 lines but the novel that includes, in addition to the poem, Charles Kinbote's foreword, his commentary, line 1000 in the poem, and even the index.

At first glance Kinbote may himself seem the author of the *apparatus criticus*.[6] After all, given his incredible ability to sustain his identity as Charles the Beloved while employed as a teacher-scholar, he might even be regarded as the ideal Nabokovian character—one who suspends himself in those complexities and contradictions of experience which finally result in the richness of text. A cursory response to Kinbote's perception of specific texts, in fact, tends only to support the conclusion that he is at least the equal of Shade in the matter of textual theory. At one point in the commentary, for example, while addressing what seems to him a deliberate but "ignoble" trickery in several of Eystein's portraits (Eystein sometimes questioned the nature of reality by inserting real material elsewhere imitated by paint), Kinbote observes that " 'reality' is neither the subject nor the object of true art which creates its own special reality" (*PF*, 130). The comment seems very urbane, and when taken together with his later comment on "the miracle of a few written signs being able to contain immortal imagery, involutions of thought, new worlds with live people, speaking, weeping, laughing" (*PF*, 289), there is strong reason to believe that Kinbote perceives as clearly as Shade himself the epistemological and ontological limitations that underlie any attempt to fashion an art by way of pigment or words. In the same breath of the second comment, however, Kinbote goes on to define himself as a "true artist" (a term that is, from Nabokov's perspective, laden with terribly ironic overtones): "I can do what only a true artist can do— pounce upon the forgotten butterfly of revelation, wean myself abruptly from the habit of things, see the web of the world, and the warp and the weft of that web" (*PF*, 289). What is interesting about this comment is that Kinbote actually believes that he can approach the "web" and even "the warp and the weft of that web"—a notion that is, of course, tantamount to believing that he can possess *the text* that underlies and gives substance to the character of the universe, i.e., the text that defines him as Charles the Beloved. Such a belief, however, reflects only Kinbote's rather unimaginative faith in God and his foolish awaiting of the confirmation of a divinely inspired text in which he emerges as king.

The fact of the matter is that Kinbote, like all men, inhabits not the Zembla in which he is king but the Zembla that is most noted for its mirrors and reflections. Kinbote may want to be the king, but because he has no experience in kingship, he can only conceive of Zembla in terms of the literary clichés with which he is familiar. Despite his cagey hints and references to himself as Charles the Beloved, Zembla finally represents only the projection (or the mirror reflection) of his clichéd self into a world beyond his grasp. To be sure, in that world of Zembla, where language according to the great Conmal was "the tongue of the mirror"

(*PF*, 242), Kinbote does play out the drama that is dear to his heart and for a time even seems to enjoy some sense of self-realization. Because Zembla exists only as a mirror world, however, he eventually becomes the victim of the very dream-text that he regards as so crucial to his well-being. Initially he may merely try to fix his credentials as the displaced king whom the Shadows are so relentlessly pursuing, but while he thus manages to explain to his satisfaction his present tenure as a teacher and also his increasing sense of paranoia, the details of his dream-text are not so easily established. Given the extraordinary lengths to which he must resort in order to play out the plot of regicide, in fact, even he must gradually have developed some awareness of the fact that what began as a dream has ended up consuming all of his energy. With Kinbote the solipsistic madness that underlies all of Nabokov's English fiction turns to horror, for the more determinedly he pursues the specifics of the cherished dream-text, the more he becomes the victim of his own limitations of mind and imagination. Despite the apparent richness of imagination that emerges in the intricacies of his commentary, he remains a one-dimensional man who knows little of that profound texturing of experience which is at the heart of Shade's genius. His one significant hope is that he can, by manipulating the great Shade, achieve the realization of his dream-text in one of Shade's poems. For him such realization would be the consummation devoutly to be wished.

Kinbote's expectation that Shade's poem will reflect, not Shade's world of experience, but Kinbote's own Zemblan world of kingship, is, of course, mad. Like the solipsist who does not reckon in any appreciable manner with the inherent limitations of his perspective, Kinbote throughout the novel remains fully trapped within the vision of significance that has, over the years of his academic career, become the principal source of his joy and consolation. For him the vision of Zembla, of himself as king, has turned into the only reality worth talking about,[7] and he fully expects Shade to share that view. The discovery, therefore, that Shade has written "an autobiographical, eminently Appalachian, rather old-fashioned narrative in a neo-Popian prosodic style" (*PF*, 296), yet completely void of Kinbote's Zemblan "magic," momentarily jolts him, and in the sudden surge of self-doubt there is even a chance that he enjoys a glimmer of his own folly and insignificance. After the momentary loss of composure, however, this one-dimensional scholar, without at all recognizing the character of his new manipulations, immediately commits himself to an exorcising of Shade's poem. Rationalizing that in his rambles with Shade he may have failed to impress upon the poet the significance of the Zemblan material, he, now that he possesses the poem himself (he assumes full control over the editing of the poem following Shade's death), forces the poem into that textual configuration which he has anticipated from the moment he has discovered that Shade is writing a new poem. It is now, therefore, as reader and *editor* that he gains the marvelous text that he for so many years has pursued: "What was that dim distant music, those vestiges of color in the air? Here and there I discovered in it and especially, especially in the invaluable variants, echoes and spangles of my mind, a long ripplewake of my glory" (*PF*, 297). For Kinbote, it is clear, the poem that has initially disappointed him shall now survive only as a poem—text—of his own making. Shade may have released an autobiographical poem, but in Kinbote's hands the poem's principal glory shall lie in its presentation of Kinbote's biography. For Nabokov, this act of displacement serves as the crucial ground of the novel.

In his foreword to the edition of *Pale Fire*, Kinbote has characterized his interest in the poem as a desire to establish its definitive text. In reality, however, because his pursuit of the dream-text as Charles the Beloved overwhelms all concern for professional responsibility and decorum, Kinbote's handling of the poem reflects the contamination of self-interest. More than that, Kinbote's deliberate nudging of the poem from a Shadean autobiography to a Zemblan history creates an incredible tension between the author and his critic that is tantamount to a desperate struggle for the possession of the text. When Kinbote, looking for hints of Zembla in Shade's strange poem, initially contents himself with the suggestions hidden in such phrases as "gradual decay" (l. 209) and "Tanagra dust" (a variant to l. 596), both of which serve as indices to Gradus's progress in his pursuit of Charles the Beloved, his slight manipulation of the text may seem rather innocuous. As Kinbote gains some confidence in his venture of distortion, however, he begins to turn these slight and rather arbitrary citations into an accomplished aria: "But Gradus should not kill kings. Vinogradus should never, never provoke God. Leningradus should not aim his pea-shooter at people even in dreams" (*PF*, 154). With such an aria Kinbote obviously pits his art against Shade's. That he does so is even more apparent in his note on the misprint of "fountain" for "mountain," which had figured so prominently in Shade's larger appreciation of an art of texture. Kinbote's note includes the following statement: "A newspaper account of a Russian tsar's coronation had, instead of *korona* (crown), the misprint *vorona* (crow), and when next day this was apologetically 'corrected,' it got misprinted a second time as *korova* (cow)" (*PF*, 260). What is striking about this correlation between the two series, crown-crow-cow and *korona-vorona-korova*, is that it enables Kinbote to surpass Shade, who had cited only the double coincidence of fountain-mountain. It is true that Shade's appreciation of language and of the games based on language (e.g., the word-golf shift from male to mare to Mars to mass to lass) remains superior to Kinbote's. After all, Shade's appreciation shows a genuine pleasure in words, in their possibilities for combinational delight, whereas Kinbote—despite having gained through his textual manipulations an awareness of the artistic uses of language—never regards, at least in a significant sense, language as the principal playfield of his art. Shade, furthermore, pursues the nuance and the striking combination, but Kinbote actually sacrifices his own, sometimes considerable, subtlety with words to his futile efforts to transform Shade's autobiography into his preconceived text of Zemblan history. Kinbote, nevertheless, because he demands that language mean before it delights, assumes complete possession of the text for himself: he distorts the text as he sees fit.

The liberties whereby Kinbote dominates Shade's text probably emerge most clearly in the problem of textual variants—a problem that obviously reflects the larger struggle between two men who would give different readings to the text. Two-thirds of the way through the commentary, in a note appreciatively addressed to the word *debris* in l. 550, Kinbote seems, at least momentarily, to face up to the unreliability of his editing:

> I wish to say something about an earlier note (to line 12). Conscience and scholarship have debated the question, and I now think that the two lines given [as a variant reading] in that note are distorted and tainted by wistful thinking. It is the *only* time in the course of the writing of these difficult comments, that I have tarried, in my distress and disappointment, on the brink of falsification. . . . I could strike [those lines] out before publication but that would mean reworking the entire note. . . . I have no time for such stupidities. (*PF*, 227–28)

The tone of the note, however, particularly its edge of weariness, indicates how Kinbote's concern for editorial exactness has disappeared under the pressure of trying to establish the text of his own royalty. More than that, having admitted his contamination of the text in this instance, Kinbote must hereafter be suspected of having manipulated the text in other instances as well—and, perhaps, of having even altered the body of the poem itself. Once it is clear, in fact, by Kinbote's own admission in the Index, that three of the seventeen variants are his own contributions, textual reliability in this edition of *Pale Fire* can only be regarded as highly unlikely. Nabokov's reader finally possesses no adequate means for defining the precise nature and extent of Kinbote's contamination of Shade's text. Because he does know that Kinbote has thought nothing of edging the text of Shade's poem into a configuration that it did not initially possess, he must conclude that there is a profound and somewhat hopeless sense in which, as a result of Kinbote's contamination, Shade's poem has become Kinbote's as well. It is in this context, of course, that Kinbote's decision, based upon his desire for that "symmetry" of meaning which has constantly eluded him, to supply the poem's missing last line by recapitulating the poem's first line, achieves its greatest effect: with that decision the Kinbote who is an undisciplined editor, and who lets his own needs influence editorial procedure, fully assumes the mantle of authorship and thus possesses the text entirely for himself. At least so it appears.

Despite his best efforts, the Kinbote who has organized his life around the possession of a specific dream-text eventually must discover that such possession is beyond his reach. In the process of editing Shade's poem, which he regards as the formal statement of his life as Charles the Beloved, he seems momentarily to achieve such possession, but even then, because he does not have the necessary stamina to maintain by himself his extremely complicated world of heroic meaning, he shows signs of succumbing to the failure of his dream. The fact that he repeatedly alludes to the noise of the amusement park that is distracting him from his work suggests that all his effort will finally come down only to a sense of exasperation and desperation as he tries to prevent the text upon which he has worked so long from leaking through his own fingers. But leak it must, for no matter how carefully he may have intended to pursue good bibliographic procedure (remember, here, the care with which he describes the manuscript in the foreword), he has taken liberties with the text and thus has sabotaged that very editorial process upon which not only his reputation as a scholar but also his very identity as Charles the Beloved depends.[8] In order to be king, the ruler of his own universe, he requires a stable text upon which he can rely. By making a travesty of his editorial procedure, he becomes his own worst enemy. In these terms the irony in Kinbote's commentary lies not only in the fact that under his editorial aegis Shade's text has become steadily more insecure, but also in the fact that his own life, which depends upon a stability of text, has turned curiously marginal.[9] In other words, while Shade had contented himself with the unpredictable and surprising play of texture and, as a result, received the incredible gift of text (if only in retrospect), Kinbote, by setting out to establish a preconceived text of a very specific character, gets lost in the complications of such assertion, and eventually turns mad.[10] He loses both text and sanity.

If this view of the novel is at all convincing, however, one major question still remains to be answered: why is it Shade rather than

Kinbote who dies at the end of the novel? The best approach to this
question is probably to conceive of the novel in distinct literary terms. If,
as I have suggested, Shade is the author-poet who recognizes the
impossibility of texts while Kinbote is the editor-critic who tries finally,
not to appreciate Shade's poetry, but to establish himself in the security
of his own reading of Shade's text, then what Shade—who is surely the
originator of the game between himself and Kinbote—attempts in the
novel as a whole becomes much clearer. By providing a fairly
straightforward text of his own experience, Shade deflects the reader's
attention away from the relationship between the author and his text to
the complicated relationship that the editor-critic (or any reader) develops with the text. Kinbote, the editor who is primarily conscious of his
own needs, obviously distorts Shade's poem for his own purposes, and in
the process he provides another, perhaps the most crucial, instance of
the dilemma surrounding textual ownership in Nabokov's fiction. A
Shade who is sensitive to the epistemological and ontological limits of
texts in the twentieth century, and who is sensitive especially to the
increasing decline of the author's authority in view of those textual
limits, must himself finally face up to the fact that it is his critics and
readers who too often (and maybe always) dominate and thus possess his
texts.[11] Whereas he has throughout his life maintained a fairly tenuous
relationship to his texts in view of their essential inadequacy, he knows
that in recent times, with authors and readers no longer united in
sympathetic perspective, many critics and readers distort the texts that
they come across until those texts conform to their own expectations.[12]
Such distortion nullifies authorial intentions, and finally what a critic-
reader such as Kinbote does to a text, in the process of manipulating it,
is to destroy it.

Near the end of the foreword Kinbote himself, although unwittingly,
admits this destruction: "Let me state that without my notes Shade's text
simply has no human reality at all since the human reality of such a
poem as his . . . , with the omission of many pithy lines carelessly
rejected by him, has to depend entirely on the reality of its author and
his surroundings, attachments and so forth, a reality that only my notes
can provide" (*PF*, 28–29). Because he fails to appreciate the subtle
process, the "combinational delight," that underlies Shade's accumulation of a text, Kinbote has little choice but to give his own text priority
over Shade's. There is, perhaps, a sense in which Kinbote's brutalization
of Shade's poem defines any act of reading. No matter how neutral or
objective a reader might be, there is very little chance that he can
completely avoid contaminating his acts of reading with the character of
his own personal affairs. The crucial matter here, however, is the

reader's attitude—whether he will try to suspend himself in the author's texturing or whether he is determined to impose his own text upon the author's. If the editor-critic-reader cannot suspend himself in the act of reading, there can be no question that he shall never approach the text before him with the semblance of neutrality that will finally enable him to expropriate for himself a genuinely new text, i.e., the author's text of experience. Kinbote cannot suspend himself, and it is this failure which leads both to his brutalizations of Shade's text and, if only in a figurative sense, to the murder of Shade.[13]

In the end *Pale Fire* as a whole represents a dialogue between author and reader. After writing his poem, which celebrates the notion of "combinational delight," Shade decides to enrich the texture of that poem by providing, through a character of his own creation, a commentary that calls into question his own poetic achievement. In fact, just as Kinbote has projected himself into Zembla, so Shade projects himself into Kinbote's world in an effort to gain a deeper appreciation of that act of reading which separates all authors from the possession of their texts. Because they both indulge themselves in acts of projection, Shade may initially seem only to be another Kinbote, but here there is a critical difference. Whereas Kinbote regards his Zembla as a specific and necessary content, Shade knows that his own Zembla, the projection of himself into Kinbote, is only the shimmering mirror world that belongs to all victims of solipsism, i.e., to all men. Kinbote regards Zembla seriously, but Shade plays with Zembla as if it were only a game. In another, perhaps deeper, sense, Kinbote serves primarily as Shade's escape valve—as his opportunity for separating himself from the necessary reduction of his own experience to the conventional yet inadequate structures of language and poetry, of content and meaning, of prosody and chronology. By creating a Kinbote, Shade complicates the act of his poem and thus achieves a greater art. No matter how one responds to the relationship between Shade and Kinbote, however, it is clear that as a novel *Pale Fire* is an exercise in what amounts to colossal irony: the brilliant poet, who initially exists in the shadow of his editor, finally regains his stature when Nabokov's reader recognizes that Shade, far from being dead, has actually played out his own death only to realize the full extent of Kinbote's tyranny over the text.[14] While Kinbote falls victim to his own madness, Shade actually remains the chief magician of Nabokovian art.[15] Near the end of the foreword Kinbote himself describes this magic:

> I am witnessing a unique physiological phenomenon: John Shade perceiving and transforming the world, taking it in and taking it apart, re-combining its elements in the very process of storing them up so as

to produce at some unspecified date an organic miracle, a fusion of image and music, a line of verse. (*PF*, 27)

Substitute "a richness of texture" for "a line of verse," and the comment wonderfully characterizes Shade's achievement within *Pale Fire*. This novel is about the character of imaginative transformations, and it is Shade's artistry that underlies it all.

5

Ada: The Texture of Incest

One of the crucial facts that distinguish *Ada* from *Lolita* and *Pale Fire*, which end in the rather ambiguous deaths of Clare Quilty and John Shade respectively, is that *Ada* merely concludes on the note of a ninety-seven-year-old Van "merging" with a ninety-five-year-old Ada. In addition, because *Lolita* and *Pale Fire* both depend for their ultimate effects upon the struggle for textual dominance enacted between Humbert Humbert and Clare Quilty and then between Charles Kinbote and John Shade, it is worth noting that *Ada* as a novel seems to lack such a significant conflict. Van and Ada, to be sure, having had to rely upon each other's memories in order to fill the gaps of narrative dealing with their early summers together, may in a limited sense be seen to be struggling against each other for the final authority to provide the text with its peculiar "shading." In actuality, however, Van Veen is always willing—with hardly a break in the text of his narrative—to allow Ada the chance to comment on his recollections, to supply diary and epistolary material for events he has largely forgotten, and even to create a narrative texture of her own.[1] Thus, no matter what contradictions surface in the text between Ada's and Van's views of the past, it is clear that they are not frustrated by the same dilemma that leaves Quilty and Shade dead at the end of their respective novels. Even if, as is the case, Van should serve as an exhibit of the essentially unstable character of consciousness, especially in its dependence upon the processes of memory, in the end there is no doubt about his primary control over the text. He (with Nabokov) is the source of the text.

There is, nevertheless, a comment at the end of *Ada* that does tend to parallel what has occurred in *Lolita* and *Pale Fire*. Immediately before the concluding summary of the book's contents, Ada (in the final speech of the novel) suggests that Van's and her failure to love Lucette enough and particularly Van's failure to marry Lucette has led to much of their own heartache over the years. Ada imagines what might have been, had

Van married Lucette: "I would have stayed with you both in Ardis Hall, and instead of that happiness, handed out gratis, instead of all that we *teased* her to death!" (*A*, 586).[2] It is the emphasis here upon Van's and Ada's mistreatment of Lucette that is interesting. I am not about to argue, of course, that the teasing of Lucette to death constitutes a murder that recalls the ends of Quilty and Shade, for Lucette's death by way of suicide finally does not match up precisely with what happens to Quilty and to Shade. Quilty and Shade subject themselves to the ambiguities of writing and thus experience what amounts, in Nabokov, to textual suicide when Humbert Humbert and Charles Kinbote press the significance of their stories and in the process manage to dominate the texts of those two novels.[3] Lucette, on the other hand, is only an object in an ambiguous game of sexuality whose texture has been developed by its two principals, the young Van and his cohort Ada. Finally, therefore, when Lucette becomes the victim of a game initiated by others, her death must belong to another order. In light of the fact that the deaths of Quilty and Shade serve as important keys to what transpires in their respective novels, however, there is still a chance that Lucette's death does serve as a key for understanding Van's handling of narrative in *Ada* as a whole. On that assumption, then, let me develop those background considerations—particularly the relationship that exists between Van and Lucette—which have some bearing on the reader's response to her death. My starting point is the relationship between Van and Ada.

At first glance Van and Ada appear to be remarkably alike in attitude and sensibility. During their two summers at Ardis Park (1884 and 1888), both display a cleverness of insight and wit that largely separates them from the others present in the country house. To be sure, nearly everyone, with the possible exception of Lucette, who is yet a child, has become engaged in some pursuit of originality. After all, at the dinner table a great deal of Ada's lively conversation on botany and Lepidoptera originates in her attempt to deflect either her mother, Marina, from launching into a discussion of the theater, or her governess, Mlle Larivière, from recounting the progress of her latest story. In such a context, it is true, Ada's lively chatter may strike the reader as merely another manifestation of the artificial atmosphere of self-indulgence that seems to characterize all life at Ardis Park. Ada, nevertheless, by virtue of her nearly encyclopedic knowledge of fritillaries at the age of twelve and her seemingly limitless ability to see relationships between the flora and fauna in Ardis and in literature, is genuinely a marvel—a fact that a number of critics, appalled by the character of her relationship with Van, have been reluctant to acknowledge.[4]

When Van has first appeared in 1884, in fact, Ada has immediately introduced him to her shadow games (he finds them boring) and then has acquainted him with the "little system" of "real things," "things," and "ghost things" that in various combinations become "real" or "simple" or "ruined" bridges or towers. Already at that tender age Ada has with her unique container of philosophic insight become quite comfortable in a world that is not real—where shadows dominate all play and where words must, consequently, remain limited gestures that cannot contain what is finally beyond verbalization.[5] In Ada's world, as in the worlds of Nabokov's other original characters, texts do not enjoy concrete, absolute status. As she says at one point, when alluding to the terrible odds against the development of reliable texts, "In 'real' life we are creatures of chance in an absolute void—unless we be artists ourselves" (A, 426). Artistry is for her, as for Nabokov, the only possible solution to the profound inadequacy that attaches to all attempts to define or to categorize human experience. She is herself an artist, and like other Nabokovian originals (e.g., Pnin, Quilty, Shade), she plays with the texture of her experience—rather than seeking the ultimate text that she knows shall never materialize. Indeed, as a result of her constant play she has not only become very adept at puns and at assorted word games (especially those based on etymology and Scrabble), but she finally represents everything that her principal predecessor, the conventional Lolita, could not become. Whereas Lolita, despite having had to deal with both Humbert and Quilty, never progressed beyond the games of the fledgling, Ada has achieved a sophistication well beyond her years. She is Lolita pushed to a profound key of originality.

Where Ada's character really shines is in the area of sexual play. During a first reading of the novel she may appear the innocent, uninitiated virgin who in her inimitable fashion transforms her first contact with Van's penis into a moment of scientific observation: "Now what's this? The cap of the Red Bolete is not half as plushy. In fact . . . I'm reminded of geranium or rather pelargonium bloom" (A, 119). By the time the reader reaches the end of the first summer, however, at which point Ada is refusing to swear fidelity to Van because she is "physical, horribly physical" (A, 158), the reader has good reason to suspect that in fact Ada is already quite experienced. For it is then that certain details, such as the specificity of Ada's interest in the early phallic stages of metamorphosis within the fritillaries or the two lovers' inability to remember the exact circumstances in which Van had "deflowered"

(*A*, 129) Ada, converge in the reader's mind, and he begins to realize that Ada has long ago surrendered to her mentor in fritillaries, Dr. Krolik. What is important in this convergence of detail, of course, is the reader's recognition of Ada as a girl of spirit who responds to her feelings and who thus delights in the spontaneity of whatever imaginative and emotional texture the present circumstances will allow. She is the one youngster in Nabokov's fiction who has already, at the point of puberty and adolescence, learned to avoid the constrictions of containment, of an established text. Committed, in fact, to the continual extension or expansion of her world of play, she has come to regard her personal freedom as a necessary condition of her existence that not even her love for Van must be allowed to violate. It is in light of this fundamental necessity that the contradiction, late that first summer, between her insistence that she can never love another as much as she has adored Van and her rejection of Van's request that she swear fidelity achieves some resolution. Ada cannot accept the text of fidelity, which is a text of containment, because she knows that, at least for her, the spontaneous creation of texture is everything.[6]

Initially Van appears to belong to the same mold as Ada. He may not be a champion at Scrabble (his game is chess), but he is an original (as is apparent in his performances as Mascodagama), and like Ada he does enjoy a wide assortment of verbal effects, all of which eventually surface in the complicated, bewildering texture of his narrative many years later. Like Ada, moreover, he seems comfortable in the world of shadows, for when he returns to school following that first summer, he increasingly devotes his attention to the study of Terrapy, the science that examines the hazy relations between Terra and Antiterra (Demonia). Finally, however, despite his demonstrable sophistication, Van ignores Ada's example and commits himself to establishing stable texts that belie the essential mystery underlying all Nabokovian experience. Whether it is the matter of his own relationship with Ada or that between Terra and Antiterra, Van hopes to inhabit a realized world, one that he as an accomplished editor has come to dominate. Such a hope, especially in light of Humbert's and Kinbote's editorial follies,[7] must strike the reader as misguided.

Take the matter of Van's relationship with Ada, for instance. The two of them are frequently separated for long periods of time, and yet Van wants to establish a continuity in their relationship that the vitality of their lives will only negate. Indeed, merely by forcing Van into a conservative posture despite whatever play of mind he may initially have seemed to possess, his determination to remain faithful during long absence must prey on his relationship with Ada and eventually wreck whatever chances the two lovers have for a life together. Beyond that problem, it is also true that just as Ada is unfaithful to him, so he—despite his professed intentions—turns out to be unfaithful to her. That fact proves rather troublesome, for the knowledge of infidelity on his part makes him even more the enforcer of his desired text: he becomes the jealous lover who, suspicious because of his own betrayals, badgers Ada with the necessity of remaining true to the text that he has prescribed for their love. The upshot of this jealousy becomes apparent toward the end of their second summer together, in 1888, when Van is especially conscious of his suspicions concerning Ada's infidelity. At that point one of the maids at Ardis Park, in a pique of jealousy, acquaints Van with the facts of Ada's complicated infidelities. The situation is marvelous, for at that point, when Van finally believes himself to be in possession of a concrete text, he discovers—ironically—that he cannot "endure the agony of consciousness, the filth of life, the loss, the loss, the loss." Van is a character of mind, of texts that he has himself constituted, and in this instance, given a text that his own suspicions had warranted, he discovers that in order to handle his profound grief he must sabotage that very text by "the magic method of not allowing the image of Ada to come anywhere near his awareness of himself. This created a vacuum into which rushed a multitude of trivial reflections. A pantomime of rational thought" (A, 294). Obviously ironic, at least in the face of Van's previous attempts to identify Ada's lovers and thus the specific text of her infidelity, this passage goes a long way toward locating the essential folly of Van's orientation toward experience. Having sought the prescribed text of fidelity, Van has made himself vulnerable to those relentless processes, apparent even in himself, that militate against the very possibility of a world of fidelity. In these terms, of course, the pursuit of stable texts, of secure relationships so well defined that they must turn rigid, is in Nabokov's world not only foolish but pernicious. A wonderfully vital Ada cannot provide Van with the secure text of a fixed relationship, and the Van who expects such a text must be disappointed.

Once Ardis Park has become the scene of his textual disorientation, Van has no choice but to flee. Typically enough, while departing, he—still the editor trying to fix the character of his experience—imagines what Ada must look like as she leans against a tree observing his departure. His text of the departure requires that she be grieving. In actual fact, however, although she does feel some grief, Ada also feels some relief over having successfully avoided Van's textual domination. Momentarily at least, she is again free to play out her own textual constitutions. Van, however, faces yet more problems. Once outside the park, he compounds his present folly by immediately committing himself to an act of revenge against the two lovers whom the maid has identified. As yet he does not have any appreciation at all of the fact that Dr. Krolik was probably his primary rival for Ada's affections. While traveling by train in pursuit of Philip Rack and Percy de Prey, furthermore, he without provocation offends a Captain Tapper who has only the most remote of relationships to Ada[8] but who, in the succeeding duel, nearly deals Van his death. The circumstances are ludicrous, especially when added to the fact that the two principals upon whom he seeks revenge have already been dispatched. It is as if Van, despite his determination to wreak his revenge, cannot gain control over this pursuit any more than over his previous pursuit of faithful love. First he gets involved with the wrong man and is himself wounded (rather than vice versa). Then he discovers that Philip Rack is already dying, poisoned by his wife, in the same hospital in which Van is himself convalescing. And finally he learns that Percy de Prey has been killed only two days after arriving at the front—far out of Van's reach. What should become evident to Van in this situation is the fundamentally haphazard nature of all experience— and thus the folly of committing himself to specific textual prescriptions that the hazards of chance will only overthrow.

Van, nevertheless, cannot as yet escape the rigidity of his reliance upon his own prescriptions. Even when Ada addresses a series of letters to him, a series that could serve as an opportunity for shifting from those prescriptions to an appreciation of the incredibly complex texture of all human experience, Van stoically keeps his silence. At the beginning of the first letter, when she points to her own difficulty in discussing what has happened to them, Ada herself identifies the nature of Van's problem. She alludes to the fact that in their final confrontation she had told him that she would rather write later than try to explain herself in the midst of difficult circumstances, and in her letter she now states, "I could not utter the proper words [of explanation] at short notice. I implore you. I felt that I could not produce them and arrange them orally in the necessary order. I implore you. I felt that one wrong or misplaced word would be fatal" (A, 332). The point here, at least given the fact that at the moment of separation Van continued to demand the fulfillment of a text that he then knew Ada had frequently violated, is that Ada could say nothing. Even later there is little that she can say. The contradiction between Van's prescribed texts and her acts of free and expansive play, a contradiction at once so immediate and so overwhelming, requires imaginative understanding, not verbal explanation. In the face of Van's determination that she present a text of explanation at the moment of separation, an astute Ada knows that she does not possess the construction that would mitigate—at least in terms of Van's prescriptions—the circumstances of her "betrayal." Say what she will, she can only conclude, as she does in a letter some two years later, that "I cannot logically explain my behavior" (A, 335). At that point she may also, having finally recognized that Van will not be satisfied with anything less than that prescription of fidelity in which he has so heavily invested, accept the hopelessness of the situation and admit her "infidelity" (a term that primarily belongs to Van's vocabulary). Even then, however, still wedded to texture rather than to text, she herself continues to swear that in her encounters with other men she has at least avoided the acts of possession (if not of "pollution") except for "one messy occasion" when she was half-taken by force. In a sense, perhaps, Ada might here be accused of merely temporizing, but in the context of her whole experience (and of Nabokov's fiction) what she attempts here is to recover the larger sense of her personal fidelity in that period in her life when, according to Van's narrow view, she was grossly unfaithful. In terms of fidelity to the imagination Ada clearly comes off very well.

Not surprisingly, given his determination, Van's dependence upon his prescriptions continues into the next period of his relationship with Ada. It is true that after another four-year separation, i.e., in 1892, Ada does confront Van with her continuing desire to live with him, and that Van, still devoted to her presence, agrees to a reconciliation. This agreement, nevertheless, is as problematic as their relationship in the summer of 1888, for despite the passing of time Van has not changed in any essential way—and thus Ada quickly finds herself in the familiar and untenable position of having to bend to Van's constructions of their relationship, both in the past and in the present. There is no question that she recognizes the extent of the problem she is getting into. Already before she rejoins Van, for example, she herself destroys the incriminating photographs from 1888 that would confirm her repeated infidelities and thus cause Van great pain. Then in Van's presence she repeatedly insists that their first summer in the gardens of Ardis had become "a sacred secret and creed" (A, 409) for the people living near the estate—as if, somehow, the experience of that summer was inviolable and thus a solid foundation, a secure text, for building their future together. Instead of allowing Van's attention to drift toward the raw edges of his past suspicions, where the security of such a text immediately disappears, Ada shrewdly concentrates upon fleshing out the character of their love in the summer of 1884, if not that of 1888. What all such effort on Ada's part comes down to, of course, is the fact that by holding the relationship together through such calculated means, Ada herself begins to give textual prescriptions precedence over the imaginative play that has made her experience so rich. In 1893 this shift in Ada may not emerge in full dress, for when Demon intrudes into the Manhattan apartment and terminates the relationship between these sibling lovers, the transformation of Ada's character to an orientation that matches up with Van's is not yet complete. Indeed, because the reader's attention is in the scene upon Van and his response to Demon's horror, Ada and her recent adjustment of perspective tends to drift further into the background. Van momentarily surprises the reader (and probably Ada herself) with what is for him an uncharacteristic suggestion—that since nature is kind, "we can afford to be careless in every sense of the word" (*A*, 442), even in terms of incest. Here Van ignores the world of moral prescriptions and, much in the fashion of Ada herself, insists on the freedom of the imagination to create its own webs of experience. Van's light touch, nevertheless, although a clever ploy to escape the literal freight of the situation, does not impress his father. Demon's horror over their transgression of a taboo prevails, and in the face of that horror Van finally—and, rather typically, because he does not even consult Ada— calls the relationship off. Again, although this time only because of his father, Van bows to a prescription, and the immediate result is another period of separation—one that promises to be long because there is a real question not only whether Van will ever achieve the Nabokovian ground of imaginative play but also whether Ada will manage to recover for herself her previous enjoyment of such ground.

For thirty years, then, from 1893 to 1922, Van Veen the editor, the maker of texts, allows himself to wither away—alone, lost in his philosophy, a man who generally has lost all contact with the enthusiasms of his youth. Only in 1922, with the reinstatement of his relationship with Ada, does he again begin to enjoy a resurgence of his former energy and vitality. By that time, however, the restoration of the old relationship is not easy. A pedantic, rather boring, and now fifty-two-year-old Van actually finds himself wary of involvement with anybody—and especially with an Ada whose physical attractions have now long since considerably diminished. Surrounded by the generally comfortable, if merely academic, routine of his philosophic inquiries, Van is almost content to leave the past alone. Ada, too, has her reservations. After her long devotion (from 1905 to 1922) as a nurse to the stupid Andrey Vinelander, whom she has married once it is clear (in 1893) that she can never expect to live with Van, she surely recognizes the difference in style that separates her distant past (when she played with the textures of imagination) from that past which is more recent (when she has known, as a result of her experience as a nurse, only the constraints of duty). In 1905, to be sure, she has tried to break free of her marriage and rejoin Van, but it is precisely at that point of separation that Vinelander has turned invalid—and the narrow text of marriage to Vinelander has turned into the even more restrictive text of nursing him. Once in the Vinelander text, Ada seems increasingly unable to extricate herself from the burden of literalness. It is in this light that the full extent of Van's earlier influence (his reliance upon firmly edited prescriptions) becomes most evident in Ada's life as well. With Vinelander's death in 1922, Ada does regain her freedom and, perhaps, even the opportunity to recover the wonderful character of her adolescence. The question for her, however, is whether she can retrieve her imaginative vitality without Van's assistance. On the other hand, should she again become involved with Van, the editor who has already caused her so much difficulty, she must anticipate even more distress than she has known in the past. Despite such reservations, none of which is fully developed from Ada's perspective in the novel, she does plunge ahead.

What brings Ada around to accepting Van, I think, is her belief that he, the most prominent figure of her adolescence, still represents— despite his limitations—her best opportunity for recovering that vitality which she, over the years of marriage and nursing, has completely lost. By the same token, Van seems to accept Ada on the grounds that he, having over the years become steadily more withdrawn in his academic pursuits, also must alter the present character of his experience or risk losing what little vitality remains to him. He recognizes that his career as a philosopher has brought him, instead of success, only the profound sense of being "unbeloved by his austere colleagues, unknown in local pubs, unregretted by male students" (A, 507). For him, therefore, 1922 becomes the crucial turning point in his experience. Not only does he desert the practice of philosophy and its concentration upon editing texts and establishing the authority of those texts, but, once more in Ada's embrace, he finally suspends himself—in a fashion beyond his ability as an adolescent—in the complicated texture of human experience. That Van makes a shift in 1922 from a career in philosophy and the editorial pursuit of stable texts to a career in literature and its acts of unpredictable play becomes more clear, however, if I now return to the original question of this chapter—the question of the significance of Lucette's death.

During Van's long separation from Ada in the 1890s, it is Lucette who represents his principal opportunity for exploring the world of texture. Van may originally have known Lucette as the intruder, as someone who prevents, in 1884 and 1888, his easy access to Ada's attentions, but in

the narrative of the return journeys[9] following the birthday picnics from
those two summers there already appears a suggestion that the natural
progression for Van is from Ada to Lucette. After the picnic of 1884, it is
Ada who rides back to the house on Van's "hard lap." Van obviously
finds that ride delightful, for, as he later recalls, he has had to endure
the pressure of Ada's weight while it is "responding to every bump of the
road by softly parting in two and crushing beneath it the core of the
longing which he knew he had to control lest a possible seep perplex her
innocence" (A, 87). By shifting Ada's bottom to his right knee, Van
removes the pressure that has been giving him so much pleasure and
thus avoids the moment of release. Four summers later, this time with
Lucette on his knee, Van seems to experience much the same pleasure.
In this second instance, however, Lucette's weight serves principally as
a goad to Van's exercise of memory and to the recovery of the specific
character of the previous picnic. For with Lucette in his lap he suddenly
finds himself "in the quicksand of the dream-like, dream-rephrased,
legend-distorted past" (A, 280), and at that point he can no longer avoid
transforming, or reducing, the moment with Lucette into his familiar text
of love for Ada. Eventually, in fact, having closed his eyes in order to
indulge himself with "the golden flood of swelling joy" (A, 281) and thus
having approached the imminence of a release rooted in the past, he
finds that he must chide himself for having tried to substitute "a little
pauper" (Lucette) for the fairy tale princess (Ada). In a certain sense the
outcome of these two rides is the same: both with Ada and with Lucette
Van stops just short of the fullness of pleasure. What is most striking
about this deliberate paralleling of episodes, however, is the fact that
Van, at least in textual terms, makes the second instance dependent
upon the first. If given equivalent status the two episodes develop, I
think, an implied, almost natural, progression from Ada to Lucette, but
in view of Van's consistent refusal to consider Lucette seriously, such
progression never has a chance of materializing. The prescription of
fidelity to Ada completely dominates Van, and finally the one-
dimensional character of that prescription must be said to underlie his
curious but deliberate rejection—twice—of release. Clearly the Van
who possesses some inhibition in relation to the potential openness of
sensuality is a man who exists outside the Nabokovian world of texture.

The fact of the matter is that the young Ada and the young Lucette are
both far more ready to indulge themselves in sensual pleasure than is
Van. Ada, for example, not only enjoys the attentions of a series of lovers
but gets involved with girls as well—a fact that becomes apparent to Van
himself when, during a visit in November 1892, Lucette acknowledges
that she herself, at the age of fourteen (and while Ada was making a

movie in Arizona), has learned certain practices from Ada that she had never before imagined. As Lucette suggests with an eye toward the unusual texture of the situation, "we interweaved like serpents and sobbed like pumas. We were Mongolian tumblers, monograms, anagrams, adalucindas" (A, 375).[10] Back in the summer of 1888, when Ada and Van first introduce Lucette to some presumably rudimentary aspects of sexual play, Van himself seems to possess some of the same sensual openness. Consider, for example, that classic encounter in the garden which occurs as Marina argues over a movie script. While Van "struggle[s] to rise," Ada and Lucette busy themselves "kissing him alternatively, then kissing each other, then getting busy upon him again" (A, 205). Despite the rich texture of this episode, however, Van has eyes only for Ada. He may have allowed Lucette to participate in his sexual play with Ada, but he never allows himself to recognize her as a genuine player in the game. For Van, it is clear, such allowance would require an expansion of the game's text and thus, presumably, an even further enriching of its texture.

What readers of the novel must realize here is that Lucette, as a result of the gaming in 1888, has come to expect sexual (or is it textual?) privileges similar to those of Ada. While such an expectation may at first seem rather extraordinary in the middle-class environments of contemporary America, within her sense of the game itself the expectation is understandable. Consider, for instance, the fact that, in the presence of Ada and Van, Lucette has seen little that might signify the existence of constraints. In their summers together Ada and Van may make some pretense of concealment, but in reality they pursue their play quite openly—even to the point of becoming a myth of love in Ardis Park. During their separations, furthermore, each of them becomes involved with other lovers, thus complicating the game already established—at least from Lucette's perspective. Given these circumstances it is not surprising that Lucette should regard sexual experience generally as a function of desire, as an enriching of texture, rather than a matter of constraint. Indeed, in these terms her expectation that Van will surrender to her desire should carry great weight even for Van himself, for he represents the one element in the texture of the original threesome that has not yet played out its full function. Van, however, continues to resist Lucette's attention, and the poignancy of this fact becomes fully apparent late in 1892 when Lucette joins Ada and Van one final time in a frolic in Van's Manhattan apartment. In this episode Ada undresses Lucette, and then she and Van give Lucette special treatment: "Ten eager, evil, loving, long fingers belonging to two different young demons caress their helpless bed pet" (A, 420). When Van suddenly climaxes

(Ada's hair has been tickling his "local curio"), however, Lucette snatches up her nightdress and flees the apartment. The episode possesses a richness in itself, but for Lucette the close proximity to the completion of the original and still longed-for text (consummation with Van) is more than maddening. Nine years later, when she sees Van in Paris, she is in the same straits. In a moment of banter she may acknowledge that she is still a "quarter-virgin," but in the next breath she is quick to urge, "Oh, try me, Van! My divan is black with yellow cushions" (A, 464).[11] Van in that instance permits her to sit on his lap for at least a minute; on another occasion he even allows her to slide the knuckles of her gloved hand lightly across his genital area; but always he sets a limit on his play with Lucette and thus not only frustrates the completion of Lucette's expectation but also prevents himself from achieving new levels of understanding.

It is possible, perhaps, to counter the argument here on the grounds that Lucette's expectation is unrealistic in the face of Van's consistent refusal to respond to her attentions. In a certain sense she seems as "stuck" in a one-dimensional text as Van. And yet, if it is true (as I think it is) that Lucette can never regard Van's refusal as a genuine condition or circumstance in the game as it was originally constituted, then her expectation must be accepted as quite compelling. Indeed, when the reader realizes that Ada herself has from the beginning regarded a relationship between Van and Lucette as the normal outcome of the play initiated in 1888, then there can be little doubt that Van is playing out the game in a far different fashion from the manner of the two women. Following that bewildering frolic in the Manhattan apartment, Ada will even suggest, after insisting that she will never allow Van to harm Lucette, that "Van, Van, somewhere, some day, after a sunbath or dance, you will sleep with her, Van!" (A, 421). Ada offers the comment with some enthusiasm, certainly with no derision, but Van never does sleep with Lucette. In 1901 a surprisingly urbane Lucette will confront Van with this striking possibility:

> Everything is quite simple. You marry me. You get my Ardis [which Lucette has inherited]. We live there, you write there. I keep melting into the background, never bothering you. We invite Ada—alone, of course—to stay for a while on *her* estate. . . . While she's there, I go to Aspen or Gstaad, or Schittau, and you live with her in solid crystal. (A, 466)

Many years later, at the end of the novel, Ada will still be lamenting the fact that Lucette fails to convince Van of the feasibility of this unique conception, which is again—like the original game—predicated upon a rich sense of the texture of human relationships. In 1901, however, a Van who has devoted himself to philosophy is generally incapable of responding to such a bold proposal. Only on the ship voyage of that same year, when it is clear that his separation from Ada promises to be very long, does he begin to respond in any serious way to Lucette's attention. By then, of course, it is far too late. Even if he should reconcile himself to sleeping with Lucette that fatal night and thus finally play out his function in the original game of 1888, he delays the consummation until the two of them have watched *Don Juan's Last Fling.* That delay proves to be Lucette's undoing, for when the film visually confronts Van with evidence of Ada's betrayals, it propels him, still the jealous victim of a one-dimensional text, to the privacy of his room for a double release by way of masturbation. Lucette, once more deprived of the fruition she has long awaited, and this time left to the company of the strange Robinsons and to the relief of drink and drugs, goes overboard—presumably by design.

It is impossible to conclude, on the basis of this rehearsal of the facts, that Van "murders" Lucette, but it is clear that he has caused her, just as Ada before her, great stress. The issue of Van's mistreatment of Lucette aside, however, it is even more clear that Van has suppressed the range of his own emotions and has thus deprived himself of the enriching of imaginative experience that was his merely for the asking. When Van meets up with Lucette shortly before the fatal ship voyage begins, he knows that he is in difficult straits. At that point he is even questioning the meaning of his existence: "What was he? Who was he? Why was he? He thought of his slackness, clumsiness, dereliction of spirit. He thought of his loneliness, of its passions and dangers" (*A*, 471). The fact remains, however, that it is not until 1922, two decades later, when a much-altered Ada reappears in his life, that Van finally begins to open himself up again to the riches of imaginative play that were once his as a child. At that point, completely bored with the tasks of philosophy that have occupied him for so many years, he points himself in a new direction—one that in 1957 shall result in an altogether new conception of writing (and thus in the recovery of his adolescent vitality): "why, then, did he not let himself go, why did he not choose a big playground for a match between Inspiration and Design" (*A*, 578).[12] For Van this conception of a new playground for himself obviously constitutes an important moment of realization. What must disturb the reader about such a moment, however, is that it was already available to Van, half a century earlier, in his relationship with Lucette. There is little doubt that Van's life has been rich in opportunities for playing with texture, but having squandered all such opportunities away in his pursuit of a career in philosophy that has failed to satisfy him, he is left with the difficult task of trying to recover the vitality of adolescence when it is almost too late. In a profound sense, at least in Nabokov's eyes, he has come very close to throwing his whole life away.

Once Ada and Van restore their relationship in 1922, however, Van embarks upon the shift in writing from that rather pedantic philosophical style which he parodies in part 4[13] to the complicated texture that is prefigured in Ada's verbal excursions at the dinner table in 1884 and that eventually becomes the basis for his handling of the family chronicle. Ada's presence is crucial, for while Van in 1922 may no longer be obsessed with establishing precise relationships between Terra and Antiterra, it is her encouragement and assistance that enables him to fashion that rich texture of consciousness, that amalgam of memory and imagination, which has to that point eluded his grasp but upon which will surely rest his achievement as a writer of genuine distinction. Merely by taking their own experience in 1884, 1888, and 1892–93 as the nodes of an inquiry into the character of human existence, Ada and Van initiate a process that, although resulting in little definitive statement of a philosophic character, does develop a resonance that fully engages their powers of imagination and originality and thus recovers the wonder of their peculiar experience. Without full notes and diaries at their disposal, to be sure, they find that they frequently have to rely upon "oral tradition" or upon residual impressions from a haze of memories, and at times the consequence for their inquiry seems to be more confusion than a rich recovery of the past. The two of them, nevertheless, continue to surrender themselves to the process with enthusiasm: "Calendar dates were debated, sequences sifted and shifted, sentimental notes compared, hesitations and resolutions passionately analyzed" (*A*, 109). In light of all these difficulties, Van and Ada eventually recognize and embrace the proposition that it is impossible to fix the character of the past—especially the character of human consciousness in the past. At the very least they come to appreciate the extent to which past events are necessarily transformed by the peculiar character of succeeding events and how, consequently, the past is always re-created in the present. From the beginning of their inquiry, then, they increasingly learn to content themselves with the understanding that it is the texture of their narrative, not the exactness of the text, that matters. In addition, Van, the scholar who was originally wedded to the precise editing of texts, discovers that such understanding is also bound up in an appreciation of the notion that it is the "originality of literary style . . . [that] constitutes the only real honesty of a writer" (*A*, 471). With Ada's help he finally, if only late in life, achieves the stature of author—rather than that of editor.

Despite Ada's and Van's increased understanding, however, the matter of incest still remains. If, early in the novel, that matter enjoyed the traditional status of a taboo, the question is, what has happened to the concept of incest at the end? Already fairly early in the novel, while citing the opinion of a Judge Bald, Van has argued that the proscription of incestuous cohabitation was an "infringement of one of humanity's main rights—that of enjoying the liberty of its evolution, a liberty no other creature had ever known" (A, 134). Such an argument may seem specious, but what is at stake here, I think, is the essential contradiction of human experience. In the world of texts, where logic prevails, where laws (and the taboos supporting the laws) provide a set of boundary conditions that enclose the world, the incest between Van and Ada must be regarded with horror. In the world of texture, however, where illogic prevails, where the imagination extends itself beyond all set boundaries and thus opens the world up to the unpredictable, the matter of incest takes on an altogether different character. Clearly Nabokov is not arguing in Ada that a dose of incest will lead to new freedom or to heightened imaginative experience. Incest, in fact, frequently results in the opposite. What Nabokov is suggesting, however, is that the pattern of incest in this novel does serve as a metaphor for one of the fundamental contradictions of human experience: while man desires facts, a logic of stable texts, in the end the essentially subjective (and profoundly incestuous) character of all his perceptions and impressions prevails. Because man cannot escape his subjectivity, in fact, Nabokov seems to regard as the test of a man's genius and originality his awareness of his own peculiar subjectivity. For a long time, of course, Van fails the test. In 1922, however, he begins to come around, and eventually he joins Quilty and Shade as one of the sophisticated proponents of Nabokov's incestuous art.

6

Barthelme: The Essential Contradiction

In Nabokov's fiction the problem of establishing a text dominates the artist. Nabokov himself may not desire a fiction of content, but all his narrators seem to resort to strikingly unusual postures in order to establish a narrative coherence that will tie their efforts up with the long fictive tradition that has preceded them. Clare Quilty plays himself off Humbert Humbert, John Shade plays off Charles Kinbote, and the aged Van Veen plays off his younger self. It is true that by introducing this strategy of dialogue, which essentially reduces to a struggle between each set of contestants for possession of Nabokov's text, Quilty, Shade, and the elder Veen establish an ironic relationship between themselves and that fictional tradition which, recently, seems to have exhausted the possibilities of a vital personal vision. Earlier in this century the modernists felt that a significant vision was no longer available to them, but they at least continued to explore whatever curiosities were left to them in their rather restricted frames of perspective. Their narrators, to be sure, never offered up a statement of universal significance, yet in the absence of such a statement they did manage—regardless of the complicated epistemological difficulties that surrounded their exploration of personal perceptions—to nudge as best they could the character of their own perspective to the achievement of a limited art. In the end, of course, the efforts of these narrators finally resulted in, above everything else, the culmination of that solipsistic tendency which had, ever since the rise of romanticism but especially during the modernist period itself, been stalking the author committed to substantiating the authority of his perspective. With Nabokov such verification is no longer possible. In his fiction the neuralgia of a narrator who no longer possesses even a personal platform from which to speak takes over the operation of creating all texts. The upshot is that artifice, rooted in a sensitive awareness of the complicated relationships among the various textures of human experience, replaces content as the focus of the text.

To a large extent Barthelme merely expands on the dilemma at the heart of Nabokov's fiction.[1] Certainly there is no question that his narrators, because they inhabit the same limited ground as do Nabokov's, feel the oppressive weight of solipsism as they seek to create texts of even the most limited vision and significance. Despite this essential similarity, however, Barthelme generally avoids Nabokov's reliance upon intricate forms—or upon an artifice that tends to establish a residual content in the text. Nabokov's novels never succeed in removing all content, for despite the limited ground that Quilty, Shade, and Veen all inhabit, the texts of their three novels ultimately achieve some sufficiency at least as examinations of the imaginative configurations of the narrators themselves. Even *Pale Fire,* seemingly the most disjointed because of its use of an *apparatus criticus* and its strained tension between poem and commentary, enjoys—if only in the reader's imagination—that wonderful moment of convergence when all the elements of the text meld together in a powerful, albeit limited, statement about the character of Shade's experience. Barthelme's fiction generally lacks such coherence. Instead of exploring further what seems virtually inescapable, i.e., the solipsistic nature of human perception, Barthelme tends to reject the self-critical (Quilty vs. Humbert, Shade vs. Kinbote, Veen vs. Veen) nature of Nabokov's texts and refuse his narrators and characters the luxury of any vision at all—not even that vision which is intensely personal, idiosyncratic, or mad. Thus, whereas Nabokov's novels all possess an intricate, finely wrought structure, Barthelme's fiction tends to dribble away, as if in the absence of vision there can be no meaningful artifice or structure in experience.

Barthelme's fiction exists in the void, in the chasm that appears following the bankruptcy of all the romantic and especially the modernist emphasis upon the ability of the individual mind to create a meaningful vision out of personal experience. In Barthelme man no longer possesses the illusion that he can understand the variety even of his everyday experience, and thus his short stories and novels emerge only as hopeless efforts to contain what is already acknowledged to be uncontainable.[2] Instead of the author or his narrator establishing himself securely in the text, as in Nabokov's fiction, the maker of a Barthelmean text finds himself in the difficult position of trying to capture a text that is, in his own mind, always dissolving before the awareness that his perspective can never be considered sufficient—whether for himself or for others.[3] Not surprisingly, therefore, his texts generally reveal an irresolute and hesitant character that serves only to magnify the silence that surrounds the text and that even seeps into the very heart of the text by way of the lacunae existing among its various fragments.

There are, to be sure, a number of strategies that Barthelme himself employs in the face of this problem of the dissolving text. Before I examine them, however, it might be helpful, especially in light of the previous discussion of Nabokov, to address Barthelme's own view of the artistry that is available to would-be writers of the present. Like Nabokov, Barthelme is very aware of the collapse of traditions that has fragmented so much twentieth-century fiction and art, and at rare moments, again much like Nabokov, he even seems to wish that the fairly stable perspectives that had supported the act of text-making in the past were still in place. To be sure, in a couple of early stories— "Florence Green Is 81" and "The Dolt"—he satirizes those would-be writers who prepare for a traditional application of their profession either by enrolling in the Famous Writers School or by taking the National Writers' Examination. Both stories portray writers, Baskerville and Edgar respectively, who, lacking imagination because of their deter- mined preference for the models of the past (which essentially reflected the more stable perspectives on human experience then available), never escape their rather pedestrian unsuitability for the careers they crave. Baskerville wants to write a novel entitled *The Children's Army*, and in an age that resists overt formalism and structures of coherence he, at least marginally aware of the new developments in literature, manages to commit himself to writing what he considers to be a "new" novel. Finally, however, his notion of a new literature never surpasses the following concept: "The aim of literature . . . is the creation of a strange object covered with fur which breaks your heart" (*DC*, 14).[4] For Barthelme himself, the artist who can suspend himself in the void of models and perspectives, such a definition might stand, but for the Baskerville still wedded to the traditional application of fiction the definition leads only to an achievement of the most common and unimaginative kind. It is true that Baskerville's narrator is conscious of being in the predicament of a patient who fears boring his psychiatrist and who thus "strives mightily to establish his uniqueness" (*DC*, 8), but Baskerville himself is not aware enough and bright enough to be "elected . . . on the strength of [his] glamorous remarks" (*DC*, 13). On the other hand, he does write his own novel, and thus his situation may not be as trying as that of Edgar, who completely fails to muster the middle of an old-fashioned story for which he already possesses the beginning and the end.[5] Baskerville, too, nevertheless fails to understand and thereby surmount the fundamental limitations that permeate the craft of fiction- making in the present. Like Edgar, who deliberately chooses archaic words in an effort to introduce strange effects into his narrative, Baskerville never fully suspends himself in the problems of the contem-

porary writer, and thus his text never realizes the wonder of an art that
has ventured beyond the pale and reached new ground.

Nabokov, the writer who was a genius at suspending himself in the
limited ground of the solipsist, surely avoided the limitations of a
Baskerville or an Edgar. A writer such as Barthelme, however, who is
fully aware of the extreme artificiality in even the smart solipsist's ground
(e.g., Quilty's or Shade's), cannot content himself with Nabokov's
achievement—at least not without turning himself into a writer who,
much in the fashion of Baskerville and Edgar, merely parrots what
earlier writers have already accomplished. At the same time that he
satirizes the limitations of these pedestrian would-be writers, therefore,
Barthelme himself remains very sensitive to the crucial problems confronting all writers who seek to come into contact with what is new in
their times. There are three stories, I think, that especially illustrate
these difficulties. In "See the Moon?" the narrator at first suggests that
he hopes his "souvenirs . . . will someday merge . . . into something
meaningful" (*UP*, 156) and then concludes that "fragments are the only
forms I trust." Like any first-person narrator, he is interested in
presenting the details that give character to his life, but because he also
recognizes that at this point in Western civilization there can be no final
logic to his recitations, he deliberately keeps the details of his experience very sketchy. It is as if, in an age of the incredible event such as a
lunar landing, he knows that the details of his life not only cannot
generate serious attention but also that they cannot achieve that containment which smacks of sufficiency. To be sure, while taking stock of
his life, he does reach the significant conclusion that his own job of
writing "poppycock, sometimes cockypap," for a university president is
pointless and that he himself is no longer a "promising" candidate for the
system. That conclusion, nevertheless, rather than providing him with a
solid perspective for future action, merely plummets him further into the
difficulty facing all contemporary writers—the knowledge that he lacks
"a point of view kinky enough to call [his] own" (*UP*, 166). In this story
the reliance on personal peculiarity as a measure of originality may
initially seem an appropriate means of counterbalancing the marvels of
moon shots, but finally such reliance must lead to a very disquieting
irony. The reliance on personal idiosyncrasies has already defined the
efforts of Nabokov's best narrators—Quilty, Shade, and Veen—but in
those novels there still existed the illusion that the artist could create his
own world of artifice. In Barthelme's "See the Moon?", on the other
hand, the narrator, at the very same time that he believes himself to be
free to promote whatever interests him at the moment, is convinced that
he is completely insignificant. Unlike Nabokov's narrators, therefore, he

must deliberately and somewhat blithely choose, say, to classify the cardinals of Rome in the very face of his recognition that there exists no justification for doing anything whatsoever. The result is that his art then exists as an even more profound contradiction of itself than does Nabokov's.[6]

This contradiction also appears in the story entitled "A Film." Again, as in the previous story, the technological achievements of the space program profoundly affect the manner in which the filmmaker perceives his art. At one point in the making of his film he focuses the camera on the rocks retrieved from a lunar landing: "We set up in the Moon Rock Room, at the Smithsonian. There they were. The moon rocks. The moon rocks were the greatest thing we had ever seen in our entire lives! . . . They scintillated, sparkled, glinted, glittered, twinkled, and gleamed" (S, 77). Given the character of the previous story, the reader can conclude here that the incredible aura of the moon rocks is essentially a function of the filmmaker's awareness that the rocks represent a world that, because of its inaccessibility, convinces him of the fundamental limitations of his own. The filmmaker, to be sure, in the face of confinement within his narrow world, hopes that he can escape the depression of personal inadequacy by emphasizing the play of his own originality. As he himself remarks, the idea behind making his new film is that "it not be like other films" (S, 73). The fundamental fact of the matter, however, is that the marvelous achievements of the space program—and the presence of that other world—diminish whatever original sequences he might include in the film. In the end, consequently, this story becomes an analysis of the filmmaker's exploration of his options as he tries to upstage what cannot be upstaged. He wants to achieve great art, but despite the seemingly infinite variety of options open to him in an age of artistic license, he finds himself falling prey to self-doubt. Eventually, fully separated from the confidence traditionally available to the artist who is conscious of the strong relationship between his artistic achievement and prevailing social perspectives, he hires an expert consultant named Ezra and thus secures for himself the consolations of what has come to be regarded as the committee decision. Despite this insuring of his undertaking, however, his doubt only increases: "What if the film fails? And if it fails, will I know it?" This filmmaker wants to create, but no matter what procedures he follows, he is finally conscious only of failure: "I wanted to film everything but there are things we are not getting" (S, 79). He cannot upstage the moon spectaculars. He may conceive of ending the film—in fairly recent Hollywood fashion—with a colossal scene of air flight, but the huge scale of that undertaking, instead of vying with the moon shots, finally only underscores the absence of a confident and sensitive perspective that might engage its viewers in a shrewd analysis of man's lot in the present. The air scene basically represents only a gratuitous gesture—the attempt to be "grand" when there exists no justification for it. The filmmaker fails to resolve the contradiction before him, but with the story itself Barthelme at least provides a brilliant excursion into the problematic character of much recent art.[7]

In the third example, entitled "The Flight of the Pigeons," the narrator elaborates on the problem of originality by citing such marvels as an abandoned palazzo, the Numbered Man, the Sulking Lady, or even My Father Concerned About His Liver—all the citations serving as the basis for his unleashing of three propositions:

> The public demands new wonders piled on new wonders.
> Often we don't know where our next marvel is coming from.
> The supply of strange ideas is not endless. (S, 139)

For a writer like Barthelme, who has separated himself from a comfortable reliance upon the strangeness of first-person narration common to modernist fiction (the culmination is Nabokov), the three propositions must embody much of his own thinking. Lacking a comprehensive perspective with which he might ground his own experience, he cannot easily determine, any longer, what a marvel actually consists of. In an age of lunar exploration, of widespread technological change, and of increasing reliance upon mass media, furthermore, he finds that originality quickly exhausts itself in the effort to keep up with the explosion of civilization. For the narrator of "The Flight of the Pigeons," the succession of wonders has accelerated so rapidly that he, again in the manner of Barthelme himself, must even toy with the notion of "folding the show—closing it down" (S, 139). Such a notion may seem radical, but to the extent that it would allow the artist to relax from the pressure of his need to formulate something new, it represents an attractive alternative to the prevailing confusions of contemporary art. The tradition of artistic achievement, nevertheless, dies hard. With the disappearance of the "pigeons" or the données upon which the artist has for centuries relied, that tradition may now require drastic revision—but die? Hardly, even in Barthelme's fiction.

Barthelme himself seems to perceive the current state of fiction as largely an open field in which the author generates new materials in an effort not to dominate the world but to respond to its essential strangeness. In his two balloon stories, both of which focus upon the situation of contemporary visual art, Barthelme expands upon this idea in an effort to demonstrate that perspective is not as crucial as it once was to the making of art. In "The Balloon" the first-person narrator recounts the effect of observing a balloon that covers approximately forty-five blocks of Manhattan below Central Park.[8] The balloon, with its "deliberate lack of finish," its "rough, forgotten quality," initially evokes quite a bit of reaction, but finally the people of New York temper their response because they have already learned to distrust all questions of "meaning" except in cases involving "the simplest, safest phenomena" (*UP*, 16). The upshot is that the New Yorkers limit themselves to very personal, and quite idiosyncratic, responses to its presence. Eventually, in fact, the view that "what was important was what you felt when you stood under the balloon" (*UP*, 19) achieves a large currency. New York critics may continue to argue about proper responses, but the New Yorkers themselves see the balloon only as a geographical sign that offers each individual "the possibility, in its randomness, of mislocation of the self, in contradistinction to the grid of precise, rectangular pathways under our feet" (*UP*, 21). For people locked into the stresses of technological specialization the balloon serves as the occasion not only for that "spontaneous autobiographical disclosure" which provides at least a momentary sense of personal creativity but also for that deliberate suspension of self which relieves them of the commitments that organize their everyday lives and which, in addition to serving as the dominant mode of Jerzy Kosinski's fiction, becomes the basis for such Barthelmean stories as "Daumier." Let me allude to "Daumier" for a moment.

The narrator of "Daumier," himself concerned with the problem of originality, eventually concludes his story with this assessment: "The self cannot be escaped, but it can be, with ingenuity and hard work, distracted. There are always openings, if you can find them, there is always something to do" (*S*, 183). That "something" in this story may merely be the creation of surrogates that seem more attractive than the self, but in an age that lacks the means of verifying the self, the self can take pleasure in its insatiable ingestion, by way of deliberate mislocation or suspension of itself, of new modes of experience.[9] The narrator of "Daumier" recognizes that the self is "always, always hankering. It is what you might call rapacious to a fault. The great flaming mouth to the thing is never in this world going to be stuffed full" (*S*, 163–64). And instead of regarding this trait of the self as a quality that must be suppressed, he encourages the notion that the self should be allowed to meddle, to get involved in as many things and activities as possible. In "Daumier" the Nabokovian distinction between text and texture does apply: the self may initially lack a coherent text, but by developing a rich texture of things and activities, eventually a wonderful text does emerge—if only in retrospect.[10] The implication for both Nabokov and Barthelme, however, is that the self must at least be willing, like the artist, to indulge himself in the act of suspension. Thereafter the process of creation shall take care of itself.

The people in New York who relish the mislocation of self occasioned by the balloon, therefore, gain for themselves some of the stature of the contemporary artist who is interested in the openended examination of the processes of language and perception. What this stature is, is even more apparent in Barthelme's other balloon story, "The Great Hug." In that story a first-person narrator generally recounts how a Balloon Man creates balloons of seemingly unremarkable events. This Balloon Man clearly conceives of himself as an artist, for when he refuses to sell his balloons to kids and then also refuses to have his picture taken because he does not want others "to steal his moves," the fact that he has a high opinion of what he is and what he makes is fully evident. That is not to say that he believes he has gained possession of a significant content. On the contrary, he seems to regard the making of a balloon as being all "in the gesture—the precise, reunpremeditated right move" (A, 46). What interests the narrator beyond the stature of the Balloon Man as artist, however, is what will happen to the Balloon Man when he meets up with the Pin Lady. In his view such a meeting will bring two artists accomplished in the open-field gesture into serious conflict for attention, and thus the result promises to serve as an exemplum of what transpires throughout a western culture that has lost its underpinnings and that has virtually forced all imaginative men to adopt an aesthetic posture. The narrator at first imagines a kind of wrestling down the hill, two falls out of three defining the victor, but eventually, taking further stock of the situation, he realizes that the match will probably turn out to be rather inconsequential—because the art of the two principals is essentially the same. As the narrator suggests, "Pin Lady tells the truth. Balloon Man doesn't lie, exactly. How can the Quibbling Balloon be called a lie? Pin Lady is more straightforward. Balloon Man is less straightforward. Their stances are semiantireprophetical" (A, 48). Balloon Man may establish a firm position, *"But I insist that these balloons have a right to be heard!"* (A, 48), but Pin Lady's creations possess the same right. Whatever happens in this confrontation between equals, there is little chance that it will make much difference—to them or to anyone else. Again, as in "The Balloon," the principals lack that sufficient perspective of experience which would allow them to assume a role of artistic domination. At the end of "The Great Hug" the Balloon Man merely looks over to a man in a black cloak and suggests, "The Balloon of Perhaps. My best balloon." In this story, and in Barthelme's fiction in general, "perhaps" is everything. Without a significant perspective to rely upon, with only the mislocation or the suspension of self as the basis for creative effort, the artist faces a career of tentative gestures—of gestures that extrapolate out of the medium "something," but a something that knows no *a priori* conception of human experience.[11]

An especially good illustration of Barthelme's model for the artist appears in the story entitled "City Life." In that story one of the main characters describes the predicament that an apparently well-informed artist faces as he stands before a succession of empty canvases. Each day the artist initially delays his confrontation with the canvas by reading the *Times* as thoroughly as he can. When he does face up to the task before him, however, it is with little purpose and intention: "So (usually) he makes a mark on it, some kind of mark that is not what he means. That is, any old mark, just to have something on the canvas. Then he is profoundly depressed because what is there is not what he meant" (*CL*, 165). The problem is that, in a world where everything is so tentative, he cannot know what he meant. More than that, however, after lunch—having painted out the first mark—he again builds himself up to the moment when he must decide "whether or not to venture another mark." He does venture the mark, and again, as with the first mark, he suffers from the sense that the mark lacks significance. Finally, of course, after a series of "wrong moves and the painting out" of those moves, the canvas does begin to appear somewhat interesting—but only because it is no longer empty: "A something has been wrested from the nothing. The quality of the something is still at issue. . . . It's not where his head is, and he knows that, but nevertheless he—" (*CL*, 166). In spite of himself, and only because he has surrendered himself to his medium, art—or at least "something" of the sort—has emerged on the canvas. The art may not represent much, if anything, but it does capture the difficult character of perception and of language that lies at the heart of recent art activity.[12] What is on that canvas is at least a small indication of the artist's own awareness of the processes of creativity that define his innermost being. Despite its lack of representation or content, the canvas must serve as an eloquent comment on the present character of art achievement.

In the end texture counts for everything in Barthelme's fiction. There is, as I have already indicated, a sense in which the principle of texture, rather than that of content, has also established itself as the center of Nabokov's fiction. For no matter which of his great novels one cites, it is clear that Nabokov, even though still committed to the exploration of perspective, has carefully avoided reductive assertions of value and has thus edged himself very close to the emptiness of contemporary art. In fact, because his protagonists never finally comprehend and control their destinies (the philosopher Veen devotes half his life to an examination of space and time but never achieves a significant understanding), they must learn to suspend themselves imaginatively in the processes of human experience and to take heart in the texture that emerges, over the years, in the interplay of memory and the imagination. In Barthelme, of course, the influence of memory is much less pronounced. There the act of suspension tends to occur only for want of something else to do, not because the actor is playing out a complex game of association between the past and the present. The artist in "City Life," for example, merely explores the texture of his experience from day to day by playing out a gesture, then considering the nature of that gesture, and finally reacting with further gestures that reflect his increased sophistication.[13]

That having been said, however, it is also true that Barthelme continues to recover that residual content which lingers on in the affairs of men. Whether one cites his short stories or his novels, what gives his fiction focus is generally the fragile content of a primary relationship— e.g., the relationship between a husband and wife, or father and son, or psychiatrist and patient. Like the Nabokov who creates a content about the problems of text-making even though he has hoped to avoid all contents, Barthelme has involved himself in a significant and largely inescapable contradiction. He may have avoided the more obvious elements in Nabokov's strong reliance upon perspective (as, for example, in the disjointed presentation of narrative in *Snow White*), but it is also true that, with the exceptions of the conversations between Julie and Emma in *The Dead Father* and some of the dialogues in *Great Days*, he has not opened his texts up in the manner, say, of Jerzy Kosinski's bewildering *Steps*. Barthelme relies upon disorientation in his fiction, whether of his characters or of his readers, but generally his texts still limp home with some sense of purpose or meaning. What that meaning usually is can, I think, be established in light of this fundamental contradiction.

Throughout his stories and novels Barthelme's characters are above all conscious of their limited stature as agents of their own fate. Whether I cite the dwarfs in *Snow White* or the implied dwarfism of the Dead Father's followers in *The Dead Father*, the characters seem constantly to be responding to their inability to achieve a vision of coherence that would allow them the grace of substance in their lives. Because the characters never do gain such vision, in fact, at least not in focused form, they tend, in their hyperconscious awareness of their limitations, to regard themselves as failures who cannot straighten out the character of their lives. The more astute among them, such as Thomas in *The Dead*

Father, even regard themselves as murderers. The character of murder here is, of course, more metaphorical than literal. In a limited sense it even builds upon the kind of murder that attaches to Nabokov's texts. For just as the murders of Quilty and Shade (and to some extent even of Lucette) serve as metaphors for those narrators' surrender to the enervating sense of engaging in the impossible task of writing, so Barthelme's privileged characters become aware of words and deeds as arbitrary acts that constitute a type of murder—the imposition of attitude and value upon what knows no firm structures.[14] In Nabokov, to be sure, narrators such as Quilty, Shade, and Veen all remain conscious of themselves as creators within a broad tradition of art and philosophy, and thus for them murder largely functions only as a rhetorical device whereby they can explore the contradictions of self that emerge in the practice of their art. In Barthelme's work, on the other hand, murder constitutes a much more radical act. Because his characters generally labor in what one of them calls "the most exquisite mysterious muck," a muck that "is itself the creation of that muck of mucks, human consciousness" (*CL*, 167), the characters have little chance of separating the various strands of their consciousness as a means of approaching (and defining) the essential acts of the self. The self never becomes clear, and in the unmanageable confusion that surrounds it, Barthelme's characters can only regard their lives as hopelessly arbitrary and necessarily artificial. They never understand the nature and the ground of their experience, and the consequence is that, if only to stay alive physically and mentally, they must accept themselves as the murderers who have imposed themselves upon the things and the people about them.

In the end the profound sense of arbitrariness that underlies the experience of most of Barthelme's characters must radically affect all their acts of communication and relationship. There are, it is true, some characters in Barthelme's fiction who never face up to the problematic nature of their acts. Generally, however, his fiction exists as an attempt to defuse—by confronting it—the anxiety that attends any structuring of a text. Because he regards all texts as arbitrary gestures, as acts of communication that disregard the void and thus murder both the sender and the receiver, he has even concluded that man's one hope lies in an enlightened communication (and a web of relationships) that is based, beyond the widespread hypersensitivity to the fundamental arbitrariness of the universe, on a turning down of texts—i.e., upon a lessening of their value and import so that both text-makers and text-receivers will enjoy more freedom to explore the widely varying, yet frequently ignored, facets of their experience. Real freedom in Barthelme is never possible because no one is ever freed of the necessity of text. Men make texts, and they receive texts, and if they expect to live fully, they do both in an incredibly complex, mysterious way. The question for Barthelme (and his readers) is whether, in the process of handling their texts, men can appreciate the manner in which they become—at the very same time—both the victimizer and the victim within that complicated process. For Barthelme hope lies only in awareness.

7

Barthelme's Short Stories: Ironic Suspensions of Text

One of Barthelme's early short stories contains this quotation, which is Robert Kennedy's comment on Poulet's analysis of Marivaux:

> The Marivaudian being is, according to Poulet, a pastless futureless man, born anew at every instant. The instants are points which organize themselves into a line, but what is important is the instant, not the line. The Marivaudian being has in a sense no history. Nothing follows from what has gone before. He is constantly surprised. He cannot predict his own reaction to events. He is constantly being *overtaken* by events. A condition of breathlessness and dazzlement surrounds him. In consequence he exists in a certain freshness which seems . . . very desirable. (*UP*, 46)

This passage serves nicely as a touchstone for an introduction to Barthelme's short fiction because it addresses, with remarkable fullness, the matter of the timeless present that generally serves as the fundamental boundary for all human activity. It is true that Barthelme's stories frequently focus upon characters who are profoundly conscious of past achievements and/or of future goals, as if time were a continuum within which they can carefully stage their lives. Nevertheless, because these characters also know the terrible difficulty of trying to substantiate themselves, of verifying their perspectives as real, this consciousness of past and future tends to submerge in the overwhelming pressures of facing up to the present. The characters cannot know themselves in any final, absolute way, and for them, therefore, the question of their existence comes down to whether they possess the courage to acknowledge their insufficiency and, even more than that, whether they possess the vigor and freedom of mind to participate in a full dialogue with the present. In the process of "being *overtaken* by events," the characters have a wonderful opportunity for observing the nature of their own

reactions, to perceive the emergence of a texture that is both unanticipated and imaginative, and thus to explore that mode of Marivaudian
being which has become the foundation of so much recent art.

In Barthelme's fiction time ultimately surrenders all authority. To
some extent this surrender is already present in Nabokov—at least in the
sense that, having freed his narrators to explore the bizarre character of
their imaginative being, Nabokov develops a narrative texture that
appears to be dominated by the succession of time but that finally only
recovers the specific mingling of memory and the imagination in the
present. As a result of the tricks of both memory and imagination,
Nabokov's narrators always have some difficulty in maintaining strong
coherence within their conceptions of themselves, particularly when they
unleash their Humberts and Kinbotes, but in the end the dialogue of
selves that underlies each Nabokovian text does stabilize in the narrators' increasing understanding of themselves.[1] In Barthelme, on the
other hand, the narrator generally possesses a more fragile, and sometimes very tenuous, relationship to a conception of self; and thus, always
worried about the character of his identity, but at the same time
recognizing that the identity will never cohere, he must engage in
deliberate acts of suspension that allow him to come into closer contact
with that complex world of the present which surrounds him. The
narrator, or the character, who manages to avoid full organization "into a
line" (where plural instants of time develop some pattern), gains a
genuine, albeit limited (because he will never fully understand it),
opportunity for freedom, for fresh personality, for spontaneity—for that
"condition of breathlessness and dazzlement" which is crucial to retaining life's intensity. Man's deliberate surrender of authority for himself to
the processes of being in which he is "overtaken by events" is for
Barthelme, then, the key to the overthrow of time's authority and thus of
those psychological obstacles which prevent man from remarking and
even relishing the strangeness of whatever surrounds him. Quilty and
Shade and even Veen manage this surrender only through the contriv-
ances of narrative stance. In Barthelme, however, this surrender is the
possession not only of certain obtrusive narrators, but also of all those
characters who have avoided lives of content by maintaining full contact
with the marvelous texture of the everyday experience that is theirs by
birthright but that is so frequently lost in a misguided determination to
establish a web of significance for experience.

Poulet's analysis of Marivaudian being serves as a nice touchstone for
Barthelme's fiction because it isolates the fundamental consideration
that underlies all of Barthelme's techniques. So often readers of Barthelme tend to dismiss him as a master of the parody, as a writer who is

particularly adroit at capturing and mocking the absurd character of contemporary experience, but his ability in creating brief yet effusive forays into the quirks of the present is actually better evidence of his awareness of the impossibility of what has gradually become the postexistential position. For the postexistentialist, vision (even if created and sanctioned by the individual) is virtually a contradiction of itself: regardless of what one may accept as a framework of significance and value, the framework exists on quicksand because it can never contain all the perceptions that impinge on any human consciousness. The postexistentialist, therefore, like Barthelme's resourceful characters, cannot expend himself in anxiety over the consistency of his responses to the environment (as did many of the existentialists) but must, instead, freely indulge himself in the marvelous quiddities of the moment. He may not always regard those quiddities with enthusiasm, but at the very least he must accept as the source of his vitality and energy his contact with what in any ultimate sense represents the unknown but what in the immediate present is an opportunity for the unleashing of his being. Like the beings of Marivaux, Barthelme's characters extend themselves in what amounts to a negative space—negative because the space is not dominated by the characters' categories of thought—and thus come into touch with the deeper structures of their experience. That this is the case becomes even more evident if I now turn my attention to several of Barthelme's stories in which he, by employing a question-and-answer methodology, appears to pursue the reverse, i.e., positive (filled) space.

In "The Explanation" the exchanges between Q. (the questioner) and A. (the answerer) seem to be focused upon the desire for a full understanding of life's mysteries. The questioner is from the beginning, however, so overwhelmed by the monumentality of the task that he has great difficulty sticking even to one topic. As he shifts from subject to subject, in fact, from machines to blouses to literary questions to Maoism, the story turns into a rather exciting venture because its lacunae seem to swallow up the questioner's intentions, thus giving the story an unexpected texture in which negative space counts rather heavily. The black square that punctuates the story, apparently at random, probably serves as the best image of this negative space, but in the end all the verbal exchanges in the story (much like the exchanges between Julie and Emma in *The Dead Father* and the dialogues in *Great Days*) accomplish nothing and thus themselves rival the importance of the black square. Toward the middle of the story A. at least gives the reader a hint of what is happening when he comments on the advantage of Q.'s Socratic method: "I realize that [the method] permits many valuable omissions: what kind of day it is, what I'm wearing, what I'm thinking. That's a very considerable advantage, I would say" (*CL*, 73). A.'s comment goes to the heart of the matter, for by allowing the lacunae within and between the bits of conversation to take over the story, Q. has effectively avoided the folly of establishing a model that purports to explain all human experience. Later the shrewd A. seems to figure out what underlies Q.'s method, for during a conversation about madness and purity A. suddenly observes that "the content of right reason is rhetoric."[2] In other words, what A. seems to realize is that any system of understanding is dominated, not by "right reason" or unassailable models of logic, but by the persuasive powers of rhetoric—by the attitudes and assumptions that allow a logic to emerge. In and of itself, of course, rhetoric possesses no sufficient ground. It is merely the means (largely a technique or style) whereby a content is established. In Barthelme's fiction, because there is no category of absolute content, rhetoric—technique and style—lacks its usual function but at the same time becomes all the more important. Near the end of the story Q. rather urbanely points out that "the issues raised here are equivalents. Reasons and conclusions exist although they exist elsewhere, not here" (*CL*, 78). Reasons and conclusions generally reflect the use of an established, consistent rhetoric, and in the absence of such a rhetoric, as in this story of open-ended juxtaposition of questions and answers, there seems nothing to control the exchanges and thus organize the conversation. The exchanges in such a situation can only represent equivalent moments in time. Despite the lack, however, of a traditional rhetoric, one that supports the conventional acts of communication, this story does achieve its own imaginative, even supralogical, rhetorical character.

In "The Agreement," a brilliant tour de force, the answers actually disappear. In the story, which is merely a long series of questions, the questions emerge out of the narrator's paranoia concerning his ability to complete the "task" (which is never specified), and they generate a nearly incredible realization of the anxieties latent in his awareness of the fundamental solipsism that attaches to human consciousness. Consider, for instance, the following sequence:

> Will I deceive myself about the task that is beyond my abilities, telling myself that I have successfully completed it when I have not? Will others aid in the deception?
> Will others unveil the deception? (*A*, 62–63)

This passage clearly addresses the horror of the narrator's inhabiting of a world of hypersensitivity where the personal splitting of hairs has become the modus operandi. Try as he may to establish for himself a stance of some courage and determination, he is always left only with the enervating sense that the assumptions underlying any stance he might choose lack sufficiency. The upshot is that, instead of accepting the limitations that attach to any formulation of experience, he increasingly finds himself the victim of a paranoia that has as its sources both his sense of the "mess" out there and his sense of his own inadequacies before the fundamental dilemmas of contemporary epistemology. As he recites the case, "If I embrace the proposition that, after all, things are not so bad, which is not true, then have I not also embraced a hundred other propositions, kin to the first in that they are also not true? That the Lord is my shepherd, for example?" (A, 64). Clearly this narrator desires the positive space of secure, i.e., rationalized, ground, and in its absence, instead of courageously accepting the challenge of Marivaudian being, he finds himself the victim of such nagging anxiety that finally he approaches the necessity of deliberate self-deception. Paranoid about himself, he even finds that he has no choice but to resort to social activities and associations that can convince him of his self-worth. Such deception will, however, depend heavily on "aid" from others, for given the extremity of his paranoia this narrator now requires the corroborating evidence of others in order to recover his pose of esteem. His is obviously a thoroughly unsatisfactory situation. At the very end of the story he may quote at length—and rather wistfully—the twelfth article of his divorce agreement, an agreement that seemingly spells out in detail the "rights, obligations and causes of action arising out of or under this agreement," but even that agreement cannot give him the stability and exactitude that he desires. The divorce agreement, in fact, serves only as another illustration of his inability to rise above his paranoia, to surrender to the world of the present.

If in "The Explanation" the avoidance of strict logic and rhetoric makes possible a life of Marivaudian being, "The Agreement" points to the difficulty of achieving a separation from logic and rhetoric that will allow one to suspend oneself in the processes of unfolding experience. The first story exposes an eloquence of being; the second story, the failure to achieve the same. In a third story written in the Socratic method, "The Catechist," the difficulty of establishing sufficient appreciation of one's "deeper structures" becomes even more clear. In the story the first-person narrator, himself a priest, encounters another priest who, while holding a text on church doctrine, daily catechizes the first priest about his use of alcohol and his relationship with a woman with dark hair. In order to deflect the catechist's concerns, the first priest alludes to the presence of alternative interpretations within any situation—a theme that causes the catechist to refer to his book, where he finally discovers the response, "*A disappointing experience: the in-*

adequacy of language to express thought. But let the catechist take courage" (S, 122). Intellectually, prompted by the text on doctrine, the catechist knows the problem of language and thus the corollary inadequacy of any rhetoric that presumes to fill the lacunae within all verbal statements, but there is little sense in the story that this knowledge has profoundly opened him up to experience. Rather, he is still clinging to as much structure as the church can provide. When the first priest proceeds with his "self-defense," in fact, by professing to know nothing even of the theological virtue of love, the catechist immediately refers to several theologians whose views have established the ground for his own experience of that lofty emotion. Unquestionably the catechist requires a stable world of language and meaning that is no longer available to the first priest. In a certain sense what the first priest provides the catechist is an opportunity to come into contact with the deeper character of human experience—that character which lies beyond definitions wedded to doctrine. The catechist, however, fails to open up.

On the other hand, at least once he has given himself up to emotional realities beyond doctrinal limits, the first priest experiences only a compulsion to write inconclusive letters ("one does what one can") or to submit to "analysis terminable and interminable" (S, 125). He has surrendered himself to the deeper character of his experience but in the process has lost his comfortable grasp on "reality." When the catechist questions him about his call to the priesthood, for example, the bewildered priest can only admit that he "heard many things. Screams. Suites for unaccompanied cello. I did not hear a call" (S, 125). The catechist has failed to appreciate his having been trapped within a theological rhetoric, but the first priest, presumably more perceptive and imaginative, has failed to establish a creative relationship to a new, presumably more open, style that would allow him to accept the character of each moment in time as sufficient in itself. At the end of the story, to be sure, the priest does return to the woman with the dark hair. The woman, however, is married to a psychologist who is engaged in measuring "vanishing points" in an effort "to define precisely the two limiting sensations in the sensory continuum, the upper limit and the lower limit" (S, 126). Much in the fashion of this psychologist, who, despite his learned awareness of the limitations of perception and language, tries to quantify what is surely variable from person to person, the priest still hopes for some understanding and thus fails to surrender fully to the unstable nature of his experience. Instead of embracing from moment to moment a process of being that is inexplicable and thus unpredictable, he—despite his sensitivity—still thinks in terms of defining the limits of his own understanding. He has moved beyond the catechist's dilemma, but he is not yet free.

The most interesting feature of these three stories is that their method virtually contradicts what Barthelme seems to have concluded about human experience. The very posture of questioning, because it entails the construction of answers, frequently prevents the questioner from achieving that final gesture of liberation in which he, having recognized the unavailability of answers, turns his experience into the creative play, not of content, but of mere being.[3] The principals in "The Explanation," because they recognize that there is no explanation, gain such imaginative ground. The principals in "The Agreement" and in "The Catechist," on the other hand, display varying degrees of hysteria because they fail to separate themselves entirely from the need for understanding. Even the narrating priest, whom the reader might not initially associate with hysteria, lacks the perspective that would introduce him to a radically new sense of being. What happens in these three stories, of course, generally characterizes the heart of almost all of Barthelme's fiction, where there is never much effective communication or human understanding. Whether I cite *Snow White*, which focuses upon problems of communication among peers, or *The Dead Father*, which focuses upon problems of communication between generations, the difficulty of substituting a new openness for the limited grounds of the past leads to the failure of all the principal characters. Trapped within their own solipsism, these characters know only a profound sense of personal inadequacy when dealing with the world of people about them. In order to broaden my discussion of this sense of inadequacy in Barthelme's fiction, I want to examine briefly four stories in which the husband-wife, the father-son, and the doctor-patient relationships serve almost as paradigms for man's fundamental need for a suspension of self as a means of countering his deeply felt anxieties.

In the first story, entitled "The Big Broadcast of 1938," the principal character, Bloomsbury, manages to retain his hold on reality following a divorce from his wife, Martha, only by sounding off as the rather peculiar owner of a radio station. Repeatedly, and in an incantatory manner, he singles out in his broadcasts, "for special notice, free among all the others, some particular word in the English language, and repeat[s] it in a monotonous voice for as much as fifteen minutes, or a quarter-hour" (*DC*, 67). On occasion such repetition discloses in a word "new properties, unsuspected qualities," almost as if the repetition were introducing the speaker to a new level of eloquence, but because Bloomsbury has actually intended only to fill up the time with such repetitions he never realizes that new dimension of experience which is rooted in a shrewd appreciation of the function of language in his life. That this is the case becomes more apparent when Bloomsbury devotes himself to a series of radio "announcements" that he directs at his wife. One of these announcements toward the end of the story gets to the heart of the matter: "You [Martha] veiled yourself from me, there were parts I could have and parts I couldn't have. And the rules would change, I remember, in the middle of the game, I could never be sure which parts were allowed and which not" (*DC*, 77). What Bloomsbury wanted in his relationship with Martha was stability, i.e., a stability that matched up with his conception of what a marriage should be. What he fails to realize here, however, is that short of defusing the normal processes of perception and language, stability will always remain an impossible goal. Stability is basically a function of content, and in a world where content is secondary to the actual processes of perception and language, stability cannot serve as the object of a relationship. When a dissatisfied Martha openly took another lover, therefore, the unimaginative Bloomsbury, who required above everything else steadiness in his life, completely fell apart. Having fashioned himself a "reckoner," someone who could tally up the events of life and thus establish its significant quality, he could not deal with a situation that lay beyond his tally sheet. His experience without Martha is hardly much different. By his own reckoning Bloomsbury may have been "an All-American boy," but now, following the collapse of his marriage, he continues to display the All-American failure to acknowledge the fundamental limitations of his childhood patterns of perception and language. Threatened, even cornered, by his recent experience, he resorts to the expedience of concentrating on words like *nevertheless*, or *assimilate, alleviate, authenticate, ameliorate*, or *matriculate*—all words that by virtue of their suggestiveness seem to offer a subtle and imaginative comment on his life—but finally these words fail to enlarge his understanding of that eloquence which lies at the heart of Barthelme's fiction.[4] The story concludes with the termination of Bloomsbury's broadcasting career in the interruption of electrical service as a result of an arrears in his account. His propensity for reckoning has entirely failed him.

In the second story, "Views of My Father Weeping," which serves as a brilliant analogue to *The Dead Father*, the relationship shifts to that of father and son. In the story the son, who has always felt powerless in the presence of his father, sets out to determine the facts of his father's death (the father has been run over by an aristocrat's carriage). From the beginning of the story, however, it is clear that he has had great difficulty establishing a perspective of his father when alive and, now, cannot establish a perspective of him when killed. He cannot, for example, ascertain whether it is his father who was lying in bed weeping or whether it is his father who, by virtue of drinking, was at fault in the carriage accident. The first issue, that of a perspective on his father when alive, explodes only in a series of unrelated images—such as the father wearing "a large hat (straw) on which there are a number of blue and yellow plastic jonquils" (*CL*, 13) or "peering through an open door into an empty house" (*CL*, 14) or "weeping" in bed (*CL*, 14) or "attending a class in good behavior" (*CL*, 15). Clearly there is no coherence in the images. In fact, the only moment of intensity that the son remembers in his dealings with the father, a moment that presumably might solidify his character, occurs on a hunting trip when, in the absence of "a long list of animals" (*CL*, 13) to shoot at, the two of them "hunkered down behind some rocks, Father and I, he hunkered down behind his rocks and I hunkered down behind my rocks, and we commenced to shooting at each other. That was interesting" (*CL*, 13). It is a strange scene—but not so strange, perhaps, in the absence of a coherent perspective that might bind father and son together. The son and his father are separate, and thus after the father's death the son still feels the difficulty of verifying the nature of his father. He never succeeds. The other issue, that of verifying the father's responsibility for the accident, would appear to reach a similar conclusion, but here the story takes a new turn. The son may establish the identity of the aristocrat's liveryman, but he also finds other witnesses to the event who both affirm and deny the father's blame. Even when the son visits the aristocrat's house, he hears in one moment the liveryman deny any responsibility for the tragedy and in the next a dark-haired girl rebuke the liveryman for being "an absolute bloody liar" (*CL*, 16). The son, like the questioners and catechists, can never get to the heart of the matter, at least in a preconceived sense, for the real problem in this situation is the limitation of all perception and language—a fact that depreciates the value of content and reinforces the importance of developing the ability to suspend oneself continuously in the processes of experience. The story concludes on the simple note of "Etc." and at that point the fundamental question before the reader is whether the son has embraced this principle of suspension.[5] Given the style of the story, one of Barthelme's finest and one narrated by the son, I think it probable that he has. A Bloomsbury he is not.

In the third story, "The Sandman," which is essentially a letter from the narrator to his girl friend's psychiatrist (the Sandman), the importance of suspension in life's processes rather than adherence to a content is unmistakable. In his letter the narrator accuses Dr. Hodder, who has judged Susan to be a voyeur, of allowing "norms" to "skew" his

view of Susan's problem (S, 92). What is interesting about the accusation, of course, is that the narrator, privy to Barthelme's basic attitudes,
recognizes that the reliance upon norms introduces a content that may
have little, if any, validity in its application to Susan. Hodder's belief,
for example, that Susan might "become an artist and live happily ever
after" profoundly troubles the narrator not only because such a belief is a
commonly accepted norm for creative people but also because, at least in
his eyes, "the paradigmatic artistic experience is that of failure" (S, 93).
In his view Hodder's juxtaposition of Susan and a happy career as an
artist constitutes an incredibly naive and arbitrary formulation of a
"content." The narrator, presumably because he is more sensitive to the
dilemmas of perception and language, shrewdly recognizes that the artist
deals fundamentally in failure because "the actualization [that he seeks
in his art] fails to meet, equal, the intuition" with which he initiates his
work. For the narrator, Hodder's associating of Susan, or anyone with an
imagination as alive as Susan's, with the "content" of an artist is
pointless because the artist finally deals not in content but in the
processes that surround and support his being—and that resist easy
classification and understanding. Distressed by the confusion or,
perhaps, the absence of content in her life, Susan may herself have
sought Hodder's assistance, but at the same time, as the narrator is
quick to point out, she has taken care to avoid the easy content of such
"instant gratification as dealt out by so-called encounter or sensitivity
groups, nude marathons, or dope" (S, 94). Regardless of Hodder's
appraisal of her dilemma, therefore, it is clear that her imaginative world
lies well beyond a dependence upon his limited formulations. Eventually, in fact, having routinely seduced Hodder (he is himself clearly open
to "instant gratification"), she recognizes that he possesses no real
solution to the basic doubts that have momentarily diminished her
self-confidence. She thus initiates her withdrawal from Hodder, and it is
at that point, having patiently waited for Susan to master her own
problem, that the narrator writes his letter in order to squelch any further
interference in Susan's life that Hodder might be considering. As the
narrator remarks about Susan, "Susan is wonderful. *As is.* There are not
so many things around to which that word can be accurately applied" (S,
95). It is an astute observation. The imaginative being who develops his
own technique and style, his own eloquence of being, despite the failure
of all content, is genuinely a marvel.

There is another early story that parallels, but with a significant twist,
"The Sandman." That story, entitled "Alice," is noteworthy not only
because of the narrator's general suppression of punctuation (an act that
destroys the fragile border between coherence and chaos) but also

because of the narrator's indulging of himself in daydreams that center on a desire that compromises his professional ethics. In this story the narrator is the doctor, here an obstetrician, who in the course of his practice falls prey to an overwhelming desire to "fornicate with Alice" (*UP*, 119). The obstetrician is aware of the potential impact of such a relationship upon both his own and Alice's marriages, but influenced by the intellectual atmosphere of the New School he easily manages to regard " 'good' and 'bad' as terms with only an emotive meaning" (UP, 125). Like the psychiatrist in "The Sandman," the obstetrician with an air of sophistication tries to create a clever game whereby he might calm those moral qualms which hinder the fruition of his desire. Toward the end of the story, however, having already fantasized his release from the bonds of moral perspective, this obstetrician continues to consider such facts of his past experience as his having "followed obediently in the footsteps of my teachers" (*UP*, 126). Obviously, even after long consideration, he is having difficulty overthrowing his deep-seated moral scruples. His fantasies may turn to the crudeness of "chewing" on Alice's breasts, but by the end of the story, with no fruition of his desire at hand, he has managed only a sensitive examination of his situation— yet an examination that surely surpasses the psychiatrist's rather easy formulations. Here is the obstetrician's appraisal of himself:

> possible attitudes found in books 1) I don't know what's happening to me 2) what does it mean? 3) seized with the deepest sadness, I know not why 4) I am lost, my head whirls, I know not where I am 5) I lose myself 6) I ask you, what have I come to? 7) I no longer know where I am, what is this country? 8) had I fallen from the skies, I could not be more giddy 9) a mixture of pleasure and confusion, that is my state 10) where am I, and when will this end? 11) what shall I do? I do not know where I am (*UP*, 127)

Unlike the psychiatrist, the obstetrician does not possess an easy ground for initiating extramarital affairs. No matter what stance he adopts in relation to his desire for Alice, he cannot avoid the terrible sense of violating the moral field of his past experience. The reader who is impatient with his temporizing might even be tempted to accuse him of having allowed himself to be victimized by a rather narrow perspective of human relationships. And yet, particularly if one recalls the nature of Bloomsbury's possessiveness, there is good reason to argue, here, that the obstetrician is in fact very sophisticated in his examination of his personal situation. Indeed, instead of merely violating his past, or instead of merely discounting the significance of a relationship with Alice, he shows a wonderful ability to sustain himself in the very complicated addressing of the contradictions that have surfaced in his feelings. To be sure, he may never resolve the contradictions, and thus he may never fully escape his present confusion, but at least he has come into contact with the fundamental notion that human beings are not simply empty vessels but consciousnesses with peculiar imaginative configurations—configurations nurtured in childhood, sustained in maturity, and thus open to many contradictions. To some extent maturity does open the doctor's fields of moral experience, but finally some of the limits from his past will remain. Having realized this much, the doctor is a privileged character—confused yet eloquent.

The progression from Bloomsbury's life of narrow content to Susan's and even the obstetrician's lives of complex style points finally to the need, in Barthelme's fiction, for an ironic suspension of self. Whereas the son who tries to figure out the nature of his father is only beginning the process of suspension, Susan and the obstetrician have already committed themselves to its necessity. Barthelme's fiction in general reflects the same imaginative suspension, and as a fiction principally of technique and style it remains, at least theoretically, a matter of infinite variation. As an artist, of course, Barthelme may seem to limit the possible variation by his preference for certain stylistic traits. Despite his use of his own peculiar styles, however, his fiction continues to possess a remarkable openness that suggests that his stylistic variations shall know few boundaries. There is no question that style counts very heavily in Barthelme's fiction—witness, here, the final two selections of *City Life*.

"Brain Damage," a story replete with the ominous headlines reminiscent of *Snow White*, on the surface provides an excursion into the cerebral litter of contemporary society—from the promise of ESP to the enthusiasm of the flower culture, from the priesthood of waiters to that of university professors. Throughout the story, however, people are caught up in the confusions of the present, and at the heart of it all is the narrator who works for newspapers "at a time when I was not competent to do so." In Barthelme's world, it should be clear, no one is competent to report content, and thus the reader must not be outraged when the narrator elaborates on his incompetence: "I reported inaccurately. . . . I pretended I knew things I did not know. . . . I misinterpreted. . . . I suppressed. . . . I invented. . . . I faked. . . . I failed to discover the truth. I colored the truth with fancy. I had no respect for truth" (*CL*, 138). At the very point (in its development as a medium) that the newspaper has so much varied content to offer its readers, it has—rather ironically—become a generally unreliable source of information. The narrator knows that any source of information is inadequate, and, aware of the arbitrariness of all truth, he even goes so far as to argue, "Some people feel you should tell the truth, but those people are impious and wrong, and if you listen to what they say, you will be tragically unhappy all your life" (CL, 145). The long tradition of attempting to fix truth has in his view resulted in brain damage, and because Americans continue to be prone to the need for establishing "truth," he has come to the second conclusion that "this is the country of brain damage." In the narrator's world there are surely others besides Americans who know the dangers of content, but because the brain damage that originates in the pursuit of content is so widespread and even sustained in those American centers of learning that should avoid such contamination, he is hardly hopeful about the possibility of any real escape from the dilemma: "You can hide under the bed but brain damage is under the bed, and you can hide in the universities but they are the very seat and soul of brain damage" (CL, 146). For the narrator there is no escape. He is himself damaged, and in his own writing and howling, in his moans, he may ask repeatedly "WHAT RECOURSE?" but the answer is pale at best: "RHYTHMIC HANDCLAPPING SHOUTING SEXUAL ACTIVITY CONSUMPTION OF FOOD" (CL, 141). Even his question, as a question of content, exposes his lack of redress. In the end "Brain Damage," like much of Barthelme's fiction, coheres only at its seams. While each of its fragments continues to unleash a furious comment on life's inanities, the story as a whole tends toward an awesome silence that mirrors the lacunae separating its fragments and thus again reinforces the importance of style.

"City Life," the final story in the volume of the same name, is probably one of the best examples of the substitution of technique for content in all of Barthelme's fiction. In the previous chapter I have already recounted Charles's description, late in the story, of the artist who manages to wrest something from his canvas only after a long series of seemingly false starts. Generally the story, which hinges on the complex and shifting relationships among Elsa, Ramona, Charles, and Jacques, achieves little more in terms of content than what the artist gains on his canvas. For as it explores the dilemma of men and women launching careers presumably of substance (in business and in law), it is continually pulling back in the face of the principal characters' discovery that the "content" that they have pursued is largely a hoax.[6] Charles, for example, despite his grand intentions, loses his commitment to a promising business career in Cleveland. Elsa, in turn, quits law school in order to satisfy another desire, that of marriage, and Ramona, although continuing her legal education, finally sees the law as a joke that genuinely deserves the affront of her virgin pregnancy. Eventually all of the principal characters find themselves inhabiting a world of contradictory impulses—a world in which even such institutions as racetracks and art galleries merge and thus a world in which the most rigorous of distinctions and categories finally dissipate. Victimized by the loss of the framework that has traditionally supported the acts of civilization, the characters all seem to have misplaced their sources of energy, especially the energy necessary for sustaining a relationship. As Ramona rather succinctly remarks, the world of "City Life" is a place where "one couldn't sleep with someone more than four hundred times without being bored" (*CL*, 159).

In this apparent void, to be sure, Moonbelly writes his songs as if there were still something to be said and sung about human experience. Organized as comments upon contemporary life, the songs' very titles reveal Moonbelly's determination to establish some "content" for his existence: "The System Cannot Withstand Close Scrutiny" and "Cities Are Centers of Copulation." The songs, nevertheless, instead of supporting human vitality, tend only to reinforce the emptiness that has reduced the characters of the story to postures of ennui. In the end, in fact, the songs have less imaginative value than the achievement of the artist whose struggles with his canvas results only in a busy quality of surface. In the final section of the story, when Ramona alludes to the fact that the people of the city "are locked in the most exquisite mysterious muck" (*CL*, 166), a muck that "heaves and palpitates" and "is itself the creation of that muck of mucks, human consciousness," there is no longer any question that the pursuit of "content" is, in the context of urban complexity and contradiction, a hopeless venture. Ramona herself, unable to identify the father of her baby (is it Vercingetorix or Moonbelly or Charles?), simply indulges herself in the possibility that she is the chosen one, the vessel of light, the second virgin who will give birth. Such indulging is ludicrous—all the more so when a law student begins to defend her position—but as she herself recognizes, that ludicrousness is all she has: "What was the alternative?" (*CL*, 168). In Ramona the madness that lies near the surface of "Brain Damage" finally breaks out. She is the character of unleashed style. If, in the process of playing with the surfaces of her existence, she does end up with a content of flagrant madness, it is a content that is marginal at best. In the city style is everything.

The best example of the eloquence of style, however, is Barthelme's brilliant "A Shower of Gold." In this story an artist named Peterson, while considering the possibility of appearing on a TV program suggestively entitled *Who Am I?*, confronts in rapid succession a number of instances of his own negligibility: a president who mutilates his—

Peterson's—latest piece of sculpture in order to make him think; a barber-philosopher who insists that "in the end one experiences only oneself"; and a cat–piano player who obfuscates the issue of personal choice by confronting Peterson with the dilemma of whether he chose the cat or the cat chose him. The narrator of the story very cagily blurs the distinctions between dreaming and consciousness, and thus while it is apparent that Peterson wants the freedom to be the artist, it is also evident that the lack of a world that stands at attention, with strong outlines and moral purposes, prevents him from achieving such freedom. As in the two stories that conclude *City Life*, Peterson seems only to enjoy a choice of which brain damage or muck he wishes to associate with, for regardless of whatever achievement he gains as an artist, he remains the victim of an inescapable solipsism. In his own mind he may continue to hope for the circumstances that will allow him to establish his credentials as a man who can dominate the world about him, but those circumstances never arrive. In addition to the intrusions of the president, the barber, and the cat–piano player, his gallery director abuses him by neglecting to display his work and then by suggesting that Peterson might sell more of his work if he were to cut it into two—make the pieces smaller. Circumstances are never propitious, and Peterson is not much of a man. When he makes his TV appearance and there witnesses the humiliation of the other contestants, nevertheless, he rises above his strong sense of failure and manages to turn the absurdity of the situation into a running commentary that the announcer cannot terminate. Significantly the commentary is one of hope: "In this kind of world, . . . absurd if you will, possibilities nevertheless proliferate and escalate all around us and there are opportunities for beginning again" (*DC*, 183). The barber may have earlier reminded Peterson of Pascal's comment that man's condition is so "wretched" that he must be inconsolable, but now an eloquent Peterson, having earlier despaired of achieving the appearance of substance, does Pascal one better by counseling his audience to "turn off your television sets, . . . cash in your life insurance, indulge in a mindless optimism." In the face of brain damage and muck Peterson himself now indulges in what amounts to the act of poetry:

> My mother was a royal virgin . . . and my father a shower of gold. My childhood was pastoral and energetic and rich in experiences which developed my character. As a young man I was noble in reason, infinite in faculty, in form express and admirable, and in apprehension. . . . (*DC*, 183)

If with Ramona's announcement of a virgin pregnancy in "City Life" there is a strain of pessimism about the ability of the mind to manage its prison of solipsism, in "A Shower of Gold" there seems to be some real hope. The narrator may conclude the story by suggesting that in his last comments Peterson "was, in a sense, lying, in a sense he was not," but there can be little doubt that Peterson's new style finally represents a marvelous, perhaps the only marvelous, ground of human experience left to a Barthelmean protagonist.[7]

In a recent story, "What to Do Next," Barthelme expands on the nature of Peterson's experience. In the story the narrator is providing counsel to someone whose life has apparently fallen apart. After citing such instructions as adopting a new attitude, traveling, writing a will, etc., he concludes his counsel by suggesting that the person in distress must become "part of the instructions themselves," thus turning the person (and his style) into a creative act:

> we have specified that everyone who comes to us from this day forward must take twelve hours of you a week, for which they will receive three points credit per semester, and, as well, a silver spoon in the "Heritage" pattern. . . . We are sure you are up to it. Many famous teachers teach courses in themselves; why should you be different, just because you are a wimp and a lame, objectively speaking? Courage. . . . You will be adequate in your new role. See? Your life is saved. The instructions do not make distinctions between those lives which are worth saving and those which are not. (A, 86)

Here the person who accepts his status as maker, regardless of his stature as a man, becomes the standard for those about him—clearly a distressing situation and yet an astute observation of recent times. In a world that lacks a consistent metaphysical framework, eloquence becomes a matter of developing as much vitality of perception and language as one can.[8] Because no one owns a corner on truth, every person alive, at least theoretically, enjoys a genuine chance of becoming the arbiter of the world in which he lives. In these terms human existence becomes, above everything else, a test of a man's courage to be "adequate" in his own role—and thus to enjoy his own limited yet profound sense of truth.

The madness of "Brain Damage" and "City Life" seems to conflict with the more confident and optimistic[9] character of "A Shower of Gold" and "What to Do Next," but by returning to another story in the Socratic method, "Kierkegaard Unfair to Schlegel," I think it is possible to capture the quality that unites all four of these stories and that also makes the emphasis upon individuality in the latter two more palatable. In this story A. seems at first to be interested in establishing how and why Kierkegaard is unfair to Schlegel. Later, however, he acknowledges that he is merely annihilating Kierkegaard "in order to deal with his disapproval" (*CL*, 90) of the character of such lives as A.'s. A. knows that Kierkegaard is in fact fair to Schlegel, but by establishing the reverse he gets himself off the hook of Kierkegaard's argument that religion is necessary for a "reconciliation with actuality." Because A. cannot accept the religious stance, he must subject Kierkegaard to the irony inherent in his own—A.'s—insights into the matter. In reality, nevertheless, as Q. is quick to recognize, what A. is about is merely "the unavoidable tendency of everything particular to emphasize its own particularity" (*CL*, 92). For Barthelme, it appears, the location of any irony, of the contradictions that permeate even the simplest of contemporary experiences, becomes the source of an important grace: as long as man can establish a peculiarity of personal vision, if only in terms of irony, he can warrant himself as vital and still thinking for himself.[10] It is a limited grace, but surely it is its realization that enables such different characters as Ramona and Peterson to achieve their styles of eloquence.

In the context of all these stories that emphasize the suspension of the self in the play of style and irony, it is clear that Barthelme himself continues to layer into his fiction at least a partial content. He may, as in the Socratic-method stories, disparage the deliberate pursuit of content, but in the end—and despite the fragmented character of his stories—he introduces content by way of his thorough exploration of the ironic nature of contemporary man. As the narrator of "Hiding Man" at one point implies, there is always a content, for "one believes what one can, follows that vision which most brilliantly exalts and vilifies the world" (*DC*, 35). The precise definition of such vision always remains problematic in Barthelme's fiction, but finally, as yet another narrator (from "The Party") suggests, man must in moments of heightened consciousness reckon with his contents: "Of course we did everything right, insofar as we were able to imagine what 'right' was" (*S*, 62). In Barthelme there is no easy grace that allows his characters to escape the "brain damage" that surrounds and envelops them. At the same time that he stresses man's need for style and irony, however, Barthelme also recognizes man's continuing need for content. This contradiction underlies the genius within all his fiction.

8

Snow White: The Suppression of Text

One of the more obvious, yet one of the most important, comments on language in *Snow White* appears almost exactly at midpoint, and it is given by Dan, who will eventually replace Bill as the leader of the dwarfs. That passage, largely a parody of itself, bears lengthy quotation because it exposes the fundamental ground of Barthelme's irony:

> You know, Klipschorn was right I think when he spoke of the "blanketing" effect of ordinary language, referring, as I recall, to the part that sort of, you know, "fills in" between the other parts. That part, the "filling" you might say, of which the expression "you might say" is a good example, is to me the most interesting part, and of course it might also be called the "stuffing" I suppose, and there is probably also, in addition, some other word that would do as well, to describe it, or maybe a number of them. But the quality this "stuffing" has, that the other parts of verbality do not have, is two-parted, perhaps: (1) an "endless" quality and (2) a "sludge" quality. Of course that is possibly two qualities but I prefer to think of them as different aspects of a single quality. (*SW*, 96)[1]

What is striking about this comment is Dan's attitude. For him language has lost its purposeful demeanor, its primary function as a means of precise communication, and in the vacuum created by this loss the sludge quality of language has mushroomed so rapidly, much like the quantity of man's trash, that man's relationship to language has switched "from a question of disposing of this 'trash' to a question of appreciating its qualities, because, after all, it's 100 percent, right?" (*SW*, 97). If it is true that the question of language use in recent times must now focus upon the appreciation of its trash qualities, the character of such appreciation, of course, becomes a matter of some interest. On the one hand, weighed down by the sludge of language, man might merely learn how "to dig" (Dan's pun) the wearisome situation and, in doing so, discover that he wants "to be on the leading edge of this trash phenomenon." On the other hand, instead of merely accepting what amounts to a bad situation, he might adopt the ironic mode of Barthelme's narrator and thus, in a certain sense, turn language against itself. The choice of response, here, is a very significant choice, for the nature of man's relationship to language profoundly affects all aspects of his existence. In *Snow White,* therefore, the crucial question before the reader is the identification of those characters who, as a result of an ironic stance that reflects their sensitivity to the processes of language, manage to create some imaginative—albeit limited—ground for their experience.

To some extent, if only because of the narrator's bizarre juxtaposition of fragments, all the characters in *Snow White* seem to possess an ironic stance toward language—or, at least, toward the exhausted character of their communications. Consider, for example, the passage, again toward the middle of the novel, in which Paul, Snow White, and the seven dwarfs attend a "howling party." At the party, which is parodied much in the manner of Barthelme's story "The Party," the chatter centers upon such delectable topics as "the bat theory of child-raising" (*SW,* 116) or the reign of Harold Bluetooth "during a certain period" of Scandinavian history or even a conventional topic such as politics.[2] As in the "sludge" passage, the narrator's emphasis is upon the manner in which the partygoers fill up their time merely in order to stay clear of the void that will envelop them if they remain silent. Even Clem, who deliberately takes some "consciousness-expanding drugs" in order to separate himself from the inanities of the others' chatter, feels the terror of the void, for when he suddenly concentrates his attention upon his own thumbtip, it becomes evident that he, too, is the victim of the pressure to speak in order to reify his presence. He may only look at his thumb and ask rhetorically, "Is this the upper extent of knowing, this dermis that I perceive here?" (*SW,* 117); or he may only let his mind wander rhetorically into the territory of nonsense: "The content of the giraffe is giraffe meat. Giraffes have high blood pressure because the blood must plod to the brain up ten feet of neck" (*SW,* 117). The process of articulating nonsense, however, brings him back to the chatter of the party, where he now serves as the parody of what he had hoped to escape. Some readers might be tempted to regard Clem's discourse on the thumb or on the giraffe as an indication of a superior imagination, but finally there can be little doubt that Clem's use of language reveals as much exhaustion as the others'. After all, this Clem is the dwarf who, on a visit to Chicago, expects "something a little different" (*SW,* 23) in terms of sexual activity, yet ends up seeking a bordel in the Yellow

Pages because of a failure of both imagination and energy. At the cocktail party, therefore, he becomes the fullest image of the manner in which trash has come to dominate the communications of the exhausted. That this is the case is especially apparent when Snow White, recognizing the foolishness of Clem's behavior, separates the dwarfs from the festivity by insisting in a petulant manner: "Take me home. . . . Take me home instantly. If there is anything worse than being home, it is being out" (SW, 117). Snow White and the dwarfs had come to the party because of their boredom at home. The communications at the cocktail party, however, serve only to weary their spirits further.

What happens at the cocktail party has an important parallel at the beginning of the novel when Snow White and the dwarfs are sitting around the breakfast table. Snow White in that instance exclaims loudly, "Oh I wish there were some words in the world that were not the words I always hear!" (SW, 6). What Snow White requires, however, is not a new vocabulary but a new enthusiasm in her conversations with others. The dwarfs, especially while eating such hackneyed cereals as "Fear," "Chix," and "Rats," hardly promise the satisfaction of this pressing need. A visitor named Howard may proffer the phrase "Fish slime," as if that phrase were at least a start toward a new level of communication, but even the dwarfs see through it and thus immediately get rid of its originator. Fish slime is little better than giraffe meat. Bill then suggests the possibility of "Injunctions," a word that momentarily gladdens the dwarfs' hearts, but in the end it is not until Henry blurts out "Murder and create" and Snow White responds by saying, "That is one I've never heard before ever," that the dwarfs as a group take heart and begin to respond to Snow White's needs: "We all began to say things, things that were more or less satisfactory, or at least adequate, to serve the purpose, for the time being. This whole [problem] was papered over, for the time being, and didn't break out into the open" (SW, 6–7). In this instance it may appear that utterances unleashed from a strict context can satisfy the desire for a new vitality in language. Despite their pursuit of a language that is imaginative and original, however, the dwarfs lack that sense of rich texture which might provide their phrase-making with the character of genuine originality. For the most part their communications exist only as random gestures that underscore the lack of any real cohesiveness between themselves and Snow White—except by way of the emptiness of habit. In the world of Snow White and the dwarfs words exist either as language weighed down with sludge or as language unleashed from context, and in both instances the language is meaningless and vapid. For them there seems to exist no mediating ground between the two extremes.

This lack of mediation in the dwarfs' use of language is also apparent in the manner of their voting. Voting is one of those verbal acts which, at least in the traditions of the United States, has carried with it the suggestion of serious consequence—e.g., the effecting of an important change in the political affairs of a given constituency—but in this novel the act loses virtually all of its significance. When the subject of voting first comes up in the narrative, it is in the context of why women respond to the dwarfs. The dwarfs believe the response is predicated upon their great stature as voters: "We have voted again and again, and I think they like that, that we vote so much. We voted to try the river [of girls] in the next town" (*SW*, 15). Voting, here, seems to confer upon the dwarfs something of a macho quality—as if the dwarfs by virtue of their readiness to vote have identified themselves as men of decision. In this context, nevertheless, because the act is deprived of any real significance as a measure of choice, the act of voting represents only a parody of its former importance. This fact becomes fully evident much later in the novel when, after a long series of accusations against Bill for failing to lead, Dan pointedly remarks, "If he doesn't want to lead, then let us vote" (*SW*, 137–38). Again the suggestion of consequence is in the air, but in this instance, overwhelmed by the sludge atmosphere in which they have allowed themselves to live, the dwarfs fail even to muster the effort to vote. Toward the end of the novel the dwarfs engage a boy named Bobble to pull down all the election posters, and at that point they seem to face up to the emptiness of all their presumptuous voting:

> To hell with the whole business. Voting has turned out to be a damned impertinence. [The elected] never do what we want them to do anyhow. And when they do what we don't want them to do, they don't do it well. To hell with them. We are going to save up all our votes for the next twenty years and spend them all at one time. (*SW*, 146)

In a sludge world, where the confusions of experience have fully overshadowed the clarities, the act of decision has degenerated into a stroke of no consequence. The dwarfs may save their votes for one big election in the future, but it will probably matter very little whether they again exercise their franchise. Their lack of imagination prevents them from casting any vote of consequence.

Even more indicative of the dwarfs' lack of a mediating ground where their imagination might thrive is their limited understanding of language in general. Fairly early in the novel, when Dan and Henry talk about the definition of an interrupted screw ("a screw with a discontinuous helix, as in a cannon breech, formed by cutting away part or parts of the thread, and sometimes part of the shaft"), they completely reveal themselves as the victims of the processes of language. It is true that in this novel the dwarfs enjoy little alternative, for at the same time that language presents them with the opportunity for establishing a relationship with what is "out there," its character as the prison-house for all perception and experience limits the possible range and depth of whatever relationships the dwarfs might initiate. Dan and Henry, nevertheless, never really understand this profoundly metaphysical dilemma, which underlies all language usage. Henry, for example, genuinely thinks he can improve on the "screw" that he has just complained about:

> "This filthy," Henry said, "this language thinking and stinking everlastingly of sex, screw, breech, 'part,' shaft, nut, male, it is no wonder we are all going round the bend with this language dinning forever into our eyes and ears. . . ." "I am not going round the bed," Dan said, "not me." "Round the *bend*," Henry said, "the bend not the bed, how is it that I said 'bend' and you heard 'bed,' you see what I mean, it's inescapable." "You live in a world of your own Henry." "I can certainly improve on what was given," Henry said. (*SW*, 29–30)

Here these two dwarfs may glimpse the fundamental philosophic problem (the linguistic basis of all human perception and experience) that profoundly qualifies the "reality" within any perspective of a thing or event, and yet neither of them manages to turn that insight into the ground for a genuinely imaginative response to human experience. If Henry foolishly believes that he can improve on the situation, Dan (who the reader later discovers resists all "breakthroughs") presumably concludes that man is simply cursed in his language. Neither dwarf sees the dilemma as an opportunity to play with all language situations—to generate new enthusiasm for all their activities by adopting an ironic stance (or series of such stances) that is rooted in their deep appreciation of language as a complex act.

The behavior of the dwarfs at the cocktail party and around the breakfast table, especially when coupled with their limited understanding of language in general, marks them as men of slight imaginative stature and thus deserving of the category of dwarf. At one point in the novel, in fact, in the same breath that she is discussing the "low-grade concrete-block quality" of her life, Snow White herself rather pointedly suggests that "the seven of them only add up to the equivalent of about two *real men*, as we know them from the films and from our childhood, when there were giants on earth" (*SW*, 42). The dwarfs are clearly, at least in relation to the heroic contexts of the past, rather pathetic. That this is so is probably most apparent, throughout the novel, in their tendency to concentrate their attention, not on the matters of mind and imagination, but on objects and things—on details such as washing buildings, cooking Chinese baby food, stealing Paul's typewriter (and engaging in some "automatic writing"), or buying Snow White a shower curtain. In the larger context of contemporary fiction such attention to the material dimension of experience may not seem extraordinary, but in a novel that is presumably searching for more imaginative uses of language, this reduction of existence to a matter of "things" tends to manifest a crucial limitation in the dwarfs' lives. At times they are themselves conscious of the lack in their lives, but—as might be expected of mental dwarfs—they are at a loss as to what to do about it:

> Perhaps we should not be sitting here tending the vats and washing the buildings and carrying the money to the vault once a week, like everybody else. Perhaps we should be doing something else entirely, with our lives. God knows what. We do what we do without thinking. One tends the vats and washes the buildings and carries the money to the vault and never stops for a moment to consider that the whole process may be despicable. (*SW*, 87)

In Barthelme's fiction the dwarfs surely represent the people who, overwhelmed by the complexities of human experience, try with varying effectiveness to limit their confusion by focusing their attention on the material dimension of their lives. By filling their lives with things, and the activities that produce or require the use of things, they manage to defuse their self-doubts. They have little time to reflect in any serious or imaginative way on their limitations.

It is also true, however, that before the dwarfs found Snow White wandering in the forest the quality of their lives may have even been worse, for in the forest (the rural past now long since lost) they "lived lives stuffed with equanimity" (*SW*, 87). "Simple bourgeois" before Snow White, after encountering Snow White the dwarfs at least move in the direction of becoming "complex bourgeois" whose "equanimity has leaked away" (*SW*, 88). This slight change in stature, to be sure, does not argue a weighting of the dwarfs' sophistication. For while the introduction to Snow White might have served as the opportunity for new, perhaps original, gestures, the dwarfs, once they are in the city, actually resist the intrusion of complexity and confusion into their lives, particularly if such intrusion results in diminished productivity. In the end, therefore, uncertain just how to respond to Snow White's appearance, the dwarfs find only that a strange ambiguity has crept into their lives. On the one hand, they like Snow White's company, especially in the shower, and no matter how complicated their relationship with her sometimes seems, they recognize what her presence means to the household as a whole. On the other hand, distressed over the complications that hinder their productivity, they dream, in a "fantasy of anger and malevolence" (*SW*, 109), of cooking Snow White on a spit suspended over a big fire. The best example of this ambivalence, of course, is their purchase of a new shower curtain. Initially the dwarfs take pride in seeking a new curtain for their showers with Snow White, but eventually, much to their chagrin, they find that this search has embroiled them in the aesthetic (and epistemological) problem of verifying whether their shower curtain is "the best-looking shower curtain in town" (*SW*, 123). The very fact that the dwarfs become involved in such ludicrous speculations probably suggests that they are now "paying" for their past avoidance of metaphysical considerations. Accustomed, in fact, to a simplistic equanimity, to a perspective that does not concern itself with locating "the figure in the carpet" (*SW*, 129) or with managing the "complex and netlike" stain that has engulfed human experience in a contemporary world, they find that the shower curtain,[3] which has immediately become at least as much a source of anxiety as their quality control of, say, the vats of Chinese baby food, actually increases their resentment toward the recipient of the gift.

It is clear, then, that while Snow White has introduced the dwarfs to doubt and anxiety, her presumed superiority of imagination has at the same time little enduring impact upon their notion of existence. That fact is probably most evident in the situation in which Edward worries about Snow White abrading herself with a red towel. Edward is convinced that Snow White is a victim of self-hatred, and when Dan—the future leader—responds to Edward's concern, it is in terms that are rather familiar and certainly to be expected:

> The whole damned thing . . . can be resolved very neatly, in the following way. Now, what do we apprehend when we apprehend Snow White? We apprehend, first, two three-quarter-scale breasts floating toward us wrapped, typically, in a red towel. Or, if we are apprehending her from the other direction, we apprehend a beautiful snow-white arse floating away from us wrapped in a red towel. Now I ask you: What, in these two quite distinct apprehensions, is the constant? The factor that remains the same? Why, quite simply, the red towel. I submit that, rightly understood, the problem of Snow White has to do at its center with nothing else but *red towels*. (*SW*, 100–101)

If Dan seems at first a bit facetious, the reader must remind himself that Dan's argument only illustrates more fully the dwarfs' indefatigable tendency to scale all experience, even the most personal and emotional, down to a matter of objects and things. Never very responsive to Snow White's deeper needs, the dwarfs to the end remain entrepreneurs, not sensitive friends, and thus in the larger terms of human experience—the terms that in Barthelme's fiction are difficult to define—they must represent the casualties of a Western civilization that has lost sight of what it is to be human. In fact, with Dan—the dwarf who (unlike Bill) is not at all interested in a "breakthrough"—as their future leader, the dwarfs will probably never separate themselves from the material considerations that have supported their lives of equanimity in the past but that now also prevent them from becoming real "men."

What is most significant about the dwarfs' handling of their experience is that it reflects little sense of irony. By reducing their experience to a matter of objects and things, they manage to create the illusion of some consistency in their lives—when in fact, as is evident in the fragmented approach of the narrative, the circumstances and the events of their lives actually possess a confusing, ambiguous, and sometimes rather contradictory character. Throughout *Snow White* the narrator deliberately explores the lack of effective traditions and models for communication and human interaction. Obviously in the sections that parody, say, Shakespeare or the excesses of sociological or legal jargon, he is exposing the fragmented character of language usage in the present—the fact that a group or subculture tries to establish a sufficient model for their communication at a time when no model provides a universal basis. Language is power, and by developing their own models (essentially jargons) subcultures create circumstances in which the "initiated" can be identified and thus encouraged to rise to the top. Manipulations of language have, it is true, always supported the trappings of power and dominance, for regardless of the precise content of their communications, men have always known the importance of relying upon specific models of expression in order to satisfy, as comfortably as possible, the expectations of communicating within particular situations. People naturally use, for example, a different model while making love from that employed while buying groceries.

On the surface this fact is hardly troubling, but given the fact that the dwarfs have deliberately ensconced themselves in a comfortable materialism, with little intention of sustaining themselves in a shrewd long-term appraisal of the language in which they have invested, there is good reason to attack them as men who pervert what is crucial to human experience.[4] For Barthelme's narrator there is, above everything else, a fundamental obligation in times such as the present to be conscious not merely of the contents but especially of the character and the processes that underlie all acts of communication. This narrator may not himself possess a stable model, i.e., a set of narrative traditions, whereby he can contain his own fiction, but he does appreciate thoroughly the processes that emerge in his own narrative. Consider, for example, the difficulty readers of the novel have in establishing the nature of his narrative consciousness. Because the fragments seem to leap from perspective to perspective, and especially from those of the characters to those of this surprisingly elusive narrator, it may even be impossible to pin down the quality of consciousness that presumably unites the novel. What the narrator accomplishes with his elusiveness, however, is crucial to the novel, for it is this elusiveness that forces the reader to become aware of the narrative as a process whereby its maker assembles varying perceptions and insights into a fiction and thus establishes the process of narrative, or of communication itself, as being at least as important as any content that might emerge in the text. The narrator's accomplishment, because it is deeply rooted in his ironic stance, clearly—and rather sharply—contrasts with that of the dwarfs, who have merely committed themselves to a model in order to achieve a certain, preconceived level of comfort.

In *Snow White*, then, the brilliant character of the narrative belongs to the narrator rather than to the dwarfs. It is the narrator who, even more than the dwarfs, feels the exhaustion of what now seem the constricting patterns and models of old words and communications. This narrator may not possess any fresh models for generating fiction (the widespread creation of various subculture languages has helped sabotage the traditional language of fiction), but, sensitive to the exhaustion that attaches to so many acts of communication in the present, he can at least resort to parody in order to turn, say, the outmoded pattern of a fairy tale into a residual art. For the same reason, if only to inject new vitality into old forms, he can delight in the possibilities of the pun or the juxtaposition of two very dissimilar ideas (e.g., Alicia's pornographic pastry). The narrator is determined to test the limits of language, to make his reader so aware of the artificiality and the insufficiency of language that he must reconsider the nature of his own acts of communication (the questionaire at the end of part 1 serves a parallel function). Perhaps the best example of such testing, an example that occurs twice in the novel, is his inclusion of what appears to be Snow White's process of thinking as she responds to her lack of a real man. Here is a portion of the first example:

THOSE men   hulking   hulk in closets and outside
gestures eventuating against a white screen difficulties intelligence

I only wanted one plain hero of incredible size and soft, flexible
manners   parts   thought dissembling   limb   add up the
thumbprints. . . . (SW, 31)

Some readers may, particularly if they regard the passage as Snow
White's stream of consciousness focused upon the idea of a missing hero,
succeed in forcing these phrases into a web of meaning, but such an
emphatic interpretation must finally be resisted. What the passage
illustrates, at least from the narrator's viewpoint, is the presyntactical, if
not the preverbal, character of thought-feeling, and as such it points to
the prison-house character of language once thought-feeling reaches full,
i.e., active, consciousness. Taken with other passages exploring her
situation, this passage might at least be regarded as an indication that
Snow White has herself escaped the limitations that prevent the dwarfs
from becoming the creative agents of their own experience. In actuality,
however, this passage does more to expose the narrator's sensitivity than
it does Snow White's.

There is no question that Snow White is more concerned than the
dwarfs about becoming the creative agent of her own experience. After
all, it is she who writes a four-page poem (an "immense work" in the
view of the unimaginative dwarfs) and who, while writing the poem,
reinforces the act of creativity by switching around the tulips, the lilies,
and the Indian paintbrush. It is also she who, when queried about her
request for a glass of water, responds a bit whimsically, "Let a hundred
flowers bloom" (SW, 16), as if the flowering will support her efforts of
imagination. Like the dwarfs, however, Snow White never achieves any
excitement over the exercise of her imagination. At one point she may,
as if she has achieved at least a little originality, disclose to the dwarfs
that the theme of her poem is the theme of loss, and that the first phrase
of the poem is "bandaged and wounded," but in the end any pleasure she
might feel over the poem disappears in her awareness of the fact that
despite her apparent originality she has continued to live among
dwarfs—and thus to be defined by their standards. Because she does not
possess the ironic distance that would allow her to play with the
possibilities of the dwarfs' language, she is—like the dwarfs—
thoroughly embedded in this context of slight men. By her own assessment, in fact, her inability to generate a poem and thus to escape the
dwarfs is "a failure of the imagination. I have not been able to imagine
anything better" (SW, 59). It is an accurate assessment, and when the
dwarfs underscore the appraisal as a "powerful statement of [their]
essential mutuality," there may even be good reason to conclude that
Snow White is merely another unimaginative dwarf. And yet the bitter-

ness of Snow White's self-appraisals and the fact that she is not at all content with the comforts of the dwarfs' household suggest that she, at least potentially, possesses a glimmer of that ironic distance which might finally make of her the poet. Unlike the dwarfs, she is conscious of the fact that her "imagination is stirring." Unlike the dwarfs, moreover, she is yet trying to consider the unknown and thus may still achieve that sense of Marivaudian being which is crucial to the experience of irony.[5]

Snow White, it must be remembered, in the process of gaining a liberal education at Beaver College (with courses in psychology, literature, and painting), has apparently assumed some responsibility for rehumanizing the world in terms of traditional values. She may be surrounded by dwarfs, i.e., men who have reduced their existence to a matter of objects and things, but she is herself conscious of a need to preserve those traditions from the past which she believes will ennoble her existence. The fact that she engages in laborious attempts to keep the books clean (SW, 37) or her reputation spotless (SW, 41) in an age that values neither books nor reputations is by itself an indication of how thoroughly she has allied herself with a language that has lost most of its significance. Even the dwarfs, conscious that their relationship with Snow White has "excited no special interest in the neighborhood," know that her concern for reputation is ludicrous. When confronted with this fact, to be sure, Snow White may herself reveal some realization of the folly that underlies her continuing identification with the past: "My suffering is authentic enough but it has a kind of low-grade concrete-block quality" (SW, 41). Despite the fact that in the world of the dwarfs her existence must take on the "gray" character of her peers, however, Snow White continues to pursue the authenticity available only to the heroes of the past. Having, at Beaver College, absorbed the language and traditions of the past (in essence she has absorbed the brain damage of her teachers),[6] she may—with her expectation of a world rehumanized, full of princes and heroes, and herself the princess—even believe herself to have escaped the imaginative reduction of the dwarfs, but finally her determined entertainment of the heroic mode has merely limited the field of her imaginative play. Because her version of experience possesses little more ironic play than does that of the dwarfs, in fact, she ultimately seems to accomplish even less than do the dwarfs—who at least have their successes in business.

Snow White's fundamental problem is not only that she lives in the past but that she expects the terms of the past to regain their long-lost authority. Early in the novel, while worrying over the question, "But who am I to love?" (SW, 12), she reveals a deep-seated anticipation of the arrival of the prince-figure who she hopes will solve all her problems, particularly the "low-grade concrete-block quality" of her suffering. Such anticipation of this figure from the past, however, puts her at a disadvantage, for when the prince-figure fails to turn up, she becomes even more the victim of her nagging sense of unrest. On the one hand, she can hardly face up to the fact that the stain or sludge (or to use Jane's phrase, "the slough, sump, or slime") of contemporary experience continually overwhelms her determination to keep the household (books, oven, piano) clean. On the other hand, plumbing her deeper feelings, she is aware that without the prince-figure she will never be "satisfied" or "complete"—or her experience itself finally "sufficient" (*SW*, 135). At one point, somewhat in the fashion of Susan in "The Sandman," she may seek the help of a psychiatrist, but because the psychiatrist cannot easily change a pattern of perception that is rooted in the avoidance of the present, it is hardly surprising that the two of them turn their association into a sexual escapade that serves to intensify Snow White's unrest. Only at the end of book 2, after witnessing the repeated failure of men to climb into her window in search of the origin of the long black hair, which she has deliberately hung out of the window as an inducement, does Snow White finally approach a genuine understanding of her situation:

> No one has come to climb up. That says it all. This time is the wrong time for me. I am in the wrong time. There is something wrong . . . with all those who did not come and at least *try* to climb up. To fill the role. And with the world itself, for not being able to supply a prince . . . [and] the correct ending to the story. (*SW*, 131–32)

It is a thorough and essentially accurate assessment. Snow White is in the wrong time. Her identification with the past prevents her from developing an ironic and thus potentially playful relationship with the present. For her, even more than for the dwarfs, life is unabated suffering.

In book 3, to be sure, having acknowledged to herself that she will no longer "trudge about the house pursuing stain" (*SW*, 135), Snow White seems ready to break new ground for herself. Even then, nevertheless, perhaps in her deepest moment of crisis, with her confidence shaken as never before, she returns to the beauty of her body and asserts its princely radiance in a most grandiloquent manner. Unable to give up her stature as princess, she then flails out against fate, "Oh why does fate give us alternatives to annoy and frustrate ourselves with?" (*SW*, 157). Barthelme's fiction as a whole, of course, provides an emphatic answer to that question: the alternatives require one's contact with the present. Snow White, however, resists any sense of alternatives. To the end she holds out for the fairy-tale ending. When Hogo, for instance, in the vacuum created by Paul's absence, proposes the possibility of his love, she with all the lingering hauteur at her disposal responds: "Your blood is not fine enough. Oh I know that in this democratic era questions of blood are a little *de trop*, a little frowned-upon. People don't like to hear people talking about their blood, or about other people's blood. But I am not 'people,' Hogo. I am me. I must hold myself in reserve for a prince or prince-figure" (*SW*, 170). To the end Snow White wants something better, and to the extent that she never faces up to the fact that the terms for that "better" continue to belong to the past, she must serve as an exhibit of a character who is frozen in a language that is no longer adequate for the circumstances of the present. It is her stiffness that prevents her imagination from engaging in those free gestures, rooted in irony, which might make her life more viable.[7]

Like Snow White, Bill and Paul also lean toward the past, and the consequence is that they, too, never manage to separate themselves from the fairy-tale roles that have lost all their significance in the context of "stain." Early in the novel, when Bill acknowledges that he "had hoped to make a powerful statement" or a "significant contribution" or a "definitive account" or a "breakthrough" (*SW*, 51), he seems to regard himself as a hero-figure who must define the significance of human affairs. Despite such self-esteem, however, in his "survey of the incidence of weeping in the bedrooms of members of the faculty of the University of Bridgeport" (*SW*, 52) he reaches no conclusion at all. Such a result is disastrous, for because Bill cannot turn his failure into a moment of reckoning with the world of sludge and stain, his survey becomes the crippling blow that completely alters the character of his life. At the beginning of book 2, instead of reacting to the strand of hair hanging from the window by climbing in, Bill does recognize the fact that "each of us is like a tiny little mote of pointlessness, whirling in the midst of a dreadful free even greater pointlessness, unless there is intelligent life on other planets, that is to say, life even more intelligent than us, life that has thought up some point for this great enterprise, life" (*SW*, 92–93). And later, at the beginning of book 3, "after a life rich in emotional defeats," Bill even suggests that his present mode of conduct is based upon the fact that "now I limit myself to listening to what people say, and thinking what pamby it is, what they say. . . . Give me the odd linguistic trip, stutter and fall, and I will be content" (*SW*, 139). On the surface, perhaps, especially when taken with the fact that Bill has withdrawn from intimate contact with Snow White (besides avoiding her in the shower, he refuses to take off his pajamas in her presence), both comments might seem to indicate that Bill has adjusted to the terms of contemporary experience. Despite his increased appreciation for the stain and sludge, however, Bill never manages to make the final adjustment, that of declining further leadership. In his sudden confusion he may, much to the dwarfs' dismay, quit "realizing his potential" or "maximizing his possibilities" (*SW*, 20). He may even lose their money and become guilty of vatricide—as on the night he throws a six-pack through a windscreen. Throughout all his difficulties with the dwarfs, nevertheless, he continues to play out a traditional role of leadership, one suitable for a fairy tale. Only toward the end, having succumbed to paranoia (he fears a black station wagon driven by a nun and then a blue Volkswagen operated by I. Fondue and H. Maeght), does he relinquish his position of authority. But by that point the dwarfs have already put him on trial for vatricide and finally, still determined to sustain their record of success, they even hang him.[8] Bill thus never gains the suggestive ground of irony.

Paul, perhaps, comes off a bit better. At least some of his gestures suggest that he has perceived the implications of inhabiting a world of sludge and stain. When he first appears in the novel, for example, he is in his "baff" writing a palinode, his favorite among literary forms. As he says, "retraction has a special allure for me. I would wish to retract everything, if I could, so that the whole written world would be . . ." (*SW*, 13).[9] Paul never finishes the thought, but in the context of the novel's emphasis upon the reconsideration of the uses of language, the reader can probably assume that he is interested in wiping the literary slate clean. After all, with that slate clean the past would no longer serve to inhibit Paul's own development of language and literary forms appropriate for contemporary experience. Such reasoning surely underlies his completion of a minimal painting in the first book. The painting is "a dirty great banality in white, off-white and poor-white," and although Paul himself acknowledges that the painting possesses "some of the qualities of poorness" (*SW*, 48), there is little question that in this painting Paul has faced up to the necessity of creating his own language and art form. Like his royal father, in fact, whose "sole accomplishment during his long lack of reign was the de-deification of his own person" (*SW*, 27) so that he could merely be himself, Paul the artist is in the face of the sludge and the stain determined to scale down his art from the heroic terms of the past.

And yet, while Paul does not want to be the hero, he does continue to feel the pressure of some lofty ambitions—ambitions that he may not be able to define precisely, but that are clearly there: "Probably I should go out and effect a liaison with some beauty who needs me, and save her, and ride away with her flung over the pommel of my palfrey, I believe I have that right" (*SW*, 27). Like Snow White, he even laments the fact that he was not born prior to 1900—so that he could have ridden, say, "with Pershing against Pancho Villa" (*SW*, 78) and thus have established himself as a hero. Despite his great abilities and insights, therefore, the Paul who recognizes in himself at least the possibility of such desires shall never fully escape his role in the fairy tale of the past.[10] For a time, to be sure, he seeks a literal escape by joining an order of monks, but eventually, if only as the latent prince-figure, he again finds himself pulled back to the presence of Snow White. Once there, he deliberately scales down his role—but this time, instead of painting, he becomes a voyeur, a correspondent for *Cat World,* and an expert in reconnaissance. Not surprisingly, by this point his princeliness—especially in the eyes of Snow White herself—"has somehow fallen away" so that he now appears "just another complacent bourgeois" (*SW*, 157). At the very end of the novel Paul does manage to enact the prince's role by preventing Snow White from drinking the poisoned vodka Gibson. In spite of all his efforts to reduce himself to the status of a dwarf, he ironically succeeds in fulfilling the requirements of his role in the fairy tale. Like Bill, however, who is a sky-hero only with his hanging, Paul is a hero only in death—a hero who is, consequently, profoundly wedded to the past.

In view of the limitations of language and of imagination that envelop Snow White, Bill, and Paul, as well as the dwarfs, the reader of the novel finally finds himself looking to Jane and Hogo for an alternative experience. From the beginning there is good reason for such attention because both Jane and Hogo feel very comfortable in writing letters and addressing audiences. Jane, for example, thinks nothing of completing twenty-five letters on her Hermes Rocket in one sitting. Hogo, by the same token, when appearing among the dwarfs in response to an invitation to speak on women, unleashes the novel's longest speech supporting the notion that "the world is full of cunts" (*SW*, 74). Perhaps the best example of their ease with language, however, appears in Jane's incredible letter to Mr. Quistgaard. The letter focuses upon the problem of the individual's universe of discourse ("u. of d.") and ends on this threatening note:

> The moment I inject discourse from my u. of d. into your u. of d., the yourness of yours is diluted. The more I inject, the more you dilute. Soon you will be presiding over an empty plenum, or rather, since that is a contradiction in terms, over a former plenum, in terms of yourness. You are, essentially, in my power. (*SW*, 46)

In contrast to Mr. Quistgaard, who possesses a largely unconscious relationship to language, the confident Jane enjoys an unusual—at least when compared to the other characters of the novel—appreciation of the fundamental instability at the heart of any discourse plenum. She knows that all gestures of language are the function of many variables (some of which are unpredictable) surrounding any given language user/maker, and thus she has learned to regard language and the communication acts based upon language as possessing a fundamentally arbitrary character. For her, in fact, language constitutes only an open, i.e., free, field or "universe of discourse" in which she, if she chooses (and she does), must serve as her own agent. While Snow White, Bill, and Paul feel themselves victimized by language, therefore, specifically by a language of the past that has little relationship to their present circumstances, Jane believes herself to be in control of her language acts. Instead of being victimized, she victimizes.[11] She is comfortable as the wicked stepmother.

Having embraced her agency within the u. of d., Jane freely cultivates the malice essential to her role, even to the point of having "invented new varieties of malice, that men have not seen before now" (*SW*, 40). She may no longer, unlike Snow White, exist in the good days when she was yet fair, but she knows the satisfactions of cultivating: "I grow more witchlike as the hazy days imperceptibly meld into one another, and the musky months sink into memory as into a slough, sump, or slime. . . . I have my malice. I have that" (*SW*, 40). The eloquence of her satisfaction, here, clearly separates her from the self-doubts and hesitations that trouble Snow White, Bill, and Paul, and thus late in the novel, when the tension between Jane and Snow White intensifies as a result of Hogo's switching allegiance, it is not surprising that she acts with dispatch: "Now I must witch someone, for that is my role, and to flee one's role, as Gimbal tells us, is in the final analysis bootless" (*SW*, 158). More than that, however, instead of seeming only trapped in her role in the manner of Bill and Paul, she very calmly, and apparently as an active and creative agent, considers the alternatives before her: "But the question is, what form shall my malice take, on this occasion? This braw February day? Something in the area of interpersonal relations would be interesting. Whose interpersonal relations shall I poison, with the tasteful savagery of my abundant imagination and talent for concoction?" (*SW*, 158). What is striking about Jane's conduct is that she genuinely plays out her existence within certain limits. She may be conscious of her confinement within the role as wicked stepmother, but at least she— unlike Bill and Paul—explores the range of action that goes with the role. Toward the middle of the novel this attitude of defining the limits and then playing as creatively as possible within those limits is especially evident when Jane responds to her mother's attempt to locate a significance in the act of an apelike hand reaching into their mailbox:

"Don't go reading things into things mother. Leave things alone. It means what it means. Content yourself with that mother" (*SW*, 107). Instead of reading significance in traditional terms, Jane creates her own significance. Like Kosinski's protagonists, such as the narrator of *Steps* or Tarden in *Cockpit*, she is the adroit player who understands the limits of the games she pursues.

Hogo, too, is both fluent and comfortable in his role. That fact is especially evident in his response to Jane's question concerning the future of their relationship: "Nothing is to become of us Jane. Our becoming is done. We are what we are. Now it is just a question of rocking along with things as they are until we are dead" (*SW*, 128). When Jane objects that such an assessment is not very bright, the confident Hogo even elaborates on his statement and in terms that should be familiar to Jane herself: "It's not my picture Jane. I didn't think up this picture that we are confronted with. The original brushwork was not mine. I absolutely separate myself from this picture. I operate within the frame it is true, but the picture—" (*SW*, 128).[12] While Hogo never finishes the statement, it is clear that he, too, has defined the limits (the frame) of his experience and then has explored the various possibilities that exist within those limits. Such definition and exploration surely underlies the eloquence of his long speech before the dwarfs. At the end of the novel, however, having been rejected by Snow White, Hogo joins up with the dwarfs and begins to tend the vats. Such a switch in style is jolting, and at this point, consequently, it is necessary to reconsider what Jane and Hogo are all about.

In terms of their appreciation of language and their uses of the imagination Jane and Hogo are genuinely sophisticated, probably the most sophisticated characters in the novel.[13] In the final analysis, however, their definition of their roles may not differ as much from that of the dwarfs as I have suggested. The dwarfs, by identifying themselves as entrepreneurs, have not been as imaginative in their self-definitions as Jane and Hogo. They certainly do not play out their existence within their roles with as much verve and enthusiasm as do Jane and Hogo. But in the end, just as the dwarfs are victimized by the limitations of their role, so Jane and Hogo, regardless of how much vitality and cleverness they muster, become the victims of their self-defined roles as well. Jane, for example, having created the treachery of the vodka Gibson, must live with the fact not only that Paul is dead but also that her treachery has misfired. The reader never sees her stoop under the burden of such realizations, but here Hogo's shocking decision to join the dwarfs must have a great bearing. Try as they may to be as clever and imaginative in their discourse as is possible, both Jane and Hogo are up against the essential limitations of human experience, the limitations of perception and of language. Like the dwarfs, once Jane and Hogo have committed themselves to a perspective, they are as much the glib victims of that perspective as they are its creators. What this means for the novel as a whole, of course, is the ultimate question.

In *Snow White,* finally, it is the handling of narrative consciousness that becomes the principal matter of the novel. Indeed, given the fact that perspective is at once an asset and a liability, the elusive narrative consciousness with all of its attendant ironies must serve as an example of what might be done in order to escape the victimization that pursues all the characters in the novel, from the dwarfs to Jane and Hogo.[14] By dealing in fragments, especially unrelated fragments and fragments that work against each other by way of parody and irony (so that no real statement of authorial vision or perspective can emerge), the narrative consciousness behind *Snow White* avoids the dilemma of perspective that gave a writer like Nabokov such fits.[15] In this manner Barthelme essentially opens up the process of reading and acquaints his readers with the fundamental problems underlying all text-making. What *Snow White* finally represents, therefore, is the suppression of the text—at least the traditional text of coherence and perspective.[16] Suppression of the text is an extreme gesture, but in the context of the conversations between Julie and Emma in *The Dead Father* and the seven dialogue stories in *Great Days* it is evident that the fragmented character of *Snow White* must serve as the foundation for a new, more sophisticated, and radical text-making in Barthelme's fiction of the 1970s.

9

The Dead Father: The Turning Down of Perspective

Julie's four lengthy conversations with Emma, the ones in which logic
and coherence virtually disappear and in which, consequently, the
possibilities of language—now removed from the steel web of attitude
and feeling—rise to a new level, are, perhaps, the crucial sequences of
narrative in *The Dead Father*. For while there are refrains that punctuate
the conversations and give them a certain resonance, almost enabling the
reader to establish in them a rudimentary coherence, for the most part
the conversations seem to submerge in long moments of silence. Frequently the context of the conversation simply dissolves, and at that
point, with the individual phrases and remarks reduced to the status of
words stripped of essential meaning, the silence almost overwhelms the
reader. This dismantling of the text seems to involve, at least on
Barthelme's part, a continued determination to explore, beyond *Snow
White*, all available means of escaping the victimization of language.
Julie and Emma, for example, having both "studied English" (*DF*, 24,
62, 90, 151)[1] thoroughly, have become extremely sensitive to aspects of
language such as the following: that language requires constant "con-
struing" (*DF*, 25), that "the simplest basic units develop into the richest
natural patterns" (*DF*, 25), that speaking is "making the arrangements"
and "learning to put the world together" (*DF*, 61–62), that anything is
possible in language "when it's not important" (*DF*, 62), and that in
language "feeling is what's important" (*DF*, 148) or—if not that—"the
main thing is [merely] to get moving" (*DF*, 151). These phrases and
clauses, while wrested from specific yet largely unintelligible contexts
within the four conversations, obviously reflect the extent to which the
problem of language affects any constitution of the world or of reality.
Julie and Emma, by restricting themselves to fledgling, undeveloped
motifs, apparently hope to escape traditional language structures (later to
be associated with fatherhood) and thus to create a new texture, not
merely of language, but also of human experience. Instead of requiring

the usual coherence, in fact, they seem deliberately to observe the operations of chance—here note their use of the refrain, "Hoping this will reach you at a favorable moment" (*DF*, 23, 24, 86, 155), or their response to the "elegant way of putting chairs here and there" (*DF*, 63, 151). The question for the reader, therefore, is whether such open-ended language play, in view of its negation of perspective, can ever develop into a viable style and thus into a serious alternative.[2]

Toward the end of the novel, just before he enters the grave, the Dead Father himself asks Julie what the purpose or the "entelechy" of her life is. At first Julie cannot answer the question, but when pressed by the Dead Father she does manage to hypothesize: "Could be answered possibly in terms of the kind of life one has imagined for oneself. Or in terms of what one is actually doing" (*DF*, 169). The comment is only a hypothesis, but the Dead Father immediately applauds the two choices and even extends the hypothesis by suggesting that knowledge of the "congruence or non-congruence" of the two choices would also be of interest. It is a shrewd moment in the novel, for when the Dead Father helps Julie identify the entelechy of her life as the awareness of the interplay of perceptions, both real and imaginary, she is close to establishing the processes of perception as being sufficient in themselves. For much of the novel she may seem only the object of Thomas's and the Dead Father's desire, but by the end, conscious of the essential arbitrariness that surrounds all processes of perception and language, she seems the character most likely to indulge freely in the creative acts of the imagination. This is not to say that she is above falling back upon the old patterns. Late in the journey, when given the chance to dance with some apes, she initially seizes the opportunity because the apes at least represent something "new," but almost immediately she finds herself reducing the experience to the old conventions of initiating conversation and offering her partner some food. Julie, nevertheless, much more so than Jane and Hogo in *Snow White*, finally remains the principal exhibit of Barthelme's new dispensation. For a long time she seems to represent only the "golden fleece" toward which the funeral procession is moving, but once the Dead Father (and the principle of fatherhood) has been buried, her respect for the profound silence beyond language serves as the foundation for a new appreciation of human experience.

In light of Julie's respect for silence, in fact, the fundamental issue in *The Dead Father* becomes the turning down of traditional perspective. The Dead Father is a member of an older generation accustomed to leadership, and throughout the funeral procession he tries to validate the superiority of his perspective by manipulating all the members of his retinue. Fairly early in the narrative, for example, in a conversation that originates in the discussion of Thomas's color-blindness, the Dead Father and Thomas notice a conflict between their two stances, and there the Dead Father's presumptuous self-validation becomes especially evident:

> My criticism was that you never understood the larger picture, said the Dead Father. Young men never understand the larger picture.
> I don't suggest I understand it now. I do understand the frame. The limits.
> Of course the frame is easier to understand.
> Older people tend to overlook the frame, even when they are looking right at it, said Thomas. They don't like to think about it. (*DF*, 32)

This bit of conversation, which closely parallels a conversation between Jane and Hogo in *Snow White*, goes to the very heart of the problems of perception and knowledge. What man perceives and what he knows fundamentally depends upon the framework (the limits within his basic assumptions) with which he approaches experience. The Dead Father may talk about "the larger picture" as if that picture mattered infinitely more than the frame, but his vision, too, as shall be clear in a moment, finally remains only a function of a well-established framework. Content in Barthelme's fiction always involves or reflects perspective. Moreover, because it is the framework that enables any particular content to achieve its substance, Barthelme always makes sure that his best characters carefully scrutinize their frameworks before they commit themselves to their texts. The Dead Father generally ignores the necessity of such scrutiny, and it is this neglect that reduces him—in Barthelme's eyes—to a parody of that strength and genius upon which he has hoped to build his life. Instead of allowing, as does Thomas, the processes of perception and language more play in his life, the Dead Father has enforced a specific position (that he is the hero), and the result is that he becomes an exhibit of textual deadness.

A good example of the Dead Father's tendency to enforce the content of a specific position occurs in his conversation with the bartender. After the bartender has established the fact that the Dead Father is a family man, the bartender says, "Thought so. . . . I can talk to you. We understand each other. . . . We can parley, . . . make powwow" (*DF*, 30). The Dead Father agrees, "Till the cows come home, . . . so much are we on each other's wavelengths." What is interesting about this exchange is that before the two speakers expose their "content," they establish whether or not it is probable that their perspectives—their frameworks—will match up. Once they are confident about that probability, they unleash their tirades of assorted grievances. Clearly, because the preliminary structuring of the conversation is so patently obvious, the conversation between the two of them can only be artificial, merely a confirmation of what they already know,[3] and yet when the two men indulge themselves in the full exchange of each other's "content," the conversation develops in their eyes the binding force of "reality." The Dead Father, in fact, having become accustomed to such conversations in which his views are reified, and having ultimately come to regard his vision as a perspective of unusual weight, actually possesses no longer any real chance of perceiving the artificiality of his conversations with such men as the bartender. He is locked within his own limitations.

Consider what happens when a young, inexperienced man like Thomas resists his perspective and gives him the opportunity for new, vital conversation. The Dead Father immediately falls into the questionable posture of merely asserting his rank and privilege. As he says in his wonderful fashion, "All lines my lines. All figure and all ground mine, out of my head. All colors mine. You take my meaning" (*DF*, 19). Here the Dead Father not only regards himself as the source of all serious vision, but in the process also squelches all opportunity for learning from others. A short time later, after Thomas has neglected to respond appreciatively to the Dead Father's suggestion that he—the Dead Father—is on the journey merely "for the general good," this determined manipulator goes a step further and attacks Thomas for not having the wisdom of the father: "you never *knew*. In the fullest sense. Because you are not a father" (*DF*, 33). The attack is ludicrous because Thomas is indeed a father—specifically the father of a daughter named Elsie. The attack, nevertheless, is rooted in the question, not whether Thomas is a father, but whether he possesses the vision of fatherhood that is the equal of the Dead Father's. When Thomas objects that he is a father, the real nature of the Dead Father's displeasure becomes obvious: "A son can never, in the fullest sense, become a father. Some amount of amateur effort is possible. A son may after honest endeavor produce what some people might call, technically, children. But he remains a son. In the fullest sense" (*DF*, 33). Communication is always a game of contracts, of subtle agreements that identify the speakers of rank and privilege, but unless the speakers regard the game as fluid, with a constant recycling of rank and privilege, the game must degenerate into acts of recalcitrance. In the long journey of this novel the Dead Father is himself, in a sense, being recycled, and yet, because he refuses to accept the necessity of the biological process, his only choice as a speaker becomes that of manipulating and dominating. Repeatedly he resists Thomas's leadership and obstructs his courses of action. He certainly does not listen to what Thomas has to say.

As a novel, however, *The Dead Father* focuses upon the problem not only of the Dead Father's mistreatment of Thomas but also—to use Thomas's terms—of "fatherhood as a substructure of the war of all against all" (*DF*, 76). Fatherhood in this novel is not merely the Dead Father's, or Thomas's, fatherhood. It is the fatherhood that attaches to all well-defined perspectives that, because of their sharp definition, delimit the range of human experience. Initially, perhaps, this wide conception of fatherhood, because it is so broad, may possess only metaphoric value—i.e., there is a fatherly trait that underlies and supports any sense of perspective. When Julie, however, initiates a digression following Thomas's pronouncement about "fatherhood as a substructure," she provides an elaboration on Thomas's comment that establishes a great deal more warrant for its validity. Essentially she refers to the problem of the child: "The father speaks to it [the child]. The 'it' in a paroxysm of not understanding. The 'it' whirling as in a centrifuge. Looking for something to tie to. Like a boat in a storm. What is there? The father" (*DF*, 77). In Julie's view it is the father who fills the emptiness of preverbal silence. Earlier in the novel, when the funeral procession comes across the two children whose age together is "twenty," the Dead Father himself has heard a similar line when the little girl rebukes him: "you cannot remember what it was like, being a child. Probably you don't even remember the fear. So much of the *it*. So little of you. The lunge under the blanket" (*DF*, 15). In this instance the *it* generally refers to the undifferentiated mass that is preverbal, whereas in Julie's comment the *it* refers to the child. In both comments, nevertheless, the child is experiencing the horror of not possessing enough sophistication of language to contain his experience and thus to control his sense of horror. Julie clearly sympathizes with the dilemma of the child. Her appreciation of the extent to which the father overwhelms his child may seem sexist, but in her experience—as she retorts to Emma's query about the influence of the mother—"the mother hath not the postlike quality of the father. She is more like a grime" (*DF*, 77). Whether it is the father or the mother who is responsible for the overwhelming, however, is not the principal question. The crucial consideration is simply that by the time the child becomes aware of the arbitrariness of the content that he has absorbed from his parents, his chances of developing another orientation toward experience have largely diminished. As one of the comments in the conversations between Julie and Emma puts it, "Repetition is reality" (*DF*, 87). Fatherhood becomes a substructure precisely because fathers (and mothers) assert and repeat themselves so often that the father himself becomes an inescapable boundary in the child's world. The child may rebel, or he may shift his perspective to different grounds, but in every instance he is always responding in some fashion to the original ordering of the father. In this sense, ironically, the Dead Father is right when he insists that the son can never become the father. The father is supreme.

Much of the parody in the novel, of course, depends upon the reader's appreciation of the relationship between the Dead Father and fatherhood as a substructure of human experience. In this novel the Dead Father is the father who, not content with having fathered, say, Thomas, assumes for himself the stature of the supreme father in the class of fathers. Late in the novel, when Julie chides him for his interest in the assignation under the trees that she is arranging with Thomas, the Dead Father flings himself to the ground and insists: "But I should have everything! Me! I! Myself! I am the Father! Mine! Always was and always will be! From whom all blessings flow! To whom all blessings flow! Forever and ever and ever and ever! Amen! Beatissime Pater!" (*DF*, 156). Here the Dead Father identifies himself as the All-Father, as the source and the object of all experience. The Dead Father is in actuality only one member in the class of fathers, but in the process of identifying his perspective as "real," he has virtually usurped the rights of all other members in the class and has become law unto himself. He may, to be sure, give the appearance of some flexibility, as when—in the mechanical age—he allows one of his legs to be amputated in favor of an artificial leg. Even in that instance, however, it is not his flexibility but his "vastness" that he is stressing: "In my vastness, there was room for, necessity of, every kind of experience. I therefore decided that mechanical experience was a part of experience there was room for, in my vastness. I wanted to know what machines know" (*DF*, 13). With this sense of vastness the Dead Father overwhelms all children and all other fathers. His height of 3200 cubits by itself seems to insulate him from the fear that another being will measure up to his stature. This sense of vastness, nevertheless, eventually leads to his undoing. When Julie, for example, calls him "an old fart," he unleashes his vast wrath, slips his chain, and gains an incredible vengeance by slaughtering hordes of musicians and small animals. The vengeance is much too harsh, and its excess finally gives Thomas all the more reason to act.

In the end what is so disturbing about the Dead Father's assumption of vastness is that it leaves other people with no ground for themselves. The best illustration of this fact is probably in Julie and Emma's response to the Dead Father's recitation of the "Pool Table of Ballambangjang" (*DF*, 35). Embellished and exaggerated in order to emphasize the Dead

Father's heroic stature, this tale represents the Dead Father's most extensive effort to establish for himself a context of significant action, a myth appropriate to the hero. The story makes a big impression, and when Julie and Emma initially pronounce it to be "infuckingcredible," "unfuckingbelievable," "forfuckingmidable," and "refuckingdoubtable" (*DF*, 38), the Dead Father may have reason to be pleased with his efforts. And yet, just as the Dead Father's hyperbole has turned his tale into a parody, there is also some question whether the hyperbole of the women's responses turns those responses into parody as well. When Julie appends the comment that fathers "have this way of making you feel tiny and small" (*DF*, 38), any lingering doubt must disappear: she is appalled at the Dead Father's deliberate self-aggrandizement. In an effort to manufacture for himself a personal narrative loaded with substance, the Dead Father has aggressively encroached upon all men's space. His tale may seem little more than a joke, particularly when he concerns himself with the fathering of "the poker chip, the cash register, the juice extractor, the kazoo, the rubber pretzel, the cuckoo clock, the key chain, the dime bank, the pantograph, the bubble pipe" (*DF*, 36) and much, much more, but because he commits himself to fathering everything, to being the All-Father, he allows other men and women no space for their own creations. He is at stage center, and all other people are in the wings, with little opportunity for meaningful appearance.

What is even more disturbing is that the Dead Father cannot quit his performance.[4] Initially he may have only wanted to be the hero, but eventually, because he can never entirely avoid the fact that he inhabits an age that is no longer wedded to the heroic traditions of previous centuries, he has become aware of the clever staging of his heroic presence as a necessity of his being. Here consider, for a moment, the discussion between Thomas and the Dead Father concerning the pleasures of leadership. Whereas Thomas, the exhibit of contemporary man, frankly admits his delight in bossing people, the Dead Father continues to respond to the myth of the hero's obligation and thus plays a very cagey game: "Mostly we don't let people know. Mostly we downplay the pleasure. Mostly we stress the anguish. We keep the pleasure to ourselves, in our hearts" (*DF*, 66). The Dead Father has throughout his life "edited" his public conduct to suit all the subtle requirements of the heroic myth. In this age when the marketing of public figures has reached a new level, such editing may not seem extraordinary, but in light of the failure of myth in *Snow White* this blatant manipulation of a personal text, because it destroys the ironic relationship to experience that allows for the interaction of many texts, must represent a violation of deeper, polymorphous being. In the end the Dead Father's concentration upon one text constitutes a crucial failure of imagination and will eventually result in disaster: the man who weds himself to one text will become the victim of that text. Of this the Dead Father is a good example. Despite his apparent success as a hero he knows the bitterness of defeat, especially in the years of his advanced age, and in the moments of defeat, instead of being able to accommodate himself by way of other personal "texts," he finds himself still locked within that heroic text which he has spent so much energy establishing. His myth having fallen into corruption, in fact, he becomes a parody of the heroic order as he tries to cling to whatever trappings yet linger. By restricting the range of his activity to the pursuit of his own heroic stature, he has overlooked many of his deeper impulses and thus has contributed to his own impending doom. In a genuine sense he has victimized himself.

The final, and surely the most disturbing, feature of the Dead Father's performance is that he is never in significant contact with the biological processes of his existence. For a long time he enjoys center stage, especially after he has successfully reduced all men to the status of being his children. In the end, however, with the decline of his physical prowess his performance must lose its power and authority. Thomas knows this decline is inevitable, and thus when the Dead Father, having surrendered his buckle, his passport, and his keys, objects to the treatment he is receiving, Thomas responds, "Processes are killing you, not we. Inexorable processes" (*DF*, 158). Thomas is right. The decline of the body eventually prevails. The Dead Father may throughout his life have projected the attitudes of limitless power that he had absorbed as a boy from his own father, but in the face of the limiting processes of decay and death the staging of those attitudes has become increasingly gratuitous. In this final journey, having dressed himself with the trappings of heroism, and having defined his participation in the procession as a heroic quest of the Golden Fleece (whose "warm yellowness" will make him young and wiry again), the Dead Father may try one last time to validate himself as the hero without end, but by the end of the journey the hollowness of his claims has become apparent even to himself. It is then that the Dead Father admits to Thomas that he had known "all along" that the journey was not a quest of the Golden Fleece but a procession to the grave: "I wasn't really fooled. . . . Not for a moment. I knew all along" (*DF*, 176). In response Thomas indicates that he and Julie have themselves been humoring the Dead Father until he can accept the doom of the processes: "We knew you knew" (*DF*, 176). What is striking about this last bit of exchange is the fact that the Dead Father's line of conduct has separated him from contact with people to the very end. Having so fully dominated others earlier, at the end he is himself fully dominated by the very myth he has created. Instead of enjoying in his last days a profound sense of participation in the fundamental culmination of human experience, he is left only with the marginal consciousness of having everything slip away. Unable to embrace his dilemma openly, he appears for the most part a beaten hero.

The principal concern of *The Dead Father*, then, is the avoidance of the deadness that attaches to the concept of fatherhood. What this avoidance entails, of course, is the turning down of perspective, its influence and strength. Because it is Thomas who is stripping the Dead Father of his possessions and maneuvering him to the grave, furthermore, Thomas is probably the exhibit of the new fatherhood in the novel. Thomas's status as a father and son is very ambiguous. He is not insistently referred to as the Dead Father's son, and he does not inherit the Dead Father's estate. By the same token, while he is identified as the father of the twelve-year-old Elsie, his status as Elsie's father is very questionable in light of the fact that he has not heard from her for about four months. Juxtapose these facts with the suggestion that Thomas is still smarting from having had to wear "an orange fool's cap tipped with silver bells" (*DF*, 7)—a cap that the Dead Father has decreed he must wear until he is sixty-five—there is even good reason to question Thomas's mental acumen. In truth, Thomas at first glance does not seem much of a man. Even in his own eyes, when he looks back over his career after having been educated "up to the height of two meters" (*DF*, 57), he must seem a fool, for as an adult he has floundered around as a Navaho lawgiver, a poacher of trout, a seminarian, and a reader of philosophy. He does not possess much sense of a scintillating career. With women, too, he has hardly distinguished himself. He may have fathered a daughter, but with Julie he generally finds himself reduced to using his finger or sucking her breast or, near the end of the journey, to remaining in position A while Julie seeks whatever satisfaction she desires.

Thomas may not seem much of a man, but what the reader needs to remember is that Thomas, at least when contrasted to the Dead Father, is developing a much different sense of fathership. Thomas knows that in a particular sense (the loss of a dominating father) this journey represents for him his first real chance for legitimacy, and he is responding to the opportunity, for as he tells Julie about midway through the novel, "I am taking action, am I not? I could as well have sat at home, worn the cap-and-bells and bought lottery tickets hoping for the twist-of-fate that would change my life" (*DF*, 67). Thomas does not sit back. He recognizes that he is approaching a moment of new authority. There is, nevertheless, a profound contrast between his approaching of authority and the Dead Father's. Whereas the Dead Father was determined to satisfy the traditional strictures of a heroic myth, Thomas is merely determined to "look at everything," particularly "everything that is in front of me" (*DF*, 68). This commitment to the act of perception in the present is, of course, the key to his new fatherhood. Unlike the Dead Father, who has locked himself into the traditions of the past and thus possesses a very narrow text full of repetitions (such as the series of heroic catalogues), Thomas contents himself with a scaled-down version of himself and of his role that not only calls into question everything that the Dead Father has stood for but also allows him to respond to the many texts of his present experience. In response to the Dead Father's incredible recounting of the fathering of the Pool Table of Ballam-bangjang, a story so exaggerated that it turns into a parody of the heroic mode, Thomas offers up his own story, the Riddle of the Great Father Serpent. It is a story about lying.

Because the Riddle includes a long expository sequence about the hurting of Thomas by can openers, corkscrews, dinner forks, and finally by documents and harsh words, it may initially seem only another foray into heroic hyperbole. In the process, however, of answering the riddle, "*What do you really feel?*" (*DF*, 46), with the response, "Like murder-inging," Thomas actually does face up to the crucial problem of fathering.[5] For when he combines the act of murder with the sense of ringing, a sense that is apparent in all voicing, he essentially acknowl-edges that any commitment to a text, because it entails an imposition upon others, constitutes an act of murder. In these terms, it should be clear, Thomas's tale becomes a subtle warning to the Dead Father that his unbounded commitment to the text of heroism has made him a murderer who is now hollow at the core—i.e., dead. Beyond that, the tale also serves Thomas himself by encouraging him to appreciate the multiplicity of texts—and particularly those of the open-ended variety. When Thomas has first uttered his response to the riddle, he has wondered at "the closeness with which what I had answered accorded with my feelings, my lost feelings that I had never found before" (*DF*, 46). Unlike the Dead Father, he has been unable to establish a primary text in his life, but with the response to the riddle Thomas sees his failure in a new light and thus here accepts responsibility for the processes of developing his own multiple texts. He knows that no matter what text(s) he develops, he—merely by virtue of establishing a text that possesses no sanctions and thus no necessity—murders his experience, and that of others about him, by giving it a certain configuration that is (and must be) insufficient for containing all that he senses and feels. In contrast to the Dead Father, nevertheless, who is locked into one text, he has with his new insight the chance of playing several texts off each other. For him the multiplicity, the contradiction available in his many texts, becomes the guarantee of a life of textual play and resiliency.

A good example of Thomas's resiliency appears in his response to the men's melancholy, which seems to arise from their uncertainty about the nature of their present task. Accustomed to the one-dimensional texts of definitive leaders such as the Dead Father, these men worry about the clouded status of their journey under Thomas's leadership: "for what purpose? are we right? are we wrong? are we culpable? to what degree? will there be a trial after?" (*DF*, 92). The categorical nature of the men's concern obviously reflects their inability to adjust to the manner and style that Thomas has introduced into his relationships. Not surprisingly, since he cannot reduce himself to the Dead Father's manner, Thomas in his effort to alleviate their distress tries to nudge the men to a new level of awareness that approximates his own. First he temporizes:

> Your questions are good ones. . . . Your concern is well founded. I can I think best respond by relating an anecdote. You are familiar I take it with the time Martin Luther attempted to sway Franz Joseph Haydn to his cause. He called Haydn on the telephone and said, "Joe, you're the best. I want you to do a piece for *us.*" And Haydn just said, "No way, Marty. No way." (*DF*, 93)

As might be expected, the men, still wedded to the Dead Father's heroic notion of what is real, immediately reject Thomas's anecdote on the grounds that he has gotten "the centuries all wrong and the telephone should not be in there," etc., and yet it is in the face of their very attempt to put the traditional limits of reality upon the anecdote that Thomas gains his advantage with the men: "*There it is!* Things are not simple. Error is always possible, even with the best intentions in the world. People make mistakes. Things are not done right. Right things are not done. There are cases which are not clear. You must be able to tolerate the anxiety" (*DF*, 93). Again the issue is the problem of texts, specifically the insufficiency thereof, and while the men may continue to resist Thomas's contradictory text because it entails even more anxiety and further lack of clarity about purposes than they have been accustomed to under the Dead Father, Thomas has introduced them to the essential Barthelmean gesture, the gesture that underlies the whole of *Snow White* and the gesture that only the most imaginative ever complete—the displacement of the victimizing text by irony. Thomas's play with the text shields him from the victimization that drives the Dead Father to the folly and the exhaustion of extremes. In a profound sense, to be sure, Thomas—despite his multiple texts and his ironic relationship to those texts—continues in his own way to be a textual victim as well. But at least he understands the nature of his victimization—and its inexorable necessity.

What Thomas's understanding of texts entails appears in its fullest form in *A Manual for Sons*. The manual's translator, Peter Scatterpatter (the name itself implies a new orientation toward texts), introduces the manual to Julie and Thomas by pointing out that he has translated it "from English . . . into English" (*DF*, 108). The comment obviously recalls the recurrent phrase in Julie and Emma's conversations, and when Julie suggests that he "must have studied English," he responds, "Yes I did study English." Again the emphasis upon learning the language points to the necessity of adopting a new relationship to the fatherhood inherent in all language experience. In the manual the father, instead of inhabiting a stabilized world of heroic reality, seems to reside in an imperfect, unclear world that forces him to deliver his instructions to his sons "in a cloud of unknowing" (*DF*, 116)—a fact that immediately transforms him into a teacher of both "the true and not-true." Like the Dead Father, however, this father throughout his life continues to "leap" in an air of self-importance in an effort to establish the primacy of a particular text. He may even busy himself—by selling his children to bone factories, by imposing his voice upon his sons, by displaying his fangs, by parading his kingly presence, by kicking up his heels like a thoroughbred—with that arbitrary imposition of himself which must result in the same excesses perpetrated by the Dead Father during his lifetime of domination. By committing himself to a particular text, this father destroys the "play" of texts that would allow him to remain sensitive to others and thus to support the creativity of his own children. If this father is also a falling father, of course, one who "embodies the 'work ethic,' which is a dumb one" (*DF*, 136) according to the manualist, he will turn out to be particularly dangerous because he will "redouble his efforts" to satisfy his text whenever he experiences a "downturn"— and in the process squelch even further whatever freedom his sons possess for following their own "emotional extravagance." Like the Dead Father, the fathers in the manual do impose their texts upon their children, and thus whenever it does happen that a father loses his way, the principal problem in finding him—according to the manualist—must be the discovery of a means "to lose him" (*DF*, 137).

Like the novel, the manual takes as its major target, not the father himself, but the principle of fatherhood as the substructure of human experience. The manualist knows that fathers "murder" their children, perhaps not physically, but through textual domination. He also knows that even after the fathers have died, they remain "an inner voice commanding, haranguing, yes-ing and no-ing—a binary code, yes no yes no yes no yes no, governing your every, your slightest movement, mental or physical" (*DF*, 144). In general, therefore, what the manualist seems to want for the children is freedom from the rigidity of texts. Toward the end of the manual, for example, he suggests that the father's sense of responsibility for his children should be limited to the concern "that his child not die, that enough food is pushed into its face to sustain it, and that heavy blankets protect it from the chill, cutting air" (*DF*, 143). For the manualist, any other interaction between father and child is, in the phrase of one of Barthelme's short stories, "brain damage." In his mind there is no question that many fathers, having met the responsibility of sustenance "with valor and steadfastness," take too much delight in imposing themselves on their children—a fact that shall later haunt them when their children, in the moment of ultimate confrontation, choose their own texts. Even in the process of sustaining their children, to be sure, all fathers—including those who are the most sensitive—expose their offspring to a style of sustenance, to a set of expectations, that constitutes as much a text as any explicit moralizing the fathers might direct at their children. Finally, therefore, there can never be complete freedom from "brain damage" or from the process of "murderinging." At the very end of his treatise, in a moment when he is especially conscious of the impossibility of fully restraining the father, the manualist does consider patricide as a solution to the dilemma. He concludes, however, that such a solution is not necessary, for eventually, as in the Dead Father's case, "time will slay him" (*DF*, 145). In light of this fact the manualist then suggests that what is even more important than the slaying of the father is that the son develop a new relationship to his own texts:

> Your true task, as a son, is to reproduce every one of the enormities touched upon in the manual, but in attenuated form. You must become your father, but a paler, weaker version of him. The enormities go with the job, but close study will allow you to perform the job less well than it has previously been done, thus moving toward a golden age of decency, quiet, and calmed fevers. (*DF*, 145)

The son will in his turn, even if he avoids patricide, become the "murderinger" in relation to his own children, and thus the hope must be, as the last sentence of the manual puts it, that "*Fatherhood can be, if not conquered, at least 'turned down' in this generation*—by the combined efforts of all of us together" (*DF*, 145). Instead of requiring his words and deeds to cohere in the one-dimensionality of, say, a heroic text, the son might transform his experience, his very being, into a field of play where many attitudes and insights, many texts, exist on equal ground and where, therefore, his own sons can enjoy equal stature because they, too, possess vitality and imagination—at least as long as this son-father does not sell them to the bone factories.

The manual itself, while it does possess some logic and coherence (the writer obviously has an ax to grind), generally displays—much like Julie and Emma's conversations—a great deal of freedom from traditional structures. There are, for example, the largely arbitrary sections that list, in turn, the names of fathers (from A'albiel to Albert and from Badgal to Byleth) or the varieties of their many teachings and appearances (their voices, their colors, their types). In each of these sections there emerges little logic to tie the list or the commentary together, and taken as a whole, therefore, the manual approaches the essentially textless quality of *Snow White*. The strength of its texture or style is again that it calls attention to the very process of establishing a text—a crucial fact since the sons who expect to "turn down" fatherhood must, above everything else, be conscious of the processes of their own text-making, especially when it includes the lives of their own sons. The reader who is wedded to traditional, fatherly texts, of course, may respond to the manualist (and perhaps to Barthelme as well) as merely a deranged son, but if the reader can respond to the manual (or to the multifaceted verbal play within Julie and Emma's conversations) as a text in a new key, then there is a chance that the reader himself will begin to explore the nature of his own texts and perhaps even determine whether he has gained for himself that sense of "play" which is at the heart of Barthelme's fiction. *The Dead Father*, like *Snow White*, depends upon the suppression of texts, or at least the destruction of their apparent reality, and as such—although this tendency is even more apparent in the fiction of a writer such as Jerzy Kosinski—it serves as a challenge to the reader to inhabit new, multitextual, imaginative space.

Having set up the contrast between the Dead Father and Thomas, and having suggested how the conversations between Julie and Emma and then the manual serve as extensions of Thomas's style of multitextualism, I want to return to my consideration of the Dead Father and elaborate on the significance of his death. There is no question, at least once it is apparent that Thomas represents the character who recognizes the problem of "murderinging" and who thus turns down his own sense of fatherhood, that the Dead Father himself essentially represents the one-dimensional text that must be buried. In the penultimate chapter of the novel, nevertheless, the Dead Father unleashes a "Papsday" speech that contrasts rather sharply with all his other utterances—with the possible exception of his earlier collagelike speech on "anticipatory design." The Papsday speech constitutes the whole chapter, and thus from the beginning it exists without the staging, the framework of relationship, whereby the Dead Father has normally overwhelmed his followers. Instead of relying upon the trappings of rank and privilege, in fact, the Dead Father in this speech has only his words to fall back upon. Because he puns repeatedly, plays with phonemics, and incorporates the dreck of language into the very substance of the speech, however, his words suddenly take on a new character, at first that of nonsense, and finally—once the reader adjusts to it—that of multitextualism. Indeed, when he considers all the good times, i.e., the father's days of the past, the Dead Father even begins to face up to the fact that despite all his staging and blustering in the past he has never really understood himself: "I the All-Father but I never figured out figured out wot sort of animal AndI [the Dead Father] was. Endshrouded in endigmas. Never knew wot's wot. I reguarded my decisions and dispositions but there wasn't timeto timeto timeto. Endmeshed in endtanglements" (DF, 172). In addition to his confusion about himself, he is conscious of his ignorance about "what made the leaves fibrillate on the trees and what comity meant and what made the heart stop and how unicorns got trapped in tapestries" (DF, 172). Clearly, the Dead Father is reconsidering the nature of his past textual domination.

The Dead Father may have for years opted for the heroic text, but in actuality he has understood little about himself or about that which surrounds him. He knows that as an assertive father he has "dealt out 1,856,700 slaps with the open hand and 22,009,800 boxes on the ear" (DF, 172), and to a certain extent he may still be able to justify his conduct on the grounds that he never wanted fatherhood ("it was thrust upon me"), but in the end he comes to the recognition that as father he has not provided "a healthy endvironment." Even though he may have been "Papping as best I could like my AndI before me," he knows that his experience "could have been otherwise." As he says, "I could have refused it. Could have abjured it. Coastered along goodguying way through the world. Running a little shop somewhere, some little malmsey&popsicle place. Endeavoring to meet ends" (DF, 172). Like Thomas, the Dead Father could have turned down the intensity of his fatherhood. Because he failed to do so, however, he is merely left with the lame rationalization that he has done the "best I cud" and "no dubitatio about it." Or in his last moments, with the vitality of his "pappenheimer" completely gone, he is left with only the consciousness of his failure. It is true, of course, especially in light of his marvelous verbal play to the end, that such consciousness does represent a dramatic about-face for this stager from the old traditions. When the bulldozers arrive in the last phrase of the novel, the bull may himself be dozing—but in his last moments of breath he has finally managed to escape the limits of his style of heroic text. At that point, dead to text but alive to the play of language, he has become the liberated father who approaches the wonderful style of narrative consciousness apparent in the best of Barthelme.

Part **III**
KOSINSKI

10

Kosinski's Early Fiction: The Problem of Language

From the beginning of his career as a novelist Jerzy Kosinski has concerned himself with the novelist's familiar exploration into the nature of human consciousness. What distinguishes him from almost all previous novelists, however, is the fact that he has generally included within his fiction few overt themes or metaphors to serve as signs for helping his readers respond to his explorations. It is as if he has deliberately decided, in an age of minimal art, to scale down his fiction in order to allow his readers more opportunity for developing their own "texts" as responses to the reading of his novels.[1] Many readers, of course, have difficulty in reacting to novels that exist largely as open structures, but those readers who finally do accept the challenge of dealing with the unstable character of his fiction will eventually realize Kosinski's goal—a new appreciation for the nature of all human texts. Before I discuss this matter of the reader's realization, however, a few comments about the accomplishments of the minimal artists of the 1960s are in order.

If there is a quality common to almost all minimalist art work, it is the tendency to implicate the viewer in the artist's work. Sculptors such as Robert Morris and Carl Andre, for example, instead of layering their work with a meaningful syntax or hierarchy of relationships, deliberately prevent any hieratic intrusion into their creations and thus frustrate a viewer's tendency, developed in response to more traditional art, to seek meaning. Morris's laconic use of boxlike shapes in a shade of flat off-white and Andre's use of thin, squared metal plates arranged in squares upon a gallery floor both reveal an art in which the maker actually avoids displaying the craftsmanship of his hand. For both of them, it is as if the artist were determined to remove all signs, all statements, whereby the traditional artist's message was made apparent. Obviously, because such work divorces itself so radically from traditional expectations of art, it demands an altogether new relationship from the viewer. Like the reader responding to *Steps*, the viewer of minimal sculpture must himself carry the burden of developing significance for the work. Morris recognizes the presence of this burden when he identifies the gestalt situation underlying the boxes: the boxes challenge the viewer to become aware of the processes of perception whereby he creates a relationship with or, more rarely, within a particular work.[2] What is interesting about this burden is that it turns the viewer into a creator. If the artist does not, by layering his work, provide a comment about his creation, then the viewer alone can make something of the situation. By responding to the work in his own, somewhat idiosyncratic, manner of perception, the viewer reconstitutes the work and thus, in a genuine way, makes it his own.

The new importance of the reader/viewer in twentieth-century art is finally only another manifestation of the fact that the Western world no longer possesses convincing models of reality. Without a justification for imposing pattern upon the experience of fictional characters, the contemporary novelist tends to divorce himself from traditional rules of logic and sequence and from the hierarchical domination of narrative by meaning and mimesis. Like Barthelme (or even like Beckett and Burroughs), Kosinski, too, faces up to the dilemma presented by this crisis by serving his reader fragments that ostensibly exist outside any necessary framework or skein of relationships—but fragments that a reader, if he accepts the challenge, can reconstitute into a whole that says at least as much about the reader as it says about the fiction itself.[3] Kosinski himself, in an interview from 1971, emphasizes the importance of the reader as a respondent to his fragments: "a novelist cannot aim at conveying the most. He fits his language into the preexisting body of imagination in such a way that his language prompts those who are 'on the receiving end' to provide the rest since they clearly *can* provide the rest."[4] Here Kosinski not only separates himself from the long tradition of authorial ownership of the text, but he also fully allies himself with the minimalist proposition that "less is more."[5] Not surprisingly, therefore, he goes on in that interview to argue, much in the manner of Morris, for a gestalt experience in the reading of his fiction:

> I assume that my using the language connects me and my readers—
> whoever they are—in the most profound of ways, but I'm not giving my
> reader every detail of black and white, or of Kodacolor, with all the
> shadows in between. I am merely pointing out the tree in the field.
> Whether my reader will "see" the field or a tree or my intent to show
> them in a certain manner is something I will never know.[6]

In this "open" situation, about all that Kosinski can assume, as he himself recognizes, is that the use of language stripped of its hieratic associations "will trigger *some* response" in the reader. At the same time, however, he knows that whatever the response, the response will implicate the reader just as Morris's sculpture implicates the viewer. As he says, "Fiction assaults the reader directly as if saying: It is about you. You are actually creating this situation when you are reading about it; in a way you are staging it as an event of your own life."[7] This new responsibility for the reader is an important aspect of Kosinski's experimental mode of fiction, and its presence goes a long way toward explaining his determined desertion of content.

What the reader faces in responding to a Kosinski novel also possesses a rather strong similarity to the usual situation of Kosinski's protagonists. In their largest frame of reference Kosinski's first six novels essentially detail both the protagonists' loss of that web of social structure and individual commitment which underlies the contexts of tradition and their pursuit of stances that will at least see them through another day. In *The Painted Bird*, for example, the boy, once he has endured all the physical and emotional ravaging of the war, possesses no stance whereby he can dominate and control the events of his experience. Victimized by the horrible circumstances of the war, this wandering orphan knows only a process of emptying as he loses all the value associations from his early childhood. Once he has lost his voice, in fact, he lacks a personal stance with which to master even his day-to-day experience. At the end of the novel, having survived the war but then having become a pawn in the tension between Gavrila and Mitka, he responds with almost no sense at all of a moral identity. First, he cannot decipher the confusion that emerges from Gavrila's support of the party hierarchy and Mitka's assertion of a radical individualism. Then, once he is removed to an orphanage (and finally to his parents), his conduct displays little motive that could in any way be regarded as sustaining a consistency of self and value. Eventually he does recover his voice as a result of a skiing accident, but because that recovery occurs only in the final paragraph of the text, there is little chance for verifying whether it signals the acceptance of a new responsibility for developing a solid—and more comprehensive—foundation for his experience.[8]

A somewhat parallel case appears toward the end of *Steps*, when the protagonist (also the narrator), having left his own country, deliberately tries to escape the social obligations of interaction within his new country by adopting the charade of a deaf-mute spastic. His charade may not remove him entirely from the social contexts that have engulfed most men in the new country, but it does allow him to sever many of the peripheral connections with the community and thus to escape some of the prevailing moral chatter. While employed as a housekeeper for a woman connected with the underworld, nevertheless, he becomes involved in a situation that very nearly approaches the status of a mythic statement not only on the origin of language but also on the impossibility of escaping its web. The woman takes him to bed, and as she trembles with the currents of passion, "a rushing stream of words broke over her lips like foam" (S, 142).[9] The narrator's interpretation of this stream is the crucial point: "It was as if I were the master of all this fluid passion, and her tumbling words its final wave." Despite his intentions, despite his charade, this protagonist has yet created language. He may not have uttered a word himself, but by responding to the woman and, in the process, by generating language, he has become implicated (like Morris's viewer) in the webs of the community. By the end of the encounter, in fact, the woman becomes the image of that process which victimizes all men and thus which this narrator shall never escape, no matter how removed from the community he may seem:

> Like a joyous mare in its solitary stall, she cried out again and again, as though trying to detach into speech what had been fused with her flesh. She whispered that she veered toward the sun, which would melt her with its heat. Her sentences poured and broke, and she muttered that the sun left only the glow of stars brushing close to each other. (S, 142)

The poetry of the passage points, I think, to the passional origin of language and thus to the ultimate futility of the narrator's charade. He may deliberately separate himself from his context, but finally his body will speak out—first through the woman and then for itself. Existence in isolation and silence is impossible.

Between these two situations lies the range of Kosinski's fiction. In the first example the protagonist experiences the complete exhaustion of the language of childhood and is left with nothing—at least until the skiing accident, when his convalescence seems to provide him with the opportunity for recovering or renewing the powers of moral assertion. In the second example, having wearied of the stale manipulations of both self and other inherent in all uses of language, the protagonist boldly elects a separation from language (but only of the verbal variety) as a means of providing himself with some relief from the exigencies that underlie the exchanges of communication. For very different reasons, then, the two protagonists exist in an unusual separation from language that, presumably, will provide them with a privileged view of their linguistic acts—if only because they must generate a new, i.e., personal, voice.[10] Both of them, to be sure, do return to the acts of language, and those returns serve as the ground for their maturity, for while the reader sees almost nothing of either protagonist's "new" language (their losses of language have occurred near the end of their respective novels), the reader can probably conclude that the separation itself has made each protagonist much more attentive to the dilemma of language that is at the heart of Kosinski's fiction. The protagonist in *The Painted Bird* will surely have discovered that the language of childhood in no way controls the experience of his early adolescence; or the protagonist in *Steps* will have discovered that the use of language always serves as an arbitrary constraint upon the potential range of man's experience and thus belies what he is at heart—a mass of sub-language moods and feelings. In Kosinski's world language is never the adequate tool for formulating the nature of human experience. And yet, because language in its many varieties constitutes the only means for establishing a perspective on any experience, language represents a necessary and thus inescapable limit that no man, not even Kosinski's protagonists, can surmount.

Kosinski's third novel, *Being There*, probably represents his own attempt at surmounting the dilemma of language. With *Being There* Kosinski separates himself from the first-person narrator who dominates *Steps* by way of his ploys and games of intellect. The separation is, of course, not complete, for the third-person narrator of *Being There*, much in the manner of his predecessor, still appreciates the importance of perception as an act of mind. When he implies near the beginning, for example, that in Chance's world people "began to exist . . . when one turned one's eyes on them" (*BT*, 14), he seems to turn the act of perception, at its heart an act of intellect, into the fundamental ground of Chance's experience. In reading this novel, nevertheless, the reader quickly realizes that perception as an act, at least as it is associated with the mentally deficient Chance, possesses little more than a rudimentary character. Chance may layer his experience outside the walls of the old man's property with the experience that he has absorbed in the garden or he may deal with the outside world by relying upon the patterns that he has accumulated from his many years of television addiction, but in the end the reader can never conclude that Chance has in any essential way consciously produced or created the world he inhabits.[11] In *Steps*, as a result of the narrator's propensity for demystifying his experience, there are moments when the narrator seems to possess no comfortable terms at all for dealing with a particular situation. It is as if, separated from all the social categories and structures that usually give each moment its peculiar configuration, that narrator merely exists—without any expectations and certainly without any intention of nudging his experience into a specific pattern based on prior expectations. In certain key respects the world of Chance, which even more than that of the narrator is the world of "being there," expands upon the same kind of demystification.

Fairly early in the novel, for example, shortly after his accident, Chance reflects upon the "hidden" quality of the future: "He did not have to be afraid, for everything that happened had its sequel, and the best that he could do was to wait patiently for his own forthcoming appearance" (*BT*, 38). The key feature of this passage is its attitude. Because Chance exists outside any complex of expectations such as the woman's in *Steps*, he never feels the need for establishing his own world as a means of supporting his assumed identity. Language for him is not a necessary tool. Language continues to exist, especially by way of the matrix of relationships that develops around him in the aftermath of his accident, but the Chance who, when addressed by others, merely responds without insisting upon the character of his moral identity actually seems to achieve his identity as a result of the others' assertion. Unlike the narrator of *Steps*, therefore, who ultimately regards himself as the "maker," Chance is from beginning to end the act of "being" that precludes any necessary reliance upon language.

Chance's novel stance is probably nowhere more apparent than in his relationship with EE (Elizabeth Eve Rand). It is EE who has largely given him his new identity (Chauncey Gardiner), and it is she who consistently provides an interpretation of his experience when he in fact merely allows his experience to unravel as it will. When EE discovers her attraction to Chance, for example, she immediately begins to analyze the attraction and eventually concludes—but somewhat mistakenly—that it is rooted in the fact that she has never before encountered anyone "who relie[s] more on his own self" (*BT*, 74). Even though she never discovers "a single motive in any of his actions" (motives serving as the ground for shaping and interpreting relationships), or even though she has perceived that "nothing he said to her or to anyone else was definite enough to reveal what he thought of her or of anyone or, indeed, of anything" (*BT*, 75), she continues to respond to him as if the difference in their attitudes were of negligible proportions. For her Chance merely represents a bit of a mystery—a mystery that has begun to evoke her "innumerable selves" and in the process, perhaps, to expose her to the limits of her own conventional language. EE has a glimmer of the fact that Chance is different, but she never understands how. It is when she climbs into his bed that she reveals how fully she remains trapped in the conventional language of her past experience.

On that occasion, typically enough, Chance does not initiate any lovemaking, and even when EE cries out "brokenly, uttered ruptured sounds, spoke in phrases which barely began, making noises that resembled animal gasps" *(BT*, 113), this figure of being, rather than of action and response, appears to be conscious only of a limited curiosity in the progress of the trembling woman's passion. EE herself is momentarily disoriented by his passivity, but instead of being deprived of her customary language of passion, she quickly adjusts to the situation and resolves the unprecedented (at least for her) dilemma by pursuing the pleasures of masturbation. Later, when awake, she documents the quality of the pleasure by defining for herself a newfound freedom that is, she thinks, predicated upon his superior understanding: "You uncoil my wants: desire flows within me, and when you watch me my passion dissolves it. You make me free. I reveal myself to myself and I am drenched and purged" *(BT*, 116). In a limited fashion, perhaps, what EE remarks here is true. Chance has probably awakened in her a new dimension of sexuality. And yet, quick as she is to define the quality of this awakening, Chance has hardly served as its sole agent. Locked within her own conventional notions of sexuality and experience, which allow for the rites of masturbation, EE is essentially only playing out the language that she already possesses. She thinks that she has been awakened, but the language that underlies her awakening was actually in place long before Chance ever appeared on the scene. Because EE wants to understand all, to confine her experience within language, in fact, she in the end only turns Chance into a reflector of the language that has always been hers. If Chance is the act of "being there," then, EE by virtue of her dependence upon signification is the act of becoming—of measuring up to or playing out the expectations inherent in the conventional language that underlies all her relationships.

Finally what seems crucial about this novel is the suspicion that the mode of "being there," at least from Kosinski's perspective, can serve as a potentially creative alternative to the dilemma of language that victimizes the protagonists of his other novels.[12] Instead of being locked within a narrow definition of self that absorbs all available energy for its maintenance, Chance remains, throughout the novel, open to the unfolding of a truly incredible sequence of events, which even at the end means nothing to him. Without seeking it, he has joined the circle of the rich and the influential, and even though he does not speak their language, he feels little compunction either to adjust to their mode or to impress upon them his own mode of language and experience. Chance surely does possess a language, but because his language is not a function or product of his assertion, the language is never made to bear the freight or the constriction of motive and of intention that will necessarily establish him in a well-defined, predictable relationship with others. Chance is, therefore, a very privileged character who has avoided, by the quirk of special circumstances, the relentless cycle of renewing oneself through the daily acts of language only to discover that each renewal, like those preceding it, is insufficient—thus requiring yet another round of assertion. Chance's language may seem rudimentary and his perspective rather limited, but in the face of the incredible difficulties that the protagonists of *The Painted Bird* and *Steps* must endure, his case represents an interesting alternative. Because most men in the Western world, however, particularly those who belong to a well-educated society, have fully enrolled themselves in the strategies of self-definition and self-assertion that define EE's conduct, Chance's example hardly serves as a viable alternative.

In the novel that follows *Being There*, a work entitled *The Devil Tree*, Kosinski returns to the dilemma that had characterized his second novel, *Steps*. There are, to be sure, significant differences between *Steps* and *The Devil Tree*. In the latter novel the protagonist, Jonathan Whelan, not only enjoys a specific identity but is also turning twenty-one—the age at which he shall receive his inheritance and, presumably, assume that status of majority which entails a mature use of language. That Whelan will change during the course of the novel is, consequently, a likely bet. About two-thirds of the way through the novel, when Whelan suddenly (yet somewhat hesitantly) shifts the point of view in his narrative from first to third person, the nature of the change does emerge. In view of the fact that first-person narration, which dominates *Steps*, is the more likely mode of detailing how a protagonist develops his mature relationship to language, Whelan's shift to third-person narration is obviously rather surprising. In *The Devil Tree*, nevertheless, Kosinski is interested not only in the manner of Whelan's separation of himself from the floundering of immaturity but also in his establishing of a perspective that, even while personal and thus arbitrary, achieves some of that character of objectivity normally associated with third-person narration. In the end, therefore, what the reader must realize while reading the novel is that Whelan's experience at the beginning of the novel, which is largely a function of his having knocked about the world much in the fashion of, say, the boy in *The Painted Bird*, is subsumed in the larger perspective that he finally masters as a twenty-one-year-old in charge of an inheritance—and that, despite its third-person character, matches up rather closely with what the narrator of *Steps* must himself have encountered as a young man.

What disturbs Whelan from the beginning of his narrative is that he cannot stabilize his ideas of himself and of his relationships with others without reducing the terms of self and of relationship to such narrow limits that the terms become fraudulent at their very core. Fairly early in the novel he even goes so far as to suggest that his impulse is "not to speak or write, but to remain elusive, to present Karen [a friend] with cartoons of my fears and sexual desires rather than my real ones" (DT, 68). The comment surely reflects the problem of any act of communication—the inability of words to convey adequately what it is that the speaker is feeling—but it also seems to mirror Whelan's essential anxiety over the difficulty of establishing the character of the "real." For him the problem of communication is not so much the impossibility of matching up two differing perspectives (those of speaker and of respondent) as it is the difficulty of stabilizing the play of one's various selves so that a perspective or formulation of any given moment can achieve some sufficiency. Consider, here, the manner in which, as a result of having become attentive to the problem of stabilizing his selves, Whelan finds himself reduced to the status of manipulating a series of poses and stances. Whereas his depressions, for example, were once as natural as sex, sleep, and hunger, in the light of his increasing awareness of the interaction among his various selves they have become "completely calculated." Here is Whelan's description of one of his depressions: "I chose to enact a familiar ritual, to dull my mind and lose myself completely. I knew I was not genuinely upset the way I used to be. I was merely playing a familiar role, which I could abandon at any moment" (DT, 90). Such manipulations, if only because they are so patently calculated, obviously enjoy no sufficiency beyond the moment of their expression. They are poses, not reflections of any genuine feelings. In effect, therefore, it is as if Whelan were merely going through the motions, striking a pose as a response to immediate conditions, but enjoying no sense at all of what might bind all his conduct together and give it a character of coherence.[13] In this sense, it is clear, he is well beyond the boy of The Painted Bird, who has not yet achieved the ground of "complete calculation." On the other hand, he has also not reached the ground of the narrator of Steps, who instead of lamenting the lack of sufficiency has made a discourse of play the very heart and texture of his existence.

Eventually, in an effort to develop a better understanding of his dilemma, Whelan joins an encounter group,[14] with whose help he expects to explore more fully the difficult ground of the self, particularly the communications of that self. Almost immediately, however, he realizes that the encounter group is interested not in theory but in the stage upon which its members enact their carefully rehearsed—or calculated— roles. For him, in fact, the encounter sessions turn, not into helpful avenues toward self-understanding, but into "naive games" that mirror only the relentless games played out in his own mind.[15] One might expect, of course, a disappointed Whelan to confront the other members of the group with the folly of their "play," but because Whelan himself knows no consistency of mind or of emotion that might serve as a basis for confronting the group with the inadequacy of their games, he has no choice but to keep his silence. In his world every statement about himself contradicts another, and thus when he observes how the people in the encounter group exchange potential awareness of their terrible dilemma for the relief of a comfortable role-playing, it is not surprising that rather than confronting the others he ends up intensifying his own sense of inadequacy with the even darker perception of the fundamental dishonesty of human experience. As he says later in the novel, "We [may] know our lives are chaotic, but we insist that everything happen in an orderly way and be logically conceived" (*DT*, 149). In Whelan's view most people manage to find activities that "label" their existence and that thus enable them to see "exactly what they want to see" (*DT*, 104), but he himself is not one of them. Like Kosinski, he labors under a profound ignorance about the peculiar nature of human experience, and finally it is this ignorance that results in his profound pessimism: "No one understands anybody else. We are wandering around in dark caves, holding our little private candles, hoping for some great illumination" (*DT*, 98). The illumination never comes, and in its absence Whelan will presumably be left holding the bag for the rest of his days.

From the beginning of the novel, then, it is Whelan's profound sensitivity to the problem of language that separates him from the others and that eventually becomes the ground for his inheritance of maturity. While the other members of the encounter group expect language to assist them in becoming more precise about their well-defined problems, Whelan knows that the measure of his experience is a matter beyond language. As he points out quite early, "There's a place beyond words where experience first occurs to which I always want to return. I suspect that whenever I articulate my thoughts or translate my impulses into words, I am betraying the real thoughts and impulses which remain hidden" (*DT*, 32–33). If the measure of experience is beyond language, the subtle Whelan must obviously remain locked within the posture of a very difficult self-criticism.[16] He does. For while Karen, herself tired and lacking in spontaneity, rather timidly resorts to brief relationships packed with the old clichés of sex in order to avoid possible confrontation with her real self, the sensitive Whelan, superficially a drifter, actually pushes himself "to extremes in order to discover my many selves" (*DT*, 32) and the conversation between them. The dull Karen, instead of extending herself and her horizons, merely contents herself with the search for an ultimate climax or the insights, say, of the New Woman Society. She, consequently, never escapes the trammels of language that have always been hers. She may know disappointment, but whenever she becomes conscious of her failure to achieve the ultimate climax or a significant understanding of herself, she defends herself from despair with the easy conclusion that "no one else could ever really understand her" (*DT*, 150)—so why should she expect for herself a world of understanding? The Whelan who flounders around for much of the novel, on the other hand, manages by virtue of his detached point of view to suspend himself rather creatively in the fringes of awareness that surround the interaction among his many selves, and thus to gain some understanding. Whereas Karen seems overwhelmed by her lack of understanding, the sensitive Whelan not only has recognized that "living is an arbitrary matter and that I have every right to renounce it" (*DT*, 148), but he has also become determined "to remain oblique, to avoid making any decision about [the] future until some crisis arises" (*DT*, 68) that will engage him in a particular commitment. In other words, instead of trying to force experience to conform to some preconceived notion, as does Karen (and most of the encounter group members), Whelan allows himself to remain elusive and to spend his energy observing the play of his various selves as they respond to the emerging circumstances of his life. It is this elusiveness that serves as the crucial ground for Whelan's achievement of maturity.

Whelan may not finally understand himself—at least in an ultimate sense—any more than does Karen, but he does recognize that his selves constitute an open field of play whose fringes can expose some of his well-hidden personal subtleties. There are, to be sure, problems in such a theory of human experience. Toward the middle of the novel, for example, his father's former valet accuses him of merely creating in New York an existence of evasion, particularly since he has not wedded himself to any ostensible purpose. While disabusing the valet of the notion that he must justify his existence (Whelan recounts a series of "lewd and violent" sexual escapades), however, Whelan gets to the essential point of his manner of existence—the matter of freedom. For him freedom means "not being afraid, not disguising myself and not performing, not structuring my feelings to gain another's approval" (*DT*, 83). The question, nevertheless, is, how does the Whelan who is conscious of his many selves reach the undisguised self? Near the end of the novel Whelan recounts Susan's comment that "to say 'no' is to deny the crowd, to be set apart, to reaffirm yourself" (*DT*, 193). In certain key respects, perhaps, what Whelan learns in the process of gaining his inheritance of maturity is that he must possess the courage to establish himself in some specific way, chosen by himself. While such courage is not easily achieved, at least in light of this sensitive man's fundamental inability to support a one-dimensional conception of the self, Whelan's need for such courage is very apparent—particularly since Chance's stance of "being there" does not seem a viable alternative for himself. Whelan knows that in the largest epistemological terms any stance that he takes is at heart fraudulent and dishonest, but as a mature man, or at least a man who is now bound by the circumstances of his father's bequest, he recognizes that the deliberate adoption of a stance has become necessary.

Late in the novel, then, when Whelan finally moves his narration from first to third person, he seems in a very subtle fashion to be suggesting that he has accepted responsibility for a specific stance toward his existence. That he does so is probably even more apparent in his careful yet determined mastering of his troubling relationships with his father's corporation and with Karen. The fact that Whelan employs his own bodyguard rather than allowing the corporation to guard him; or the fact that he sets up in an apartment with quick access both to the street and to the river rather than in the mansions of his father; or the fact that he reduces his participation both in the encounter group and in Karen's life—all indicate that Whelan is no longer merely floundering around, wondering what it is he shall do with his inheritance. Whelan's new confidence and authority, to be sure, do not argue that he has fully accommodated himself to a well-defined scheme for his existence. He does allow Howmet to persuade him to join the Order, as if he were now ready to accept definition as a pillar of society, but as it turns out, his willingness to join such a group actually masks a complicated game that is only gradually emerging in his consciousness. At the end of the novel, in fact, after witnessing how Whelan murders the Howmets, the reader must still remember that Whelan has from the beginning viewed the initiation into the Order as essentially meaningless—or as one of those cartoons which characterize all human relationships. With the murder of the Howmets, nevertheless, the fundamental commitment that Whelan is building into his life seems finally to emerge, and it is at that juncture in the novel that the reader must face up to the full character of Whelan's experience.

Whelan's murder of the Howmets—an act that is apparently precipi- tated by his confrontation with Mrs. Howmet—is obviously complicated. Whelan had hoped to use some of the corporation's resources to assist the hundreds of derelicts living in the Bowery, but Mrs. Howmet had immediately objected on the grounds that "the Company should not attempt . . . an arbitrary interference in other people's lives" (*DT*, 182). In theory, the Whelan who has widely traveled around the world is probably himself very close to Mrs. Howmet's position on noninterference, and yet because he has realized that the circumstances of his vast inheritance do not allow him the privilege of, say, Chance's stance in *Being There*, he seems to have concluded that he has little choice but to do something with the resources suddenly at his disposal. In Donald Barthelme's terms, it is as if the circumstances of inheritance have now trapped him in a world of "murderinging":[17] with so much at his disposal, he must choose what he will do with those resources and thus which murders he will be responsible for. The Bowery derelicts trouble Whelan, for having traveled widely and having seen such peoples as the Peruvian Indians, who—like the derelicts—"lack ambition, don't compete, and don't plan ahead" (*DT*, 166) but who live much better because they are not surrounded by a society organized around competition and success, Whelan can only see the injustice of the derelicts' lot. For him the American emphasis upon competition and success is little more than an arbitrary social structure—but a particularly vicious structure because of its human cost in terms of derelicts and castaways—and thus it should not surprise the reader that he wants to commit a portion of the company's resources, which were accumulated by way of capitalist acts of murder, to the victims of those acts, i.e., the derelicts. Nor should it surprise the reader that Whelan murders the Howmets, once he gets them to Mombasa.

In Whelan's mind the Howmets represent, almost to an extreme, the unconscious acceptance of certain attitudes—social, political, economic—that wreak havoc upon the lives of (and thus kill) those who cannot measure up to the expectations inherent in those attitudes. While some havoc is endemic to any social system, Whelan seems to regard the capitalist system of "murder" as particularly pernicious because it does not recognize its acts of murder. A pure capitalist system recognizes only success, especially those who achieve the success, and those who fail simply disappear with nary a concern. Such a system obviously perverts any feeling for the welfare of people in general, and that is why, perhaps, during the Howmets' last breakfast, Whelan addresses the significance behind the name of the baobab tree ("the devil tree"): "the devil, getting tangled in its branches, punished the tree by reversing it. To the native, the roots are branches now, and the branches are roots. To ensure that there would be no more baobabs, the devil destroyed all the young ones" (*DT*, 196). The pointed aspect of this passage is clearly the association of the perversion of the natural (and its ultimately sterilizing effect) with the Howmets' world of capitalism where human affairs and concerns have gotten turned upside down. The successful Howmets, even if somewhat unwittingly, are much like the devil who destroys the young. Because their acts of murder are so deadly, in fact, Whelan feels that he must resort to his own act of murder, which is—ironically—predicated upon his larger respect for people, in order to free himself of the Howmets' influence and to begin the process of righting the difficulties of the derelicts.

Whelan's murder of the Howmets, however, is probably not as pat an act as I have here implied. Clearly Whelan cannot right the wrongs of the derelicts merely by killing the Howmets. Nor can he murder all the successful capitalists of the Western world in order to give the derelicts a new lease on life. One way out of this critical quandary, perhaps, is to regard the Howmets' murder as merely Whelan's fantasy played out— after all, he is suffering from a debilitating fever at the end of the novel, and the murder passage immediately precedes the fever. The murder, nevertheless, whether fantasy or not, does appear to signal Whelan's own release from the capitalist attitudes that have made a travesty of so much Western experience. Whelan cannot by himself terminate the structure of value that underlies his inheritance from his father, but by identifying himself with a new structure of attitudes, which involves him in his own form of "murderinging," he establishes himself as his own master. This rejection of his father's legacy, to be sure, initially leaves him in a vacuum, for while he does feel energy "flowing into him from outside" (*DT*, 201) following the murder of the Howmets, he is also conscious of an unintelligible and unmanageable quality in this energy: "There were times when he lived on the far side of communicable thoughts and feelings. He fought these moments, trying to tear off the membrane that seemed to enclose his mind and inhibit his will. But he was helpless and possessed, beyond self-control" (*DT*, 202). Clearly the murder of the Howmets does not immediately lead to the confidence that, say, the narrator of *Steps* possesses. Even though Whelan has chosen his own act of murder, that choice by itself hardly guarantees him a sense of his own sufficiency as he moves into the future. Confused about himself, in fact, he on the one hand decides to pursue a goal of becoming a champion downhill skier; on the other, he also begins to subject a girl (is it Karen yet?) to a pattern of sexual violence that even surprises him. At the end of the novel, therefore, still aware of all forms of experience as "empty figures without gravity or weight," he appears exhausted—a man who wants his mind turned off at the same time that he is committed to serving as the agent of his own inheritance. At that point he even considers blotting out "the flat shapes that used to have dimension and meaning in his life, and the sounds that used to have resonance" (*DT*,

207). For him the decision to choose his own form of murder has indeed turned out to be very difficult.

In Kosinski's early fiction, then, the problem of language severely delimits the protagonist's grasp of his experience. In *The Painted Bird* the protagonist loses the language of childhood as a result of the ravages of the war, and there is some question whether he shall ever recover himself enough to voice a modification of that language or to develop a new. In *Steps* the protagonist, conscious of the arbitrariness of all human formulations and especially of his own games, charades, and disguises, deliberately adopts a stance of silence, but it is a stance doomed to failure whenever he comes into close contact with another human being. In *Being There* the protagonist may come as close as possible to avoiding the problem of language, but even there, as in EE's formulations of him, he is the victim of the language processes about him. *The Devil Tree* shows, perhaps as no other Kosinski novel does, the problem at its most crucial point—the point of maturing, when it becomes necessary to establish a relationship to one's inheritance, and thus the point at which the protagonist must choose what character his own acts of murder should possess. In Kosinski's fiction, as in Nabokov's[18] and Barthelme's, language in the end must entail aggression. To speak to someone, as is especially apparent in the narrator's conversations with the girl in *Steps*, is to murder him—to have subjected him, again in Barthelme's phrase, to that "murderinging" which violates his being.

Not surprisingly, in Kosinski's best fiction *(Steps, Cockpit, Blind Date)* the consciousness of language as murder turns the protagonists into very cagey respondents to the circumstances of their lives. In *Steps* and *Cockpit*, ironically, the protagonist also tends to serve as an educator, one who attempts to introduce others to his awareness of the essential dilemma of human experience, and whose status as murderer thus achieves an almost unbearable intensity. The narrator of *Steps* or Tarden in *Cockpit* may, in fact, wish only to confront others with the nature of their victimization by the structures inherent in their uses of language, but in the end, with all their games and disguises, they both enact rituals not only of education but also of murder. To be sure, as Kosinski moves from *Steps* and *Cockpit*, where the protagonists enjoy the privileged status of superior insight, to *Blind Date*, where the protagonist exists in a context of equals, the intensity of the problem of "murdering-ing" gives way to Kosinski's greater interest in the nature and the quality of relationships between two "murderers." Despite the changing focus, nevertheless, the essential problem remains.

What distinguishes Kosinski's fiction from, say, Nabokov's and Barthelme's is the manner in which he, above everything else, separates his protagonists from the continuities of justification available to people who play within the limits of socially reified language.[19] In his portrayal of a protagonist who is conscious of the arbitrariness of all humanly constituted systems, but who at the same time attempts—despite the impossibility of the task—to be as responsible as he can for his own structures, Kosinski scales down (minimizes) the use of counters that might be taken to indicate a traditional orientation toward Western behavior. As a result, even while watching the protagonist's pursuit of a new, radical integrity, Kosinski's readers cannot avoid the sense in which his text seems to be in aggressive pursuit of them. In other words, what Kosinski's protagonists feel in their minimal landscapes Kosinski's readers must feel before the minimal text. The texts possess action, sometimes in an incredible form, but because the counters (the adjectives and qualifiers) are generally missing, the readers are largely left to themselves and the power of their own imaginations.[20] For them, in fact, these texts become a test of courage—whether or not they can recognize themselves as not only the victims of language but also the murderers. It is in this sense, of course, that Kosinski's fiction achieves its importance as a function of its readers' own ability to make art.

11

Steps: Acts of Demystification

In a certain respect the dilemma of EE in *Being There* defines the situation of all readers who respond to Kosinski's texts. Because Chance, following his separation from his dead employer's garden, responds to the new circumstances of his life in the familiar—but, for him, very neutral—terms of garden and television metaphors, EE has little opportunity to generate a subtle relationship (or act of communication) with Chance. With his inability to discover the quirks and curiosities of a new language, the mentally limited Chance has effectively—if unwittingly—short-circuited any possibility of a significant relationship with EE predicated upon the expansion of his self-perceptions. Instead of becoming aware of new acts of communication, all of which reflect his changed circumstances outside the garden, he has continued to regard himself in the timeworn, yet neutral, terms of the past. The consequence for EE, as well as for the others who come into contact with him, is that she must create the language of the relationship by herself. For her, Chance serves only as a stimulus, not as a respondent who seriously complicates, himself, the terms of the relationship. Because he remains so passive, in fact, she in the end manages to turn him into whatever she desires—Chauncey Gardiner, expert lover, astute commentator. Whatever she notices in his conduct, therefore, is finally only a projection of herself into the vacuum that his passivity has created. To the extent that she defines the language of their relationship, Chance can only become the victim of EE's desire to communicate.

Because Kosinski generally removes the counters (the adjectives and qualifiers that create value) from his texts,[1] thus turning these texts into cool, passive stimuli, the readers of his novels confront a dilemma rather similar to EE's. In the absence of a declaration of attitude in the texts themselves, Kosinski's readers seem to have no choice but to interpret his fiction in terms of their own "language." What the blatant EE does with Chance, however, hardly serves as a good model for Kosinski's readers. Instead of appropriating the texts for themselves, what those readers might better do is become aware of the possibilities for new discourse—the text of a Kosinski novel serving as a challenge to the readers to reconsider the nature and the origin of the values and the attitudes that they have layered into their lives.[2] Unlike EE, who ignores such neutralization of the self because she is so interested in projecting herself onto Chance, Kosinski's readers—at least if they are to appreciate the stark character of his texts—must become conscious of themselves as texts with peculiar configurations. More than that, they must become conscious of their response to Kosinski's fiction as a collision between two separate texts (Kosinski's and the reader's), each of which must not only be recognized but given its due. It is in this sense, perhaps, that the respondent becomes a significant artist in his own right when dealing with a Kosinski text.

If there is one objective that is consistent to all of Kosinski's novels, then, it is his attempt to demystify language and its everyday grammars and thus to make his readers aware of the context that limits—especially when they most ignore it—their freedom or the potential range of their responses to given situations. *Steps* is probably the crucial novel for Kosinski because it is the first in which the narrator fully explores the intricate relationships between language and attitude.[3] In so many passages the narrator gives the reader pause merely by forcing him to reconsider the complex of attitudes associated with a particular word or situation—such as circumcision (*S*, 31) or sex during menstruation (*S*, 53) or even blow jobs (*S*, 82–83).[4] Obviously layered with strong emotional attitudes and even taboos, these terms seldom emerge in polite conversation. In *Steps*, however, they do appear, and in each instance the narrator commits himself to neutralizing the term's (or the situation's) associations. A more extended example of this preoccupation occurs about midway through the novel when the narrator discusses the architecture of a concentration camp—surely a term that yet today possesses a great many terrible connotations. That discussion deserves further commentary.

In the passage the narrator suggests that building a concentration camp is *"just a project."* As he says, *"You could look at it from many points of view: in a maternity hospital, for instance, more people leave than arrive; in a concentration camp the reverse is true. Its main purpose is hygiene"* (*S*, 63–64). In response to this passage the reader may continue to layer the term with attitudes of horror, but from Kosinski's perspective, it seems, the test of the passage is whether the reader possesses enough imagination to accept, if only momentarily, the physical neutrality of the camp as an architectural project. Such acceptance is important, for it allows the reader, much like the viewer of minimal sculpture in the 1960s, the opportunity to reconsider the "grammar" of his own perceptions and thus the textual character that grounds his very self. The narrator goes on to suggest that for the architect himself the project required *"exceptional vision"* because little precedent had existed for such work. What this comment implies, of course, is that the architect first had to neutralize the term in order to turn the proposal into a matter of hygiene. As the narrator points out, the architect probably accomplishes this neutralization by way of analogy: *"Rats have to be removed. We exterminate them, but this has nothing to do with our attitudes toward cats, dogs, or any other animal. Rats aren't murdered—we get rid of them; or, to use a better word, they are eliminated; this act of elimination is empty of all meaning"* (S, 64). The reduction, by way of analogy, of a certain class of people to *"rats"* may still strike the reader as offensive, but once it is a given—as in Nazi Germany—that these people, like the rats, exist only to be killed, then the substitution of the term *elimination* for the term *murder* emerges as a genuine, if somewhat ghastly, possibility. The architect who designs a project whose principal function is expeditious elimination is, presumably, at a distinct advantage over the architect who designs for murder. Having neutralized the horror of the situation, he can demonstrate his *"exceptional vision"* by completing the unprecedented commission.

Another good example of the narrator's reconsideration of the attitudinal associations permeating and constricting all communication systems is his discussion of a potential sister-brother sexual relationship. The sister and brother whom he describes had considered the possibility of consummating their love for each other because of their failure to achieve lasting relationships with other people. In fact, having had a relationship with a man who accuses her, if only by implication, of being too involved with her brother, the sister even comes to believe that she and her brother would be wise to establish a relationship and thus set themselves apart as "allies against the rest of the world." At its worst, she further rationalizes, such a relationship would be no more "unnatural" than the lesbian pattern she had observed so frequently in college, and at its best the relationship would profit from the fact that she had never felt "so free, or so much herself, with any other person" (S, 41). Such easy rationalizations, nevertheless, prove by themselves to be insufficient. If the relationship between sister and brother is to be launched, the situation still requires a deliberate act of demystification, and finally the sister provides it: she and her brother "should become attached and committed to each other, and they could still treat their relation as an experiment; if it didn't work out, . . . then they could blame their failure on the fact that they were brother and sister" (S, 41). Like the term *elimination,* the term *experiment* defuses the intensity of the attitudes that surround this communication act (incest), and in this case, interestingly enough, should the experiment turn sour the two siblings still possess the lingering neutralization of the incestuous relationship that is available in the concept of the *failed experiment.* Again, as in the passage about the concentration camp, the mental gymnastics verge on the incredible.

Perhaps the best example of the narrator's reconsideration of the nature and the origin of the attitudinal associations implicit in the use of language is the episode in which he observes, during an exchange of badges and insignia at a Party reception, a scientist "pinning onto the chest of the Party functionaries round gold-colored badges" (S, 71). The badges later turn out to be foreign-made prophylactics wrapped in "a shiny gold foil," but during the exchange they serve the function dictated by the grammar of the ritual. Beyond the humor of the situation, this episode is particularly interesting because, unlike the neutralizing of terms like *blow job* or *concentration camp* or *incest,* it removes an object from one context of ambivalent associations and elevates it to a context of high association. The context clearly determines the meaning of the condom, and to the extent that the Party members visually ignore what the scientist is pinning to their breasts the reader may even conclude that the communication system of badge exchanges has degenerated into a perfunctory act.[5] To be sure, the high associations that surround this system will probably occasion, as the narrator implies, belatedly extreme reactions—outrage surely one of them. The episode, nevertheless, illustrates the extent to which the context of grammar dominates any communicative act—and thus the difficulty confronting any person who, for whatever reason, seeks to neutralize the contexts of his acts. Communication systems firmly govern all individual acts of communication.

The difficulty of neutralizing the contexts of one's acts becomes a problem for the narrator himself when he becomes involved with a woman dying of tuberculosis in a sanatorium. When the two of them reach the point of sexual involvement, the woman transfers the field of the "transaction" to a mirror: "She stood very close to [the mirror], touching my reflection with one hand. . . . She waited for me while I concentrated more and more on the thought that . . . it was my flesh her hands and lips were touching" (S, 17). Obviously this situation introduces the narrator to a mode of "contact" that sharply contrasts with his previous sexual experience. In this instance, in fact, because the new mode is so radical in its suppression of normal physical release, he discovers that he must "concentrate" very hard in order to establish even a residual identity in the mirror. Despite the difficulty of neutralizing the pattern of past experience (and the expectations based upon it), he eventually does manage to suspend himself in the woman's new language, and thereafter, whenever the nuns (who regard him as a "hyena") deny him access to the woman's room, he even extends the range of the new language by looking at his albums filled with pictures, some nude, of the woman. The fact that he has extended the range becomes apparent when he comments on the nature of his relationship to the pictures: "I looked at these pictures as if they were mirrors in which I could see at any moment my own face floating ghost-like on her flesh" (*S*, 18). What is striking about the comment is the emphasis upon mirrors—and the suggestion that in this situation what counts is an awareness of the mirrorlike character of one's own processes of perception and communication.[6] In his relationship with this woman the narrator has clearly come up hard against the notion that his involvement with others is bounded by the nature of what, for want of a better term, I shall call his self-contexts.

A parallel episode, but one that exposes the narrator's inability to escape his contexts, appears much later in the novel when an acquaintance invites the narrator to participate in an "intimate gathering" of show girls at his apartment. Upon his arrival, the narrator is directed to the room of one of the girls, and there he discovers himself in a situation that he, as an expert in demystification and neutralization, would seem to relish:

> a brightly lit lamp on the night table showed the walls and the ceiling plastered with hundreds of photographs of the same woman, all apparently taken throughout her stage career. No chronology arranged their sequence: some photographs emphasized her young, smooth body, its nakedness exuding sensuality; in others she was heavy and wrinkled, her body, often half clad, spongy and gross. With a single glance I scanned her a hundred times: voluptuously poised on stage, now at ease in the privacy of her room, frozen in every conceivable gesture. (*S*, 96)

On the surface the experience with the woman dying of TB would seem to provide a basis for the narrator's appreciative response to the room "plastered with hundreds of photographs of the same woman." And yet, although his acquaintance had forewarned that the girls would not entertain him "spontaneously," the narrator flees the situation without even taking leave of his host. At first the reader might be tempted to regard such a response as a failure of the narrator's imagination, for at the very least he seems to have failed to meet the challenge of providing relationship to the photographs. On the other hand, while the narrator has gradually adjusted to the displacement of sexual "grammar" in his relationship with the woman dying of TB, if only because he is genuinely interested in her, in this episode he finds himself propelled into a relationship with a girl whom he has never met and on grounds that are of little interest to him, and the result is that he cannot respond. What the reader must remember, here, is that these photographs largely exist outside any immediately apparent frame of reference with which the narrator is intimately familiar and through which, consequently, he might generate the rhythm of internal meaning. The narrator's acquaintance, who has known these girls in some way (if only in adult magazines) and who thus, presumably, has fantasized about them, might regard each room as a palace of pleasure, but his fantasies have accumulated a rhythm and a logic that are inaccessible to the narrator. Because the narrator cannot easily escape his self-contexts, he does not, here, achieve an even more radical adjustment of perspective than that achieved in the sanatorium episode.

The essential contradiction between the narrator's response to the pictures of the woman dying of TB and his response to the pictures arranged by his friend reflects the difference in his commitment to the two situations. At the same time, however, the mere fact that the narrator does get involved in both situations points to the propensity for gaming that characterizes his life—once he has become aware of the arbitrary structures underlying his language contexts. The narrator, when confronted with the pleasure palace of his acquaintance, may avoid participation in that particular game, but there is little question that, given his response to the dying woman, he is interested in exploring the fringes of his languages and contexts—if only to become more aware of the nature and range of his own being. I think that is why in so many of the novel's narrative modules the narrator focuses his attention upon examples of games that, as well-defined patterns (rituals), allow the participants to scrutinize the fringes surrounding their normal, i.e., everyday, contexts. Consider, for example, the game known as the "Knights of the Round Table." In that game, which sometimes results in a penis becoming only a maimed reminder of its former capability, the term *knight* and the sexuality ordinarily associated with the knight suffer an inversion that allows the participants to appropriate knighthood for themselves despite their limitations of character and position. The fact that the participants should be willing to risk their sexual well-being in a contest of physical risks may or may not reflect a lack of satisfactory sexual experience elsewhere, but it surely indicates the importance, for these knights, of achieving a grand sense of manliness that will at least momentarily separate them from the realities of their everyday experience. As they conceal their pain in masks of manliness, they enact a strategy of displacement that allows them the grace of achieving the ground of a generally unavailable heroism. Or consider the game (organized by a man from the city and attended by the narrator and fifty peasants), in which a young girl, chosen by the peasants, allows herself to be violated by an animal. In this game the peasants are not so much participants as spectators who eagerly supplement their admission fees in order to witness the animal's further insertion, and yet there is no doubt that this situation serves as a game in which the peasants can act out fantasies and dreams normally taboo but accessible here for the price of admission. Whereas the "Round Table" enabled its participants to achieve momentary self-elevation, this game, by neutralizing a particularly explosive fantasy, allows its participants to verge on forbidden territory without serious loss of moral identity.

In this novel, then, games serve the crucial function of exploring and maintaining one's contact with the languages and contexts of the fringe. As such, they provide a complication of one's experience that prevents any complete and total organization around or within one language and context, and thus they serve the valuable purpose of generating and preserving that self-consciousness (or dialogue within one's self) which is necessary to any sophisticated appreciation of the nature and the limits of one's being.[7] The "knights" and the peasants may not be numbered among the world's urbane, but by playing out their peculiar games they do manage to avoid that reduction to a linguistic one-dimensionality which is, in extreme cases, tantamount to the loss of dreams. An even better example of a game rooted in fantasy appears late in the novel with the ritual of the wheel, which the narrator describes as follows: "a great circle of naked men lying on their backs, their feet joined at the center like the spokes of a wheel" (*S*, 138). The participants in this game are "petty thieves and weary pimps," and essentially they are all awaiting, as members of the circle, the services of a heavy, ragged woman who functions in the ritual as "the healer." What is interesting about this ritual is that it not only tends to elevate the participants' view of themselves but also serves to convince them of their—what seems doubtful—sexual vitality. The woman washes herself before and after the servicing, and following her attentions the men, even beyond the sense of physical release, seem to enjoy a surrender that will become the basis for renewed vitality: "one by one they fell back, like corpses laid out in shallow coffins" (*S*, 138). The men do recover, and for them the game, by playing out fantasies of worth and vitality that they—for whatever reason—have come to doubt or mistrust, provides the kind of experience that is ultimately crucial for retaining a deep, if fragile, connection with the community.

In contrast to the knights, the peasants, the thieves, and the pimps, however, the narrator himself engages in games that require a more sophisticated and imaginative grasp of the limits of his contexts. There are, to be sure, some games in which, instead of surrendering to a situation, he merely plays out a strong emotion—such as when, in revenge, he administers the fishhooks to his master's children (S, 35–38) or tricks the student who belongs to the "paramilitary student defense corps" (S, 38–40) or arranges through a friend to take advantage of a woman who has rejected his advances (S, 97–101). Or there are the situations in which he deliberately injures or even kills someone for largely gratuitous reasons. He injures the reputation of a student theater columnist, for example, and she commits suicide (S, 77–81). Or he brazenly kills with bottles an old night watchman who has continued working despite the closing of his factory (S, 103–5). In all of these instances, whether or not the reader regards the instances as real or as the narrator's played-out fantasies, the reader must feel himself brought up short against the notion that this narrator, once he releases himself from the contexts of his everyday experience, loses almost all sense of the moral traditions normally associated with Western civilization. In the episode in which the narrator recounts what he does to his friend, the girl who has been raped by several men, this notion of the narrator unleashed from all restraint becomes particularly clear. After her release from the clinic following the rape, the girl expects to pick up the strands of her life "as though nothing had happened" (S, 57). The narrator, however, conscious that the rape has shifted their relationship to a new basis, decides to subject her "to various experiments, stimulating her response, exploring and violating her in spite of her pleas and protests. She became an object which I could control or pair with other objects" (S, 57–58). The upshot of such subjection is that at a party for some of his male colleagues the narrator suggests to the men present, by way of whispers, that the girl is his "gift to the host and to his guests; if they would devise the situation, each could have his pleasure" (S, 59). The narrator leaves the party at the point when the men grab the girl and prepare to gang-rape her for the second time.

Obviously there is a chilling air about all these instances. From even the most rudimentary of moral perspectives (at least in Western society) nearly every instance seems, at first glance, to verge on the unthinkable. And yet, if it is true that this narrator, as an especially imaginative being, becomes conscious of himself as a victim of his language context, and thus of the need to engage himself deliberately in games that will not only shock his inherited moral sensibility but also, as a consequence, nudge him toward a deeper appreciation of the processes of his being, then it might be possible to regard the excesses in his conduct as the price he must pay in order to come into more significant contact with himself. I do not advance this argument as a means for justifying the narrator's conduct. Clearly what he does, if those episodes are real, is unconscionable. Some of the episodes get fully out of hand. To the extent, nevertheless, that Kosinski himself has pointed to such episodes as the working out of his own fantasies, I think it is possible to regard a text like this narrator's as a game in itself—a game in which, having recognized that it is impossible to escape completely the trammels of language and context, the narrator attempts such disorientation of himself that he of necessity must approach the deeper "structures" of his being. By surrendering to his fantasies, if only in narrative form, he discovers, not a privileged position outside language, but those crucial acts of language (his morality) in which he is genuinely willing to invest. For him human experience must be a matter not of socially defined good and evil—such a perspective limits one to language's most restrictive prison-house—but of a deep understanding of the sensitive relationships between the structures of society and of one's own being.

The best example of the narrator's gaming is his relationship to the girl—a relationship generally confined to the thirteen italicized portions of the text. The most efficient means of characterizing this relationship is probably to list the nature of the fragments:

1. Conversation about circumcision (*S*, 31)
2. The girl's attraction to other men (*S*, 34–35)
3. The girl's involvement with another man (*S*, 42–45)
4. The girl's acknowledgment of her affair (*S*, 45–47)
5. Conversation about sex during menstruation (*S*, 54)
6. The narrator's involvement with prostitutes (*S*, 59–61)
7. Conversation about concentration camps (*S*, 62–64)
8. Conversation about blow jobs (*S*, 82–83)
9. The narrator's bugging of a woman's apartment (*S*, 127–29)
10. The girl's need for self-awareness during sex (*S*, 130–31)
11. The arrival of the drugs (*S*, 131–32)
12. The narrator's separation from past contexts (*S*, 136)
13. The narrator as another memory (*S*, 146)

The sequence in this list is rather revealing in itself, for in the first eight portions the narrator repeatedly introduces the girl to the essential neutrality of physical situations that have, as a result of the inescapable process of social layering, achieved the status of marginal taboos. Whether I cite the already mentioned conversation about circumcision or sex during menstruation or blow jobs, or especially the conversation about concentration camps, the intention of the narrator is the same: he does not want the girl—just as Kosinski does not want his audience—to remain a victim of the sentimental uses of language that characterize interaction within society. Language always victimizes its users, especially the unconscious users, and in the narrator's view it is only by questioning and perhaps removing the attitudinal overlay in one's vocabulary (especially the vocabulary of the body) that anyone ever achieves the freedom of a broadened perspective.[8]

Initially, however, the girl cannot appreciate the narrator's argument. A victim of a language that has been hers since childhood, she can only regard the narrator's discourse as shocking and, perhaps, even a bit revolting. At one point, when she surrenders in the narrator's absence to the impulse of sleeping with another man, it may appear as if she is breaking free from the constrictions of her past, but upon the narrator's return she—guided by the logic of her traditional vocabulary—merely conceals what she has done. She does not break free. In that very instance, nevertheless, the narrator, now revealing the full extent of his propensity for gaming, confronts the girl with the fact that he has had a private investigator observing her activities, and thus she gains another chance. Obviously the moment is difficult for the girl—far more shattering than the actual indiscretion with the other man. With the failure of her traditional vocabulary (which required the concealment of such indiscretions) fully evident, the girl has no choice but to shift the nature of her vocabulary from that of romance to one of neutral description. In one breath she has been emphasizing how much she prefers the narrator over other men, but in the next, having been exposed, she is struggling to rationalize an indiscretion by minimizing the significance of the act. As she says, "*An act of intercourse is not a commitment unless it stems from a particular emotion and a certain frame of mind*" (S, 46). There is, to be sure, a lingering residue of romance in this rationalization as well, but it is clear here that the narrator has the girl running toward the demystification of language and of act that he regards as necessary for mature experience.

In the end, then, the narrator's game with the girl is a function of his desire to season her perspective. Because he is the educator who possesses privileged insight, in fact, he is always encouraging her toward increasingly sophisticated moments of demystification and neutralization. Consider here, for example, the conversation that develops between the two of them concerning his own involvement with other women—i.e., with prostitutes. In the face of the girl's initial dismay, the narrator justifies his relationships with prostitutes on the basis of the effect that those relationships have upon his, and only his, awareness. He knows, for instance, that with a prostitute he can do what the girl *"would find unacceptable"* and that the opportunity to do such a thing (within the boundaries of a gamelike environment) will serve to extend his contact with himself. When the girl questions him about this part of the argument, the narrator quickly responds with an eloquent statement concerning the limits of their own sexual involvement with each other. There are limits, as he says, *"because you know me only in a certain way. And because our relationship is based on your acceptance of what I have been with you. . . . You also offer only the side of yourself which you think is most acceptable to me. So far neither of us has revealed anything which contradicts what we have both always assumed"* (*S*, 60–61). Obviously the narrator believes that even in the area of sexuality, where metaphors of darkness generally prevail, human beings remain victims of the attitudinizing inherent in their everyday uses of language. In his view, consequently, the girl will remain, at least while she continues to regard the basic awareness of herself and of her body during sex as "perverse," the victim of her own language. That this is the case is reinforced when she responds to the narrator's insistence that it can only be he himself, not she, whom he perceives and makes "real" in the process of lovemaking. In responding, the girl actually accuses the narrator of requiring her only to provide a stage on which to *"project and view"* himself. Clearly she has no intention of seeking out for herself those adjustments to the thresholds of her perception which are available in games such as the narrator's.

What the narrator provides the girl is an opportunity to turn her life into a game where the object is not only to sabotage the old rules of language and context but also to make the acts of sabotage the basis for a deeper and more sophisticated understanding of herself. Initially, of course, as in his use of a detective, the narrator enjoys the upper hand. Even late in the novel, when he considers the possibility of using drugs to free the girl "from what she had been," he continues to possess the stance of superiority. At that point, in fact, his superiority has turned rather smug: "Her addiction [to drugs] might regenerate all that had become flabby and moribund in her. . . . she would acquire new desires and new habits and liberate herself from what she thought of me, from what she felt for me" (*S*, 130). The reader never discovers whether the narrator finally uses drugs on the girl, but the comment does indicate the narrator's continuing control over her and his increasing impatience with her inability to make quick adjustments that match up with the configuration of his own perspective. Eventually, having failed in a series of gamelike gestures to impress upon the girl her need for a larger and more sophisticated grasp of the essential human predicament, he will come to regard his very departure as the one last available gesture that might create the necessary impact: *"When I'm gone, I'll be for you just another memory descending upon you uninvited, stirring up your thoughts, confusing your feelings. And then you'll recognize yourself in this woman"* (S, 146). It is true that the narrator's departure might merely reflect a pique of frustration on his part, but in the context of the novel's final pages the reader must not lose sight of the fact that having exposed the girl to a number of his games of demystification and neutralization, the narrator probably also suspects that upon his departure she will simply be unable to return to the easy sentimentality of her past. The last that the reader sees of the girl is rather ambiguous: the girl is swimming in the ocean, beneath the surface, looking up for the source of a shadow on the bottom. Drowning? Perhaps, at least if she, now that she is aware of the essential human predicament from the narrator's perspective, cannot make the narrator's games the basis for her own experience. Fledgling gamers do sometimes die. On the other hand, perhaps even taking a cue from the long tradition that includes the destructive element of Conrad,[9] one might conclude that her swimming indicates that she has finally accepted the necessity of submerging herself in the very waters of language that she now knows are so troublesome. The reader himself, an artist in his own right, must decide the nature of her fate.

Despite all of his games there is no question that the narrator himself never escapes the trammels of language that he so much despises. He may commit himself to the processes of demystification and neutralization, sometimes with terrifying results if his acts of injury and murder are to be taken as "real" and not just as the playing out of fantasy, but in the end, even though he has achieved a deeper and infinitely more complex understanding of the texture of his own languages and contexts, he never gains a privileged position outside language. The access to such a position, at least in a world where the subject defines all, is, to be sure, impossible. While the narrator disciplines himself and others in the use of language, he himself, the victim of the inescapably solipsistic character of all perception and language, shall never finally manage to identify and thus dominate all the subtle layerings and intricate structures that shape the character of his mind and imagination. In these terms, of course, no matter what his success with the girl might have been, his objective is quite hopeless. He will always remain a victim of that which he is most determined to escape.

Eventually, in another attempt to defuse the language constraints that have wearied him over the years, the narrator does try a new tack by moving to a new country and adopting the charade of a deaf-mute. What attracts him to a new country in the first place is his desire to escape the exigencies of time—particularly the language of "becoming" that the awareness of passing time entails. He wants, much in the fashion of Chance (the primary exhibit of "being" in Kosinski's fiction), to exist "timeless, unmeasured, unjudged, bothering no one, suspended forever between my past and my future" (*S*, 107). For a while he seems to succeed, for in that new country he not only avoids all acts of intention and motive, which constitute the "grammar" of behavior, but he also manages to keep his attention focused upon material considerations— e.g., the increasing shabbiness of his coat of Siberian wolf fur or the skills of handling motor vehicles. To the extent that such attention focuses upon objects, rather than upon other people, he does free himself of the heavier burdens of language. That is probably why, when he responds to the people of the slums and the ghettos in the new country, it is with no intention at all of initiating a pattern of such games as he had played with the girl. Instead of continuing his thorough analysis of the problems of language in their presence, in fact, he seems almost content to exist as an object himself:

> I envied those who lived here and seemed so free, having nothing to regret and nothing to look forward to. In the world of birth certificates, medical examinations, punch cards and computers, . . . telephone books, passports, bank accounts, insurance plans, wills, credit cards, pensions, mortgages, and loans they lived unattached, each of them aware only of himself. (*S*, 133)

This passage goes a long way, I think, toward clarifying the nature of the narrator's attitude late in the novel, i.e., his desire for a world where each man is aware only of himself and thus a world where man presumably has a chance for recovering his innate dignity.[10] At the beginning of the next major section of narrative, the narrator makes the nature of his response to the slum dwellers even more definitive: "*If I could become one of them, if I could only part with my language, my manner, my belongings*" (*S*, 136). By transforming himself into "*one of them*," into one of the unattached slum dwellers who does not possess the wide range of social languages that victimize most men, the narrator surely hopes to separate himself from the firm grasp of time—to dispel "the image of what I once had been and what I might become" (*S*, 133). Existing outside language, manners, and belongings is, for him, not a matter of deprivation but an opportunity for achieving what represents—in his eyes—the closest approximation to pure being.[11] In the world of the slums, where everything of necessity begins and ends with him, he believes that he will finally reach the point where he has "no other choice but to remain alive" (S, 133).

What all of this interest in the slum dwellers, as well as his development of the deaf-mute charade, comes down to, of course, is the fact that the narrator has tired of the games he has had to initiate and maintain as a result of having become conscious of the essential language dilemma of human existence. Try as he may to separate himself from time and the acts of intention, however, he eventually finds that he must make still another move and take his charade to another new country, where he can serve as a revolutionary (surely, in this novel, an important metaphor). The fact of the matter is that this narrator cannot achieve the style of pure being. Having become accustomed, over the years, to playing with the problems of perception and language, he for a time tries to defuse his determination to gain an increasing understanding of himself by adopting the deaf-mute charade,[12] but in the end he cannot leave off interjecting himself into the game of revolution that promises a new era of freedom and understanding. Such interjection obviously puts him at odds with himself, for at the same time that he is defusing himself with the charade he is also wedding himself to further acts of intention. The fact of internal conflict becomes painfully apparent to the narrator himself when, having exchanged his rifle for a knife in order to avoid the excruciating necessity of executing some prisoners, he suddenly discovers that the prisoners are to be beheaded with the knives. Despite serving as a revolutionary, he has tried to avoid the extremity of serving as an executioner (such status counters his prevailing tendency to neutralize all experience), but having embraced the cause of revolution, he now discovers that he has become, his deaf-mute charade notwithstanding, a pawn of that very language of freedom he had hoped to support: either he now executes one of the prisoners or he shall himself be executed. It is at this point, in one of the novel's most terrifying passages, that the narrator reaches the necessity of demystifying not only the situation but also himself:

> What I was about to do was inescapable, yet so unreal that it became senseless: I had to believe I was not myself any more and that whatever happened would be imaginary. I   myself as someone else who felt nothing, who stood calm and composed, determined enough to stiffen his arms, to grasp and raise the weapon, to cut down the obstacle in his path. (S, 145)

The narrator does manage to demystify the explosive character of this situation by reducing the execution to a matter of the felling of a tree. Despite such demystification, nevertheless, the execution has identified him as a murderer. Not only has he executed a man, but he has also, in the sense of Barthelme's "murderinging," established his intentions and assertions as the ground for human experience—all this in a world that knows no such ground.[13]

The narrator's stature in this novel is, then, in the final analysis a very difficult matter. If the reader manages to come round and to appreciate the nature and the origin of the narrator's games, at the end of the novel he is still left with the fact that this narrator has wearied of his own stance and has, furthermore, embroiled himself in a game of contradiction (the deaf-mute charade played against the act of revolution) that must leave the reader in a profound state of consternation.[14] The narrator has clearly lost control of himself toward the end of his narrative. From Kosinski's perspective such a loss of control may finally be inevitable, for no matter how sensitive the narrator is to the epistemological dilemmas surrounding any use of language, there is no way that he can escape those dilemmas and achieve a privileged position outside language. It is as if, having committed himself to the processes of demystification whereby he can come into closer contact with himself, the narrator has sentenced himself to an increasing awareness of the impossibility of his objective. With his disappearance in the last, two-page section of narrative, therefore, the narrator may be acknowledging that he is genuinely less hopeful about the possibilities of separating himself from his language, manner, and belongings.[15] Separation on a superficial level he can achieve, but the privileged vacuum of "being" that he has long desired—that he shall never gain. Only Chance enjoys that luxury. The best this narrator can hope for is a shrewd awareness of the intricate processes of language in his own life.

12

Cockpit: Games and the Expansion of Perception

If *Steps* separates its readers from their accustomed contexts and thus forces them to become aware of the processes of perception and of language whereby they themselves organize the texture of their experience, *Cockpit* elaborates on this tendency and eventually focuses upon the additional problem of establishing and maintaining a relationship in the face of the bewildering epistemological difficulties of the twentieth century. The mere fact that the narrator of *Steps* has at the end of that novel succumbed to the strain of developing games by which he can come into closer contact with himself suggests the virtual impossibility of stabilizing a relationship with another human being. For if it is impossible to come into full contact with oneself, at least in an ultimate sense, how can one expect to touch another human being? There is no question that Kosinski's protagonists tend to remain loners—and understandably so, given the extreme character, say, of the protagonist's experience in a novel such as *The Painted Bird*. Even in *Steps* and *The Devil Tree*, where the protagonists presumably possess backgrounds that would be considered more normal (Whelan's wealth is, however, extraordinary), the protagonists tend to be left to their own deserts. The narrator of *Steps* does take up with a girl, and Whelan takes up with Karen, but at the end of both novels the sense of isolation that attaches to both men is overpowering. In the end, therefore, Kosinski's readers must realize that the epistemological concerns that organize his fiction generally leave little room for the protagonists to explore the even more complicated textures of human relationship. The question of responsibility in a relationship, in fact, a question that has surfaced only marginally in *Steps* and in *The Devil Tree*, would seem an unlikely center for Kosinski's later fiction. With *Cockpit*, nevertheless, Kosinski begins to sharpen his focus upon that problem and to point toward *Blind Date*, the novel in which he comes to terms with the matter. *Cockpit* is a work of transition—a work that serves as the culmination of the games initiated in *Steps* but also a work that establishes the new direction for Kosinski's latest fiction.

One significant difference between *Steps* and *Cockpit* is the tone. *Steps* from its very beginning seems to disorient its readers. Because the narrator is so determined, at least in the thirteen italicized portions of the text, to introduce the girl to the character of his own perspective, there is a sense in which the novel might even be said to serve as a manual (a step-by-step introduction) whereby the reader can himself establish that strange Kosinskian perspective which tends toward the demystification of human experience. As a manual, however, the novel possesses a somewhat hesitant quality. The reader, for example, has difficulty deciding at the end whether or not the girl has embraced the perspective of the narrator. By the same token, he cannot be entirely sure whether the narrator succumbs at the end to the very dangers that he has been addressing throughout the narrative—or rises to a new level of under-standing. I do not want to argue here that *Steps* is a fledgling work because of the reader's difficulty in responding to it. It is not a fledgling work, for it creates its very sophisticated air precisely because it allows for the ebb-and-flow quality that surrounds any act of demystification in a world that knows no epistemological stability. The tone of *Steps* must be hesitant because its narrator is, above everything else, conscious of the insufficiency that attaches even to his own best games. *Cockpit,* on the other hand, even though it, too, is written in the first-person point of view, reflects the attitudes of a man who, more capable and certainly—if only because of his career as a spy—more adroit at gaming, has accepted the inadequacy that underlies all perspectives and thus simply finds himself free to indulge whatever whims impinge upon his imagination. Whereas *Steps* ends on a note of dismay, *Cockpit*—despite its status as a transitional work—ends on a note of genuine confidence.

On the surface Tarden's experience as a spy in the Service may not seem to have much relation to the issues of language that have so fully shaped Kosinski's earlier novels, for unlike Kosinski's earlier pro-tagonists, Tarden the mature man never seems to agonize over his stance. Whereas Jonathan Whelan has had to endure an intense period of self-examination before he accepts his status as a man of warring impulses, Tarden seems to know fully and almost instinctively what he is about. Readers of *Cockpit,* nevertheless, must realize that Tarden's confidence and knowledge, like that of the narrator of *Steps,* is rooted in his appreciation of the limits of language—especially of the fact, in his case, that the State's sanctions on language are of no more validity than his own. When Tarden discusses at length his flight from the State, essentially what he is seeking to establish is that his present freedom to create his own language, to ride in the cockpit of his own making, is largely rooted in his past rejection of the State, particularly the State's emphasis upon a bureaucratic language and structure that engulfs all people residing within its environs. Such rejection surely unites him with the narrator of *Steps* (who fights in a revolution) and with Whelan (who rejects many of the attitudes embodied in the corporation), but more importantly, it also provides the necessary connection between the past and the present that has to this point been missing in Kosinski's fiction. *Steps* had presented a mature protagonist who had already, for the most part, wedded himself to the processes of demystification.[1] *The Devil Tree* presented a young protagonist who, in the face of defining his response to a huge inheritance, finally realized that such demystification served as a fundamental and—for the imaginative man—as the inescapable ground of human experience.[2] Only *Cockpit*, however, possesses the scope that brings the experience (the youth and the maturity) of these two protagonists together. Tarden's careful recitation of his past, a past in which he makes crucial decisions about the function of language, actually serves as the key to appreciating the rich complexity of his life following his retirement from the Service. There are two episodes in that recitation which provide, I think, an especially shrewd analysis of why the boy's experience ultimately becomes the basis for Tarden's life as a spy.

The first of these episodes focuses upon Tarden's response, as a boy of twelve, to the State's resettlement of his parents and of hundreds of thousands of other families to recently annexed territory. Outraged by the meekness with which whole neighborhoods have accepted such resettlement, Tarden begins to punish such resettled families by making appointments—in a disguised voice over the telephone—for the heads of the families to appear before the authorities. One telephone call in particular goes to the heart of the boy's attitude. Having reached a Jew who has recently suffered a massive heart attack, he initially considers terminating the conversation because his father had been suffering from the same malady. Before he hangs up, however, he asks the Jew why he has not fled the country, and the Jew responds by arguing that "destiny had decreed that Jews were to live in the homes of others, even if they were enemies" (*C*, 115).[3] Not surprisingly, such a response only further enrages a Tarden upset by the "meekness" of the resettlement, and thus when he denounces the Jew's attitude by insisting that "destiny belonged to men, not men to destiny," he firmly indicates that the suffering man must keep his appointment. As he tells the Jew, the law Tarden represented "made no exceptions." Clearly what troubles Tarden in this episode, even at such a young age, is the Jew's use of the concept of destiny as a means for avoiding full responsibility for his own life. Instead of asserting his own perspective, the Jew allows a traditional language to dominate him. In the process he defuses whatever language he may have developed for himself and turns himself, at least in Tarden's eyes, into only a shell of what he might have been.

The second episode, which contrasts with the first because it adumbrates the possibility of enhancing one's language, occurs sometime later, when Tarden is in high school. In the episode Tarden has become involved with a girl, whom he has duped into believing that he has no penis. In reality, of course, Tarden has been experimenting with his "member" by forcing it into his body and hiding its position with a clamp. On one occasion, however, the girl, having become accustomed to the notion that Tarden is an invalid who cannot enjoy normal intercourse, is stunned by the realization that Tarden has "surreptitiously removed the clamp and shot into her without warning" (*C*, 129). At that point the relationship reaches a crisis. From the beginning the girl, who is apparently accustomed to fairly conventional sexual play, has had the choice of rejecting Tarden as a cripple. Once she has accepted him, however, she has committed herself to seeking with Tarden sources of release that "others might consider abnormal" but that for a cripple are hardly "perverted or repellent." Tarden, too, in the process of enduring the pain of the clamp, enjoys the discovery of a new perspective of sexuality in the "sense of harnessed power [that] made orgasm crude by comparison" (*C*, 129). When Tarden climaxes inside the girl, however, it is as if he has violated the contract that has been developing between the two of them. The girl, understandably enough, believes she has good reason to complain bitterly about Tarden's deception—especially in light of a possible pregnancy. Tarden, nevertheless, immediately defends his conduct on the grounds that he has been attempting to revive "sexual sensitivity" and that by avoiding "what we had experienced so often with so many others, she and I had made the act of sex fresh and pure" (*C*, 129). At first glance such a defense may seem mere rationalization or a clever means of reinforcing his deception of the girl, but when the girl admits that with Tarden she has felt "more sensual than ever before," and that her aggressive manipulation of Tarden had actually introduced her to a "new-found freedom" or a "new sexual identity" (*C*, 129) that was worth the risk of pregnancy, then there can be no question—unless the reader regards the girl as stupid—that Tarden's game has enhanced the awareness of language for both of them. What interests Tarden in the encounter with the girl, as in the episode with the Jew, is the subject's awareness of the boundaries implicit in her uses of language. Whereas the Jew remains the victim of those boundaries, the girl edges herself toward freedom and the drama of expanding play because Tarden has created, for her, a new basis for all her words and deeds.

Given the nature of the young Tarden's experience with the Jew and with the girl, it is not surprising that his interest in the Service, when a young man, fundamentally centers on the opportunity to play out the whole range of identities that emerges in his response to a given situation. When Tarden first comments on the origin of his involvement in the Service, he may suggest that he has joined the Service because it provides "a shield for the self I wanted to hide" (C, 64), but after observing Tarden's behavior with the girl in high school, the reader knows that it is not so much a consistent self Tarden wants to hide as it is a desire to realize his many identities (and the freedom the realization of these identities confers upon him) that has attracted him to the Service. In the end, in fact, once he has completed his career in the Service, Tarden will discover that his deliberate, sometimes facile, but frequently imaginative manipulation of a fluid identity was for him a necessity: "I have needed to change my identity so often in recent years, I've come to look upon disguise as more than a means of personal liberation: it's a necessity. My life depends on my being able to instantly create a new persona and slip out of the past" (C, 129–30). By that point, having forever separated himself from any consistent notion of himself (except in the broadest sense of "manipulator"), Tarden will have learned to rely upon the play of imagination because it is only in such play that his vitality continues to be unleashed. If, earlier, he had resorted to disguise as part of his function in the Service, now disguise serves as the ground of his being as he plays off his imagination against what little he knows both about himself and about human nature in general.[4] Tarden does not possess a conception of himself that he can regard as the bedrock of his experience, but in the absence of such a conception, the lack of which in Kosinski's fiction is the essential human predicament, his clever use of disguise becomes the means both for freeing himself from the constraints inherent in the configuration of any given situation and, furthermore, for "expand[ing] the range of another's perception." In bald moral terms, then, what Tarden the expert in disguise desires, both for himself and for others, is that freedom from any constricting notion of truth or of reality which allows for genuinely creative experience.

Cockpit is littered with episodes in which Tarden adopts a disguise in order to challenge not only his own but also others' notions of reality. Before I examine the instances that are particularly important to his own perceptions of experience, however, I want to concentrate on several episodes in which Tarden tries to expand someone else's range of perception through the use of disguise. In all such episodes Tarden takes care to give his disguise as much "credibility and authenticity" as he can muster, and then leaves it up to the other party to accept or reject what amounts to "altered truth." This fact becomes especially clear, I think, in a fairly minor episode in which Tarden challenges one of his acquaintances, a barkeeper who operates a tavern in the theater district. Tarden first disguises himself as a laborer who refuses a drink because of a dirty glass, then knocks over the second drink "accidentally," and finally mocks the display of mementos from the barkeeper's former career as a police officer. Then, after a brief appearance as his familiar self, Tarden returns in a second disguise, orders an imported beer, and begins to swear when the barkeeper cannot deliver. Twice he upsets the barkeeper, and twice he is thrown out of the bar. What is interesting about the episode is that upon being thrown out for the second time Tarden hears the barkeeper blame this incredible trouble on the appearance in the city of "so many weirdos" (*C*, 179) who are interested in securing drugs. In this instance, clearly enough, the barkeeper does not learn much, for he merely uses Tarden's conduct as a means of confirming long-held attitudes concerning weirdos—attitudes presumably held since his days as a police officer.

In another fairly minor episode, in which Tarden—now in a military uniform—confronts a boy named Tomek during a plane flight, the other party does learn. In the narrative that precedes the episode, Tarden confesses to a long-standing interest in uniforms, presumably because he appreciates the value of a good disguise. He also recounts how, when he approaches a tailor in Florence about making the uniform that he shall wear on the plane, the tailor immediately suspects that he—Tarden—is not a military officer but an actor because he has asked for an original uniform that conveys the precise mood of "restrained power" and "subdued importance" (*C*, 131). Confronted with the tailor's suspicions, Tarden initially denies that he is an actor but in the next breath contradicts himself: "[I am] a one-man theater, more likely" (*C*, 130). It is a significant admission, for with the uniform (and a hybrid military salute to go along with it) Tarden turns himself into a theater performance, the acts of which are constantly unfolding as the people whom he encounters repeatedly respond with immediate gestures of respect. Tarden capitalizes on such tokens of respect, but in his dealings with Tomek he also turns those tokens to Tomek's own benefit.

Aboard the plane Tomek has been bouncing around in the seat ahead of Tarden, and because each bounce bangs the seat into Tarden's shins, Tarden eventually threatens—in Ruthenian—to turn the boy into "a long, thin sausage" (*C*, 136) by feeding him to the jet engine. To that point in the episode the matter of disguise is of little consequence, but when Tomek then screams in fear to his mother, the mother—responding to the uniform more than to her own son—replies: "Stop this nonsense. . . . We are not in our town anymore. This officer cannot speak our language. Stop making things up" (*C*, 136). It is with the mother's response that the game begins, for once Tarden notices her "blind spot," he quietly repeats his threat to the boy, who in turn again consults his mother only to hear her repeat her admonition and add, "One more lie and I'll spank you." In this instance, as is usually the case, Tarden has the upper hand, and thus when he, shortly before falling asleep, addresses Tomek one last time, he can challenge the boy with a remark that must have an incredible effect upon him, "Your mother doesn't believe you, Tomek. No one will. Perhaps because they don't want to see me" (*C*, 137). Beyond its surface truth, the remark surely terrifies a boy who is accustomed to the security of relying upon the perceptions of his mother. Tomek, nevertheless, does a lot of growing during that plane flight. When the plane reaches its destination, Tarden wishes the boy—through an interpreter—a good time. At that point the mother, now with some evidence before her that her son might have been telling the truth, blindly encourages Tomek to respond with a "thank you." Tomek, however, the boy who has suffered some serious doubt about his mother's ability to see during the flight, cannot comply. When he screams out in rage, he reveals the extent to which his recent lesson has modified his relationship to reality: "What officer? . . . I can't see an officer here" (*C*, 137). Such a response may only confirm, for the mother, her belief that the boy is playing games of make-believe, but for the boy, even though he has not yet had a chance to sort out all that has transpired on the plane flight, the response probably serves as the beginning of an expansion of his perception—an expansion that will, if he continues the process of sorting out the discrepancies of experience, bring him to maturity.

Both the episodes, with the barkeeper and with Tomek, nevertheless, remain fairly minor—at least in the context of all the complex games and disguises Tarden employs during the course of his narrative. A better illustration of Tarden's determination to expand the range of other people's perception appears late in the novel in the sequence focused upon Tarden's dealings with a whole town. Having rented an estate upon which there is supposed to be no trespassing, Tarden immediately busies himself rigging the estate in order to frighten all trespassers. When he catches some children playing "Cowboys and Indians," however, he elevates the character of such rigging by coming up with a spectacular dummy of a dead Indian and thus playing out what the children have fantasized. Once he has convinced the children of their murder of the Indian, in fact, he immediately disposes of the body and then exacts from them a vow of secrecy that they, of course, fail to keep. The townspeople, when they hear of the children's "murder," have difficulty establishing the true character of the situation: the children may think they have played a game, but because they have also seen the dead body of the Indian, they—much like the untutored Tomek—cannot sort out the discrepancy between the real and the fantastic. The adults never manage to ascertain the truth of the situation. Indeed, because the children have vowed secrecy, there is not even the opportunity for the townspeople to approach Tarden himself for further explanation. In the end, therefore, in view of the fact that the "murder" exists as real by the only available standard (the children's), the townspeople not only allow themselves to become involved in the crime by way of complicity after the fact, but they also must regard Tarden with new respect for having saved their town from an ugly situation. The result of this strained situation is that the townspeople become victims of increased doubt about their children and themselves.

Having pushed the townspeople in the direction of self-doubt, however, Tarden decides to intensify their quandaries by playing out the game of the dead homosexuals. The shrewd Tarden knows that the introduction of homosexual women, especially if they pursue their ways without camouflage, will create a major sensation in the town. Several of the men, curious about the lovemaking of the two women, almost immediately confirm Tarden's expectations by invading the estate in the fashion of peeping Toms, and it is at that point that Tarden's manipulations begin to reach their culmination. For just as the children have encountered a "dead" Indian, so now the adults, at least in the face of some incriminating evidence that Tarden has deliberately arranged for their delectation, believe that they have discovered the "murder" of the two women. In this instance, however, unlike the case of the children, the men never see the bodies. If they seem to have discovered a murder, without the absolute confirmation of their suspicions they feel a strong reluctance to press the case for fear of being accused of trespassing. Again, therefore, as in the case of the children, the townspeople find themselves in a quandary about how to proceed. The fact that Tarden has saved their children, who exist as "murderers," is a further complication—and one that probably delays the final outcome of the situation. Uneasy before their doubt, two of the men finally bring the sheriff, and on the pretext of improving the estate's paths they begin to dig for the bodies. Obviously they find nothing. Without the director,

Tarden himself, the stage must remain bare. Whether or not the townspeople learn anything of lasting value from this episode (or from the previous one) never emerges in the text. For Kosinski's readers, however, both episodes go a long way toward establishing how the character of murder might attach, not only to the townspeople and their children, but to the magician and artist who, like Tarden, creates the webs in which people become embroiled. Tarden is the real murderer here because it is he who alone is aware of the parameters of the games and who, in both instances, completely dominates the play.

There are, of course, many other instances of Tarden's determination to expand the range of other people's perception in the novel—examples such as his "Polish poison" campaign that results in mass hysteria or his flagrant use of a skiing trick that lures champion skiers into challenges that result in terrible injury. All such instances, including those that I have already commented upon, reflect, I think, Tarden's strong moral commitment to the ethics of perception. Initially, at least in light of Tarden's apparent abuse of other people, the claim that he is morally committed may seem rather foolish. And yet, although Tarden exists without any traditional metaphysical perspective that might provide him with moral coherence in the face of life's essential chaos, readers of the novel must recognize that Tarden, as the only "hummingbird" to have escaped the Service, has learned to attribute both his survival and the present vitality of his imagination to the sensitive exercise of common sense and intuition. Above everything else, and like all other Kosinskian protagonists, Tarden is simply the perceiver—i.e., one who is committed to preserving the integrity of his perceptions regardless of the epistemological and ontological problems that attend every act of perception. In fact, while the narrator of *Steps* concerns himself with the process of demystification in an effort to establish for himself what is fundamental to any act of perception, Tarden has over the years become so adept at this process that he has given himself over almost entirely to the games and the disguises necessary for challenging others to pursue a similar integrity. In doing so, he not only accepts intellect or the mind as the key to his own being but he also makes the act of perception, particularly its honesty and integrity, the basis for his dealings with others. At one point in the novel he comments, "My sensitivity to the slightest change in my environment, and my craving for unusual psychological pressure have made me aware how little other people are aware of their surroundings, how little they know of themselves and how little they notice me" (*C*, 105). Such a comment surely indicates how fully Tarden is himself given over to the processes of perception, and as such it might almost serve as Kosinski's own clarion call to a life of responsibility rooted in the integrity of perceiving.

There is, however, one fundamental qualification of this moral stance that must be made, and that is the fact that in Kosinski's usual world of randomness there can be no contents, other than those generated by the protagonist himself. Tarden, for example, generally regards life as a sequence of random moments, each of which challenges the powers of the mind, and in the end, therefore, no matter what degree of integrity he achieves in his perceptions, he must also accept the fact that the configuration of experience that emerges in his perspective is little more than an arbitrary gesture. Perception is an act with no sanctions and with no limits, except as the perceiver himself musters some framework whereby he relates one perception to another. Here, of course, that discussion in Barthelme's *The Dead Father,* which is focused upon the relationship between a painting and its framework, might serve as a helpful key.[5] Once Kosinski's protagonists become conscious of a lack of a sanctioned framework that can provide them with contents, they—like Thomas—must become conscious of themselves as artists who, having accepted the disguises of particular perspectives, are adroit only at "murderinging."[6] A sensitive Tarden, to be sure, having become attentive even to the changes in his blood pressure, may for a time attempt "to structure an existence around the body's physiological demands" (*C,* 104), but such a structure, rooted only in physical realities, possesses little content that can serve as the ground of morality. What Tarden is finally left with, once he embraces the need for disguise, is the sense of being a murderer who creates something that exists only in the category of the limited, the inadequate, the illusory, even the false. There is nothing necessary about his framework or perspective. He may perceive and then order his perceptions, but what he achieves in such ordering—even when he is at the top of his form—is only the act of murder: he has forced upon his perceptions a configuration that is in no way sufficient for all the circumstances.

Tarden, I think, knows that he is a murderer. He may never apply the term to himself in his narrative, but in all the games in which he establishes a relationship with other people it is his character as murderer that predominates. That this is the case is probably most apparent in his wheel games. As a boy Tarden had played the game of keeping a wheel moving continuously. For him, in fact, the wheel's "very shape demanded movement," and when that movement was interrupted he "would leap up and send it on its way again" (*C,* 147). Such a game required him to be attentive to the act of guiding the wheel by way of a stick, and thus as he played the game he gradually found himself aware of nothing but a "vaulting through space" (*C*, 148). For him it was as if the surrender to the processes of the game provided the greatest intensity of experience. As an adult Tarden no longer played that particular game, but when he walked through the city, he remained conscious of the "same sense of vaulting"—this time the result of another process:

> Whom shall I draw out of the anonymous crowd of faces surrounding me? I can enter their worlds unobserved and unchecked. Each person is a wheel to follow, and at any moment my manner, my language, my being, like the stick I used as a boy, will drive the wheel where I urge it to go. (*C*, 148)

In certain respects this passage is the most crucial in the novel. As a creature of mind who is wedded to the processes of perception, Tarden is the artist-spy who, like Paul in Barthelme's *Snow White*,[7] must live alone, without depending on anyone and thus without keeping up lasting associations. Such life, however, as he himself is quick to point out, is "like living in a cell" (*C*, 148), under the constant threat of succumbing, as does Paul, to the excesses of solipsism. In order to break out of this cell, if only in a limited sense, Tarden discovers that he can make one of the anonymous faces of the crowd the basis for a new wheel game in which the face takes him "where it will." Whether Tarden gains access to others' lives by securing important papers from a printing shop or from a publishing firm or even from stolen mailbags, each new game originates in an arbitrary choice that is very unpredictable. Once Tarden initiates the game, however, and drives the wheel where he wants it to go, he accepts the stature of murderer—if only because it is he who enjoys the upper hand.[8]

A good illustration of this stature emerges in his invasion of a publishing firm in which he, good spy that he is, discovers a hoax perpetrated by an author named Anthony Duncan in order to restore a sagging public identity. On the surface, given the nature of Tarden's own games, the reader might expect Tarden to appreciate the cleverness of Duncan's game. Tarden does not, and when he calls Duncan in order to expose the hoax, he identifies himself with a quip that goes to the heart of his failure to develop such appreciation: "Let's say I'm a protagonist from someone else's novel" (*C*, 166). The quip is right on the mark, for essentially what Tarden accomplishes in all his wheel games is the working out of the novel that is unfolding in an unpredictable, nonpredetermined fashion inside his own head. At the same time, however, the quip seems to possess an edge of competition, for when he refers to himself as protagonist, a conflict immediately develops between his stature as protagonist and Duncan's stature as author of the hoax. Tarden's morality, therefore, if it is rooted (as I have suggested) in his integrity as a perceiver, ultimately comes down to the question, at least in moments of conflict, to which perceiver, the protagonist or the author, shall reign supreme. In this instance, when Tarden confronts Duncan's agent the next day and insists that there be a public disclosure of the hoax, Tarden usurps supremacy for himself. In his conversation with the agent, in fact, he elevates his stature as protagonist to that of author: "Now I'm in charge of the plot. It's my novel" (*C*, 169).[9] Tarden does have his way, and with the public disclosure of the hoax, Duncan commits suicide. The reader, of course, may regard such a result with distaste, but here, I think, the reader must remember that in Kosinski's fiction integrity in perception counts for everything. Tarden possesses such integrity in abundant supply; Duncan presumably does not (he does not, for example, regard his hoax as a mere game from which he might learn something). When Tarden "murders" Duncan, therefore, there is a sense in which Duncan gets what he deserves.

If Tarden is the murderer, however, what chance has he of sustaining a relationship with another party? At the beginning of this chapter I suggested that *Cockpit* was a transitional work because it reflects Kosinski's increasing concern over the problem of relationships. There is no question that Tarden, through his wheel games, does get involved with other people. Such involvement, nevertheless, is never easy, for what interests Tarden in these instances is the nature of the transaction between the two parties, each of whom is relying on his own resources of language and wit in order to give some personal shape to the transaction. Without a metaphysics that can provide the coherence of a stable moral vision and thus the possibility of a secure relationship, Tarden knows that each party must regard the transaction that he has arbitrarily entered into as a stage of his own making; and, furthermore, that the vitality of his existence depends upon the attention and the resourcefulness that he devotes to whatever performances he has chosen to enact. What this view of human experience finally entails is the solipsistic isolation of each party—regardless of how sensitive he is to the other party's perspective. In at least two of the novel's sequences, however, Kosinski begins to face up to this problem of solipsism and thus to provide himself with a springboard for *Blind Date*. The first of these sequences is Tarden's discussion of his relationship with the prostitute who is interested in his photographs; the second, his discussion of a relationship with Veronika.

The prostitute, of course, would seem to be a likely candidate for a relationship with Tarden. Because she is conscious, usually in very hard terms, of the precise nature of the transactions in which she specializes, and because she responds to the challenge of turning her "game" into the expertise of art, she seems especially sensitive to the problems of developing her own stage. Once she and Tarden have detailed the nature of their transaction (each climax is worth three photographs), in fact, she—shrewd artist that she is—takes it upon herself to examine Tarden's needs and to discover new ways of exciting him. Even when Tarden involves her in sexual matters that her previous clients had never even hinted at, she responds spontaneously to each of the demands and thus turns her involvement with Tarden into the occasion for enhancing the stage on which she is performing. An even better example of her sensitivity to the character of her experience, perhaps, is her use of disguise. Like Tarden, she is very clever at staging her own person. The second time that Tarden sees her, she has completely changed the style of her hair, her makeup, and her dress, yet remains "just as alluring as she had been the day before" (C, 181). Clearly she is an artist, and to the extent that she develops her art with her eyes wide open, she seems the ideal companion for Tarden. When Tarden presents her with the photographs she has earned, however, she responds, despite her hardened view of human experience, in terms that are at least mildly surprising: for her, the pictures prove that, despite her career as a prostitute, Tarden sees her as "clean and beautiful" (C, 184). Such a comment, necessarily suspect from Tarden's perspective, reflects the prostitute's continuing investment in a moral perspective that, because it has been hers presumably from childhood, she has not managed to overthrow. She is not, consequently, as clever about her art as she has initially appeared. When her pimp (can it be her brother?) destroys all her hard-earned photographs and thus reduces her to a cowering shadow of her former self, in fact, there can be little doubt that given the suddenly shallow air of her experience Tarden will have little chance of sustaining the relationship. Even if he should (as he does) gain a ghastly revenge on the pimp for his interference, he shall never, short of devoting himself to what amounts to a mammoth undertaking, free her from the limitations of language that cling to her from the past. The relationship fails because one party is not equal to the other.

With Veronika, on the other hand, Tarden takes care to develop some equality of perception and language. What has attracted Tarden to Veronika in the first place is, again, the woman's sensitivity to the necessity of creating a stage for herself: "like an actress who never lets down her guard, her every movement and gesture was studied and controlled" (C, 215). She is an accomplished actress, and as Tarden is quick to note, she—following her two divorces—is not averse to expanding the range of her experience, for it is following her second divorce that she becomes "the star performer of the wet set, a group of men with odd sexual inclinations," whose desires she presumably helps satisfy. Like the prostitute, she has become accustomed to creating for herself a texture of personal experience with her eyes wide open, and thus when Tarden confronts her with the fact that as her youth fades she will require "more and more time and money to maintain the masquerade" (*C*, 216) that she has nurtured over the years, she is very willing to listen to his proposals about what she might do in order to secure her future. Playing the wheel game again, Tarden suggests that the two of them enter into an agreement to the effect that if she will make herself available to him sexually, whenever he needs her, he will help her establish a relationship with a wealthy businessman who can provide all that she might desire. As in the case of the prostitute, Tarden carefully details the nature of the agreement (or transaction), but in this instance he also warns Veronika about the necessity of living up to the terms that they have established. He even cites the fact that he has already entered into such agreements with three other women and that he has dealt summarily with two of them, both of whom had "reneged" on their contracts. With little hesitation Veronika commits herself to the transaction.

In the third year of the contract, however, after she has married the businessman, Veronika displays some reluctance to live up to the contract's terms, and at that point, much in the style of the prostitute's pimp, Tarden goes a step farther and arranges Veronika's gang rape by three derelicts whose bodies are covered "with lesions and carbuncles" (*C*, 222). Obviously he intends to give Veronika a lesson, to warn her of the seriousness of her "lapses," and yet, after he gets rid of the derelicts, it is Tarden who is surprised to discover that Veronika has "pulled herself together" very quickly: "she had stopped shaking and her make-up was artfully applied" (*C*, 225). What is interesting about Veronika's response to the "lesson" is that it demonstrates that she is equal to the game Tarden plays. Tarden may try to force her to abide by the original terms of their agreement, but having developed a new game for herself, she reveals an almost unnerving confidence in her ability to make her game the equal of Tarden's.

Veronika's game is essentially a function of staging. She knows, as I have already indicated, the value of disguises and cosmetics in dealing with human beings. Shortly after marrying the businessman, furthermore, she has hired a press agent who is in charge of establishing her reputation as "an international celebrity" (*C*, 219). Conscious of her ability to develop and maintain a stage for herself, she even begins to flirt with the possibility of turning her marriage to the businessman into a larger and more significant stage for herself. In a letter to a lover, a letter to which Tarden the spy finds easy access, she describes, for example, how easy it would be for her "to convince the world that her husband had given her the power to run his estate" (C, 227). Clearly she has ambitions for herself, and from other details in the letter as well as from his own intuitions Tarden eventually reaches the conclusion that she is not above plotting her husband's murder. When he accuses her of such an intention, however, she boldly responds that, whatever the circumstantial evidence is, she will never be convicted of the crime because "she had worked hard on her image, . . . and a trial would only magnify her status" (C, 229). The Veronika who has from the beginning been "constantly posing" (C, 230) and who can handle Tarden so cleverly is now a woman whose games cannot be regarded lightly. The Tarden who is determined to force her to observe the original agreement now finds that he has a major problem on his hands.

In a certain sense Tarden has every right to be outraged. After all, when he had established the original agreement with Veronika, he had repeatedly alluded both to the content and to the seriousness of the terms. Veronika then entered the contract with her eyes wide open, and thus she might now be expected to observe its terms. On the other hand, because few imaginative people—and both Tarden and Veronika are at least imaginative—inhabit a stable world where every agreement retains its original force, what Tarden expects from the original agreement is patently impossible. Tarden himself knows incredible variety in his life, if only because of his fascination with the wheel game, and in light of this variety he might be expected to appreciate the necessary substitution of games that has emerged as a result of Veronika's changed circumstances following her marriage to the businessman. In actuality, however, Tarden seems determined to assert the primacy of his games, to insist on the terms of the original contract because it is that agreement which most enhances his own life. In short, instead of allowing another person an equality of mind and imagination as circumstances warrant, he usurps control of the situation in order to affirm himself and his perspective.[10] The upshot is that he engages a test pilot in a plot to subject Veronika to radar and thus to a lingering, insidious death—a conclusion that may satisfy him but that certainly brings the reader up short because it can only lead to the conclusion that Tarden's way, his whole style of existence, is not suitable for relationships. In contrast to the prostitute, Veronica is Tarden's equal, and yet because Tarden cannot accept the equality of someone else's imaginative ventures with his own, he virtually turns himself into the pimp who murders a recalcitrant call girl.

In a theoretical sense, as I have repeatedly suggested, Tarden is throughout the novel a murderer. His murder of Veronika, nevertheless, represents a nadir in his experience, for Veronika is essentially his opportunity to gain new ground—the ground of relationship. Even if he should continue to enjoy the variety of experience that is inherent in his pursuit of the wheel game, he may never recover from the mistake of retreating from Veronika's vitality for fear of losing his own. The attempt to protect his own investments has turned him into the loser—the man who had so much ends up with very little—and thereafter, consequently, his confidence as a man must be viewed as genuinely ironic. In *Blind Date,* when George Levanter becomes involved with a succession of women, some of Tarden's determination to dominate the game, to control the relationship, will linger on, but in that novel Kosinski will also discover for his protagonists a new direction. In that novel Kosinski finally frees his protagonists of the limitations of perspective that in *Steps, The Devil Tree,* and *Cockpit* had prevented the protagonists from achieving significant relationships with others.

13

Blind Date: The Resurgence of Relationships

Despite all the incident packed into *Steps* and *Cockpit,* Kosinski's novels remain a fiction without content. The narrator of *Steps* may have devoted himself to the processes of demystification and neutralization, and Tarden in *Cockpit* may have pursued as many wheel games as his imagination can contain, but in the end what the reader is left with, in both novels, is merely a sense of human—and, more specifically, imaginative—processes that Kosinski associates with maturity. In a certain sense, to be sure, these processes can be regarded as a "content," particularly if Kosinski is urging (as he seems to be) that his readers identify and then invest in these processes in their own lives. That qualification notwithstanding, Kosinski avoids layering his fiction with specific values, and to the extent that his text is free of such value and thus challenges the reader merely to become aware of the processes of perception and of language in his own experience, the text—even with its emphasis upon demystification or upon perceptual expansion—matches up rather well with what Robert Morris and other minimal sculptors have attempted in their art of the 1960s.[1] By retreating from specific contents, Kosinski essentially forces his reader to establish a new and much more active relationship to the text. It is the reader who, in the absence of the traditional signals of theme, metaphor, structure, etc., must make the associations and relationships that give the·text some coherence and significance. Ultimately, in fact, if the reader becomes comfortable with such responsibility rather than being outraged by the shocking grossness of the *apparent* content, he will assimilate for himself some of the fundamental configuration of Kosinski's own imagination. Such assimilation surely lies, as with the minimal artists, at the very heart of Kosinski's intention throughout his fiction.

What distinguishes *Blind Date* from the earlier novels is Kosinski's increasing interest in the protagonist's relationships with other "survivors" who have themselves discovered the necessity of understanding and exploring the limits of perception and of language that finally give shape to their experience.[2] Whereas the protagonists of previous novels, particularly the narrator of *Steps* and to some extent Tarden, have in part regarded themselves as "educators," as the privileged whose insights into the nature of man's essential dilemma requires dissemination among the uninitiated, George Levanter of *Blind Date* finds his role (especially beyond the first chapter) shifting from that of educator to that of mere participant in, for want of a better term, life's wheel games.[3] Like Tarden, Levanter explores as fully as he can the nature of the transactions he initiates or becomes involved in. Unlike Tarden, however, who was determined to dominate the other party in all his transactions, Levanter also manages to ally himself with others of like mind and attitude without trying, at least in a determined fashion, to turn such relationships to his advantage. Not surprisingly, therefore, *Blind Date* as a novel reveals a mellowing of tone or, more likely, an even greater narrative restraint than that of the preceding novels. It is almost as if, having fully explored the problems of perception and language in *Steps* and *Cockpit*, Kosinski can now explore the more subtle features of his fictive world.

The most subtle feature of this novel, as I have already indicated, is the matter of human relationships. That this matter is so subtle is, of course, a result of Levanter's sophisticated understanding of the processes of language in his life. Early in the novel, for example, when Levanter encounters in New York City a lovely actress who had starred in two Soviet films he remembers from his student days, he becomes conscious of a struggle within himself between at least two different languages. He wants to establish a sexual relationship with the former actress, but when he tries to express his passion in "the language of Turgenev and Pasternak," he comes up hard against what is suddenly an insurmountable obstacle: "In Russian, the language of his childhood and adolescence, he regressed to memories of parents and schoolteachers, to early emotions of shame, fear, and guilt" (*BD*, 58).[4] For Levanter, clearly enough, Russian is the language of constricting boundaries. It is the language that he, as a child, had to learn in order to approach the adult mysteries. Having learned that language, however, he is now dominated not only by its association with the painful memories of childhood but also by its inescapable relationship to the prevailing social attitudes of that time. For him, Russian was—and still is—the language that bound him up with a specific social milieu. It is only upon leaving Russia and his mother tongue, in fact, that Levanter enjoys his first significant opportunity to develop a new relationship with language. For at that point, learning English as an adult, he becomes conscious of his new tongue as a language within which he himself chooses to contain whatever desires (or personal mysteries) emerge in his experience: "Only in English could he name the nature of his desires; his new language was the idiom of his manhood" (BD, 58). If Russian were the language of his childhood,[5] then English is the language of his maturity.[6] More than that, English as a language represents, for Levanter, an opened field where the possibilities for exploring the many configurations of experience are almost limitless.[7] It is for this reason that English becomes the language in which Levanter, the victim of Russian, establishes himself as the agent for shaping the nature and the quality of his life. Later in the novel Jolene will remark that it is only newcomers like Levanter who know "how to change their lives overnight, how to develop new interests, take up different professions, generate fresh emotions" (BD, 110). It is a shrewd comment. Because he is acutely conscious of the range and the limits of the language that he assimilates in his new territory, the newcomer does enjoy a greater opportunity for becoming the agent of his own fate.

It is not merely the learning of English, however, that provides Levanter with his sophisticated perspective. Even before he has left Russia, he has deliberately trained himself (in preparation for his day of departure) in photography because of the supposedly universal character of its "language." In the course of his studies, to be sure, he has discovered that despite its apparent universality or neutrality photography as a medium actually "depended on imitating reality in an imaginative, subjective way" (BD, 54). For him, consequently, the language of photography turns out to be as unstable as any spoken word.[8] Such a discovery parallels what Tarden, too, has learned as a result of taking photographs of an accident in which a taxi hits a woman. After enlarging some of the photographs of the accident, Tarden selects shots for the cab driver that tend to prove the driver's innocence: "the woman had crossed the street in the middle of the block and tripped because of her high heels" (C, 188).[9] Then he selects shots for the woman's relatives that suggest a careless driver is at fault: "she had waited on her side of the dividing line for the cab to pass, and had fallen only after its fender had knocked her off balance" (C, 188). Clearly, despite its appearance of neutrality, photography never captures or stabilizes reality. Once Levanter recognizes that fact, of course, he has good reason, at least if he intends to be an artist in the medium, to scurry after a technique that is his alone. In that search he is very shrewd, for recognizing that he can easily duplicate the technical styles of most photographers, he deliberately commits himself to the development of techniques and a peculiar style that other photographers could not readily copy. He succeeds, but what is even more important in his careful search for a language (or art) that is all his own is his increased sophistication about the problems of language in general. At the very least he is conscious of the necessity of becoming the agent, not merely the respondent, in the complicated matter of shaping the texture of his experience.

An interesting verbal parallel to Levanter's experience in photography appears midway through the novel when he encounters Jolene. Jolene, much like Levanter, finds herself separated from her childhood context (she has fallen from Impton's favor), and when she recites for Levanter a version of her autobiography, it is in a style and method that matches up rather well with a snapshot camera technique:

> Snapshots from Jolene's album. Womanhood begins in grade school, age twelve. Jolene loses her virginity to a high school varsity basketball player, who also loses his. More dates. Click. Jolene discovers the orgasm. Click. High school. Meets Greg, law student. Local rich boy. Click. Going steady and bedding steady with Greg. Click. No orgasms with Greg. Click. Orgasms alone. Click. (*BD*, 104)

After continuing with snapshots of her marriage, of an active social life in a split-level house, and of her marriage failing, Jolene concludes her recitation of this snapshot album with the suggestion that her life was "a perfect subject for any lens to fondle" (*BD*, 104). The suggestion is surely ironic, for in the end what is so striking about the recitation of the album is that Jolene is not at all interested in justifying herself. Much in the manner of Kosinski himself, who does not provide his texts with the qualifications and the transitions that tend to contain and thus shape the content of a traditional novel, Jolene presents the episodes stripped of all subtle modifiers. Instead of trying to fix the interpretation of specific snapshots, she allows the pictures to remain in the open field—subject to Levanter's inferences. It is as if, separated from the language and thus the justifications of her childhood, she recognizes that she possesses no means for developing convincing transitions or a web of coherence for her life. Because she views herself as existing within the open field, her snapshots must remain there too.

As a result of her bewildering relationship with Greg, whose experience has remained completely within the constraints of childhood expectations, the imaginative Jolene has increasingly found herself outside the pale. Levanter may at one point remark that the people of Impton seem to notice her activities, but she herself knows that such interest is predicated only on their determination to bring her back within the pale, and thus for her the only possible response to Levanter's remark is, "What do I care what they think?" (*BD*, 105). Once she has separated herself from Greg's influence, in fact, the Jolene who has become aware of the problem of "contents" actually interests herself in techniques and styles that she can not only regard as her own but also use as a means of maintaining her distance from the townspeople. She is the woman, for example, who wears a grope suit into her husband's office—where the imaginative challenge becomes that of whether she can control the expression on her face so that no one will discover what is happening inside her as the conversation moves forward. She is the woman, furthermore, who, recognizing how most runaway housewives merely renew their old habits in changed surroundings, develops "a system for running away while remaining at home" (BD, 110). Unquestionably Jolene is one of the "survivors," an imaginative being who has found it necessary to establish her own textures of experience, but in the process of forsaking social content in favor of her own style and technique she has also pushed herself so far out into the open field that she has lost genuine contact with other human beings. When Levanter comes to town, of course, she may enjoy at least a momentary reprieve from her isolation, for despite feeling some apprehension because she knows so little about him, she recognizes that in his presence she has no reason to feel cautious: "I am not afraid to say or do anything that might displease you, as I have been with other men. I'm myself—it's the ultimate risk" (BD, 110). For her the experience with Levanter is a refreshing change, but given the snapshot character of her life, the reader must yet question whether she shall ever manage to sustain herself during her long periods of isolation. The people of Impton eventually cut her dealings with Levanter short, and at that point there must be some doubt whether style and technique are enough. In theory a life of snapshots is intriguing; in practice, however, as shall be even more clear later, such a life is exhausting and, perhaps, impossible.

In addition to the effects that the learning of English and the working out of a new photographic style have had upon him, Levanter as a young man has experienced the disorientation of a sexual relationship with his mother. The narrator, to be sure, after recounting in some detail the character of the first encounter between mother and son, backs off presenting a full discussion of this sexual relationship, but finally the narrator's silence tends only to match up with the silence that develops between mother and son—a silence that surely bespeaks their awareness of having stepped beyond the trammels of social language, and a silence that now cannot be broken without thrusting them back into that very language and its condemnation of their act. The mother and son obviously cannot escape the language of social traditions altogether, but in an effort to free themselves of the constriction within conventional boundaries the two of them have established a game or ritual for their encounters that amounts, perhaps, to a liberation of language itself: "They were together only in the morning. By sleeping in the nude and making love with him only when she had just awakened, his mother never undressed especially for him. She never allowed him to kiss her on the mouth and . . . always insisted that he caress nothing but her breasts" (*BD*, 9-10). Whether such a ritual constitutes an easy modification of their old language or an attempt to build a radically new language is probably yet debatable. There is little doubt, however, that the demystification and the neutralization that underlie the language manipulation within the ritual prepare the way for Levanter's later interest in sophisticated relationships—such as with Jolene. While the mother and the son never talk extensively about their encounters, their ritualized activity does speak eloquently of their sensitive awareness of each other, of their mutual recognition that they have crossed an important boundary, and thus of their willing acceptance of responsibility for what they have done. Even more than his learning of English or his success in developing a new photographic technique, therefore, Levanter's relationship with his mother may function as the crucial foundation for his adult maturity. The relationship with his mother has repeatedly exposed him to a risk of monumental proportions: at any moment, losing courage, his mother or even he himself might have reduced the relationship to a "transgression" defined in conventional language. He survives the risk, however, and thereafter possesses a sophistication far beyond the reach of most men.

Considering the level of Levanter's sophistication, then, the reader of *Blind Date* may have good reason to expect that Levanter will avoid the trap of domination that prevents Tarden from having, say, an enduring give-and-take relationship with Veronika. Levanter has discovered how to suspend himself in a relationship as a result of the experience with his mother, and if his attraction to the imaginative Jolene is any indication of his future preferences for women, it seems likely that he will manage to make the adjustment to the other person's perspective that will allow for the continuation of a vital relationship. Circumstances (his flight from Russia and then the interference of the Impton police chief) may have prevented the prolonging of his relationships with his mother and with Jolene, but with both of them it is clear that, instead of dominating them in the manner of Tarden, Levanter has sensitively responded to their needs. The question, therefore, is how Levanter responds when he in more propitious circumstances meets up with other women who, like Jolene, are his equals as "survivors" and thus good possibilities for sustained relationships. In the Foxy Lady and in Serena, both of whom

inhabit an imaginative world outside the boundaries of socially acceptable language and ritual, Levanter encounters at least two such women.
What happens in his dealings with them, particularly in light of his
presumed contrast with Tarden, is, however, jolting—and finally also
instructive.

The Foxy Lady is, of course, the man who has had his "tumor"
surgically removed and who then, aware of the Menopause Room as
"her" ultimate doom, relies on hormones to create from nothing a fragile
world that was not given to her at birth to inhabit. As Levanter himself
observes, her sexuality following the operation always appears somewhat
ambiguous, but from the beginning of her new sexual stature, even when
she cannot yet submit to a man's insertion of himself, she plays out her
new role with genuine verve and enthusiasm. Upon meeting up with
Levanter shortly after her operation, for example, she takes great care to
be inventive and is even determined to compensate "for the part of her
body that still had to remain dormant" (BD, 140). She is so resourceful
in her frank response to Levanter's needs, in fact, that despite the pain of
her healing she continues to unleash all his deepest feelings and
longings and then monitors "every detail of his release, anxious to know
the duration and intensity of each spasm" (BD, 142). The source of the
Foxy Lady's artistry is obviously her precise knowledge of male sexuality. It is as if, now a woman, she possessed the "language" of male
sexuality that is normally beyond the province of the woman. She may
never possess for herself the full language of female sexuality—witness
her sexual ambiguity—but in terms of responding to men she will always
enjoy an advantage over those who were women from birth. Given her
artistry and enthusiasm as well as Levanter's appreciation for the
achievements of the imagination that have involved genuine risks,
therefore, the reader might expect a thriving relationship between the
two of them. In the logic of Kosinski's fiction they are kindred spirits.
What is striking about Levanter's relationship with the Foxy Lady,
however, is the fact that he immediately retreats from her once he
discovers that she is a transsexual.

Before that discovery Levanter has actually accommodated himself to
the necessity of sharing her with other men. At that point, in fact, he
seems to have made the decision that he will allow no barrier to separate
the two of them. Once the facts of her surgery are out, nevertheless, he
immediately isolates himself from further involvement. Such a response,
at least in light of Levanter's previous relationship with his mother, must
be taken as a failure of imagination on his part, for while the Foxy Lady
develops her "act" against impossible odds (the Menopause Room),
Levanter simply withdraws on the lame grounds that he had been

intrigued by the mystery of the Foxy Lady and now the mystery has been "solved" (*BD*, 146). Apparently, as long as Levanter feels a certain ambiguousness that generates for him a sense of risk, the relationship with the Foxy Lady fully engages his imagination. With the introduction of specific content (the Foxy Lady as transsexual), however, his relationship with her withers. What that withering tends to imply is that Levanter, no matter how sophisticated his awareness of the problems of perception and language is, remains the victim of certain deep-seated attitudes that prevent him from continuing the relationship. The mystery surrounding the Foxy Lady has for a time intrigued him, and to the extent that he has accommodated himself to her "strangeness," he has demonstrated the rich character of his own imagination. Such character notwithstanding, in the end a latent but inflexible attitude—strict heterosexuality—prevents him from surrendering any further to her world. Like Tarden's, Levanter's imagination does have its limits.

These limits again surface in Levanter's relationship with Serena. Much like the Foxy Lady, Serena is a high-class call girl who not only is resourceful in her handling of men but also is rather contemptuous of the predictability inherent in orgasm, particularly when the orgasm is triggered too soon: "To her, an orgasm was a failure, the death of need. What touching was to the body, desire was to the mind: all she wanted was to sustain the passion, to make desire flow incessantly" (*BD*, 188). Serena's sophistication, nevertheless, seems to be of a slightly different order, for while the Foxy Lady has "murdered" the character of her own former existence, Serena has murdered a lawyer who had fallen in love with her and who had hired detectives to pursue her once she tried to escape from him. Whereas the Foxy Lady remains somewhat ambiguous and even hesitant, therefore, Serena appears to have become one of those Kosinskian characters who, once cut off from prevailing social patterns, must seek the challenge of the risky and the unusual—that edge where the conventions of language blur and thus where the survivor can most fully come into contact with his deep self. As a prostitute, Serena enjoys easy access to wheel games in which she might not only profoundly affect the fortunes of others but also explore the texture of that deep self. In the end, however, despite her initial appearance as the ideal Kosinskian character, one who might match up well in temperament, say, with Tarden, she tends to ignore other people and imaginative engagement with them because she encounters so few people of like mind and attitude. Much in the fashion of Jolene, in fact, she informs Levanter fairly early in their relationship that with old friends she tries to be "what they want me to be" and, consequently, that only with strangers like Levanter is she able to be "what I really feel myself to be" (*BD*,

187). There is no question that Serena is one of the survivors, but because she does not determinedly suspend herself in ventures that repeatedly expose her to risk, she is even less involved in the play of the imagination than is the Foxy Lady—who every day must muster all her available energies for the delivery of her "act." Serena likes strangers such as Levanter, whose stories and games provide an invigorating alternative to her everyday experience, and yet, always ready to listen to Levanter rather than to develop actively her own stories, there is a profound sense in which she is constantly retreating from the resources of her own imagination. There are, to be sure, moments when she does achieve some intensity. Immediately after Levanter has disposed of the body of the man who seemed to be kidnapping them, for example, Serena initiates a sexual encounter with Levanter in which the dead man's blood figures so prominently that the two of them must feel introduced to new heights of freedom and abandon. Such moments for her, nevertheless, are very rare.

Despite the fact that Serena does not enjoy all the resources of the Foxy Lady, she represents an opportunity for Levanter to develop a sustained relationship rooted in imaginative satisfaction. As long as Levanter, in fact, is unable to connect his desire for Serena to a specific attitude or longing—in other words, as long as he feels suspended in a relationship he does not fully comprehend—such satisfaction seems accessible for both of them. Serena comes and goes unpredictably. At the same time Levanter's response to her fluctuates because he cannot decide whether it is her body that he desires or "her way of perceiving him, of giving him a sexual reality that he had lacked before" (BD, 188). Serena's style is important to Levanter, and with her sudden comings and goings she provides "the only real break in his life's routine" (BD, 200). Again the presence of mystery in the relationship appears to account for almost everything vital in its character. Once Serena has identified herself as a prostitute, therefore, it is not surprising that Levanter— much in the fashion of his final response to the Foxy Lady—withdraws from the relationship. At that point practical considerations, such as the possibility of undetected venereal disease, intrude into the relationship and completely defeat its character. As a parting gesture Levanter may express his desire to open a trust fund for Serena's support, on the condition that she spend at least six months each year with him, but Serena—again revealing her stature as a survivor—flatly rejects such an arrangement on the grounds that she can earn all the money she wants, with no conditions attached. Once more, with the introduction of a specific content (Serena as prostitute), a vital relationship disintegrates because Levanter comes up hard against a limit in his imagination.

Despite his sophistication, he in two separate instances finds himself wanting. In a certain sense, perhaps, both the Foxy Lady and Serena are his superiors.

Having failed with the Foxy Lady and with Serena, Levanter seems to enjoy one more opportunity in the novel to realize a sustained relationship—this time with Mary-Jane Kirkland. When Mary-Jane first meets Levanter, she appears to be another of the survivors because of the adroitness with which she conducts the charade of being Mrs. Kirkland's secretary. In addition, she invites Levanter to her private quarters in a fashion that parodies his own earlier invitation (to the effect that she join him in his apartment), and thus she seems to possess a rich measure of that imaginative vitality which belongs to Kosinski's privileged characters. Mary-Jane, nevertheless, as a result of her long relationship to a dominant husband such as Mr. Kirkland (whom she herself describes as "master of his family, not its guardian"), does not have a history of experience—particularly of the imaginative variety—that she can regard as peculiarly hers. Unlike Jolene, the Foxy Lady, and Serena, therefore, she cannot challenge Levanter with the character of a hard-won experience that is the equal of his own. But for her money and the privileges it entails, in fact, she probably would never have gained the attention of this man who has accumulated such strange contacts. What is shocking in this situation is the fact that Levanter marries her anyway. Not only is he the first Kosinskian protagonist to enter such a conventional arrangement, but he also marries one of the women least likely to stimulate him. Marriage as an act, to be sure, terrifies him, and thus there is a chance that it is the act more than the woman that engages his interest. At the very least he perceives in such a definitive act the risk that chance will turn terrorist and punish the two of them for "trying to control their own lives, trying to create a life plot" (*BD*, 220).[10] The possibility that Levanter responds more to the act of marriage than to the woman also seems to underlie his deliberate retention of his old apartment. He may regard the keeping of that apartment as merely "a gesture to chance" (*BD*, 225), but finally such retention also implies that he has entered the marriage as if it were an experiment that may not have much duration.

What this discussion of Levanter's relationship with Mary-Jane lacks, however, and what all the previous discussions of his relationships with other women finally lead up to, is an awareness of the fact that in terms of energy and enthusiasm for the unusual Levanter has experienced a significant falling off during the novel. Levanter, it must be remembered, is the man who in the first chapter alone has established the possibility of spying through the mails, has deliberately slowed down the cross-country ski race in order not to appear inept himself, has forced three men to assist a woman down a ski slope, and finally has blown up the gondola carrying the Deputy Minister who had created "the notorious PERSAUD" (BD, 33). Like the Tarden who dominates his environment, Levanter is at the beginning energetic, courageous, and imaginative. By the end, however, he is a man much diminished—at least in terms of Tarden's spirit. He may at the end, to be sure, remain that shrewd representative of Investors International who "always did everything as well as he could" and who, when he did not live up to his own expectations, worked diligently "to improve himself" (BD, 234). Certainly his attitudes continue to reflect a claim his own father had once made—to the effect that civilization at any given moment in its history is the product of "sheer chance plus a thousand or two exceptional men and women of ideas and action" (BD, 87–88). Like his father, Levanter continues to regard those exceptional people as the "small investors," the people who risk their own energy and personal fortune in order to gain "certain unpredictable ends" (BD, 88), and in his own mind he himself belongs to that elite. At the end of the novel, however, regardless of his earlier Tarden-like stature as an investor, Levanter has lost much of the intensity that had characterized his earlier activities. There is a good reason for this loss.

In Blind Date, finally, the skill of the survivor-investor is not enough. While Levanter is surely a good match for the narrator of Steps or for Tarden, he does not possess as strong a faith in his control over the circumstances of his existence as do other Kosinskian protagonists. Like them, he is conscious of the "languages" with which he has learned to play in his life, but at the same time he is much more aware than they of the extent to which chance influences all the affairs of the universe.[11] As a boy he had heard his father emphasize the importance of "sheer chance" in the development of civilization, and then when he listens to Jacques Monod, the French biologist and philosopher who has argued that "blind chance and nothing else is responsible for each random event" (BD, 86) of the universe, he receives an important confirmation of his father's views. As a friend of Monod, Levanter realizes that, regardless of how careful he is with his "investments," chance will dominate all his words and deeds. In a world where Stalin's daughter, Svetlana Alliluyeva, moves halfway around the world and becomes his "ordinary next-door neighbor" (BD, 79), Levanter—whose friend Romarkin has been imprisoned for challenging Stalin's authority—must conclude that "anything can happen." Or in a world where physical decline finally dominates mental acumen, Levanter eventually has no choice but to back off from his earlier emphasis upon rational control: "While his mind retained its ability to consider circumstances and issue commands, his body, which had once reacted automatically, was now frequently unable to respond as expected" (*BD,* 21–22). Like such protagonists as the narrator of *Steps* and Tarden, Levanter previously had allied himself with the view that the heart merely acted "in uncomplicated, clockwork response to the sovereign brain" (*BD,* 30), but with time, especially after a succession of failed relationships, he has had to face up to the realization that he had allowed himself to fall into the trap of the French—who "confused logic with facts of human existence and emotion" (*BD,* 171). In the sense, therefore, that the relationship to Mary-Jane Kirkland represents an opportunity for Levanter to explore the "whims" of the heart, rather than the logic of the mind, that relationship may serve as the beginning of Levanter's even more sophisticated dialogue with experience. In these terms, obviously enough, the marriage represents, not a failure, but Levanter's accommodation to the fact that his determination to dominate his experience by way of the acts of the mind is not sufficient. If so, it finally makes little difference whether or not Mary-Jane is his imaginative equal. What counts is only the attitude of their hearts—and Levanter's new willingness to let that attitude achieve its own fullness, with no interference on his part.

The marriage to Mary-Jane Kirkland, then, is even more jolting than I first suggested. As a test of Levanter's ability to separate himself from an orientation toward the mind and its acts, which he now knows are insufficient, the marriage allows Levanter to come into contact with and to explore a dimension of experience—the world of the heart—that he has hitherto neglected. Levanter does in the end love Mary-Jane very much, and while he may not be able to comment on the character of that love (because the acts of the mind, i.e., language, cannot effectively contain such experience), he surely reveals the extent of his feeling in his grief over her death from brain cancer.[12] It is with Mary-Jane that Levanter finally manages to sustain a relationship, and even though her death abruptly terminates the time that they have enjoyed together, Levanter is left in its aftermath with a profound realization—that his success with Mary-Jane was the result of his having avoided his previous tendency to dominate the mystery of a relationship with an act of the mind that could only reduce that relationship, as in the cases of the Foxy Lady and Serena, to a category that no longer interested him. For Levanter, therefore, especially given the earlier configuration of his experience, the marriage to Mary-Jane constitutes his supreme act of courage (it may also represent the supreme act of courage for all of Kosinski's protagonists). What happens to Levanter following Mary-Jane's death confirms this interpretation.

At the end of the novel Levanter gets involved with one more woman—the Pauline whom in the first chapter he had taken into an underground grotto. Like Levanter, Pauline is an investor, in her case an accomplished pianist, and as she continues in an almost relentless fashion to add to the grand total of performances that she has given during her career, she has finally understood the artist's essential dilemma—the fact that, regardless of the care, the intensity, and the enthusiasm that she expends upon each of her performances, her playing never achieves the enduring sufficiency, the absolute character of genius, for which she has always striven. As she says of her concert the night that Levanter visits her, "All that's left is the recording, a memory" (*BD*, 226). It is a comment fraught with meaning, particularly for a Levanter who has recently lost Mary-Jane. Pauline herself, as an artist who has over the years invested so much energy in an effort to raise the performance level of her art, has recognized that what matters most in her art is not the pursuit of genius but the attitude, the feeling, that sustains her playing. Unlike Levanter, who through much of his life has tried to contain his experience within the acts of mind and of will, Pauline has for some time realized that such acts neither account for nor sustain whatever genius does emerge in an artist's achievement. Because her stature as a pianist, like Levanter's stature as Mary-Jane's lover, depends upon an expression of heart, she serves as a good match for Levanter following his loss of Mary-Jane.

When Pauline remarks that her concert has merely become a memory, Levanter immediately reveals his recently acquired sensitivity and consoles her with the fact that at least it is a "memory with feeling." At the same time, when Pauline asks him how he wants to be remembered, he responds without hesitation, "As a memory with feeling" (*BD*, 227). Clearly for Levanter, as for Pauline, feeling now counts very heavily. Having lost Mary-Jane, Levanter may at first seem only in search of an intensity comparable to what he had enjoyed with her. When he broaches his invitation to Pauline that she join him in his apartment for the night, however, she knows that it is not so much the need for another Mary-Jane as it is a need for genuine feeling that brings Levanter to her arms. In response to her query about why he wants her, she hears what amounts, at least for a Kosinskian protagonist, to an incredible declaration:

> I'm afraid of losing you. . . . I want you to fall in love with me. . . . Somehow, I think you're my last chance . . . to be wanted, rather than remembered. To have a fresh emotion, a sensation that isn't just a ricocheted memory. To be part of that spontaneous magic. (*BD*, 227–28)

If the extremity, here, of Levanter's emotion strikes for the reader a bit of a false note, the reader must remember that Levanter has only recently made what is, perhaps, the most significant adjustment in the whole of Kosinski's fiction. Lacking yet the confidence of responding to the feelings of his heart rather than to the logic of his mind, he probably has good justification for pursuing Pauline with such determination. Pauline, on the other hand, having recognized in him some of the intensity of her own being, opens herself to him in a similarly unprecedented fashion. Given the fact that she has never before experienced sexual orgasm, the reader can probably conclude that her contact with investors such as Levanter has been very rare. Whatever her past associations with men have been, the experienced Levanter subjects her to a variety of oral and manual play (he eventually inserts his hand up to his wrist), and finally she achieves what had never before been hers. For both of them, therefore, there is suddenly a rich measure of "spontaneous magic," and even if they should (as apparently they do) go their separate ways, their moment of "magic" is at least a sign of their present vitality and their genuine suspension in that life of feeling which now seems so important to Kosinski himself.

Blind Date, then, represents a significant revision of the novels that have preceded it. To be sure, because the novel tends to avoid any explicit moral comment—about all that can be said is that the heart must count at least as heavily as the mind—the reader of the novel may still have great difficulty establishing the nuances of Kosinski's vision. As I suggested at the beginning of this chapter, Kosinski's novels have always tended to exist as a fiction without content—a fiction in which Kosinski and his narrators have attempted to examine the processes of perception, of language, and finally even of feeling, but also a fiction in which the nature and the quality of the processes, not their contents, count for everything. Even at the end, *Blind Date* must exist as selected blocks of human experience, each of which is stripped of the attitudinal associations that in a traditional novel would have converged in some formulation of vision. As blocks of human experience, nevertheless, the novel does serve to examine the various processes whereby Levanter himself makes some connection with the world about him, especially with the people about him, and thus it can become, if not a statement of value, an opportunity for the reader himself to become more sensitive to the same processes within his own life.

14

Conclusion: Strategies of Murder

One of the important threads running through this book is the issue of murder. While I have generally focused my attention upon the manner in which three rather different authors respond to their imprisonment within, or their victimization by, language and its texts, it has repeatedly become evident that all three authors rely upon some aspect of murder for relief from the textual turmoil in which they find themselves embroiled. In fact, one of the best means, once the differing characteristics of their texts have been established, of distinguishing among the three writers is to isolate, as specifically as possible, the character of the murder that emerges in each of their fictions. As a concluding gesture for this book, let me do precisely that.

When compared to Barthelme and Kosinski, Nabokov possesses the attitude toward language that most closely matches up with the tradition of modernist fiction. By that I mean to suggest, not that Nabokov was the last of the great modernists (although a number of critics have argued thus), but that, like the modernists before him, he relied upon an intricate narrative strategy as the basis for exploring the complexities inherent in all acts of human perception and language. Nabokov, as his memoir repeatedly reveals, was profoundly interested in the relationships between memory and the imagination, and while he recognized that those relationships could never be fixed with precision (at least in the absence of a convincing theory of time), he did through a succession of narrators—and especially with Quilty, Shade, and the elder Van Veen—manage to portray text-makers who surmount the problems of epistemology and ontology by suspending themselves in the processes of assembling a text. Like the narrator of *Pnin*, who plays a cunning game of textual appropriation that profoundly disturbs Pnin the victim, Quilty and Shade both surrender themselves—by way of imaginative projection—to the working out of text that emerges in their characterization of Humbert Humbert and Charles Kinbote. The narrator of *Pnin*, to

228

be sure, appears to appropriate for himself the text of another "real" person, but what all three of these narrators accomplish is essentially the same: having little sense of a significant content for themselves, they manufacture through the play of their imagination a texture that while still inadequate and insufficient is at least interesting and provocative—particularly on the score of illuminating the fundamental problem of "being" in the twentieth century.

The narrator of *Pnin*, for example, after sensing the boring character of his own life, deliberately focuses his attention upon Pnin because Pnin strikes him as an original, as someone whose life (or personal text) possesses an intrinsic value worth the effort of exploring. Or Quilty, having written his long series of scenarios, and having in the process become conscious of his separation from a limited, one-dimensional self that requires daily reification, deliberately learns to indulge himself, almost on the spur of the moment (as when he sees a striking father-daughter combination in Briceland), in the imaginative realization of the curious texts that belong to men trapped within themselves—i.e., the Humbert Humberts. Or Shade, having developed the narrative of his autobiography (which he successfully contains within a thousand lines of neo-Popian prosody), deliberately projects himself into a critic-reader named Kinbote in an effort to expose the intricacies that underlie a text so limited that commentary initially seems unnecessary. Even the elder Van Veen, having toward the end of his life become profoundly interested in the character of his earlier relationship with Ada, shrewdly suspends himself in an inquiry that, assisted by Ada, enables him to recover the incredible complexity surrounding and permeating all his memory-texts of the past. All of these narrators, then, through varying acts of suspension that help them to weigh the subtle intricacies common to all texts, manage to achieve that text (or, as I suggested earlier, that "realized texture") which for epistemological and even ontological reasons had seemed impossible. There is, however, a price.

For the narrator of *Pnin*, the price is Pnin's friendship. As Pnin becomes more aware of the narrator's web, he—Pnin—finds it necessary to dissociate himself from the narrator's influence. The narrator may inflict on Pnin no physical harm, but to the extent that Pnin suddenly finds his own memory-texts and especially the character of his originality reduced to the narrator's terms and interpretation, Pnin must feel as if the fundamental nature of his experience, of his very being, has been sabotaged. In this instance the narrator himself inflicts the injury. In *Lolita* and *Pale Fire*, on the other hand, the narrators (Quilty and Shade), having suspended themselves in the process of recovering the character of Humbert's and Kinbote's determined efforts to realize specific texts, find themselves the victims of that very process. For once Humbert and Kinbote, under the extreme threat of losing what they had most hoped to achieve, begin to turn against their makers, it is as if Quilty and Shade cannot retreat from the monsters they have themselves unleashed. The vulnerability lies within their own imaginations: having surrendered to the complicated process of realizing the attitudes and stances that underlie the character of specific projections, the game must play itself out. When Humbert and Kinbote turn desperate in their pursuits of precise texts, their makers cannot—at least imaginatively—ignore the desperation and turn a cold shoulder. In fact, having achieved their glorious worlds of the imagination, Quilty and Shade must both reckon with the fact that thereafter Humbert and Kinbote will hound them to their graves—and thus, in fact, "murder" them forever. With Van Veen the situation becomes even more dramatic: unlike Quilty and Shade, he does not project himself into characters such as Humbert and Kinbote in an effort to realize some of the more subtle dimensions of text-making, but he does in the process of playing out his games with Ada mishandle his relationship with Lucette. By refusing to include Lucette in the games that he has initiated with Ada when Lucette was very young, Van has effectively concerned himself only with the character of his own desires and thus has sacrificed Lucette in favor of his own selfish interests. Only much later, when he and Ada are both near death, will he fully appreciate the fact that he has "teased" Lucette to death. At that point, fully aware that his relationship with Lucette could have been otherwise, he must shoulder at least some responsibility for her death.

The fact that murder can serve as a crucial key to approaching all four of these superb Nabokov novels is surely not incidental. In the end, perhaps, what is most important about this convergence of detail is that the nature of the murders points rather nicely to the character of the novels themselves. For just as all four novels finally depend upon the rhetorical strategies whereby the narrator develops a shrewd relationship with his text—i.e., a relationship that allows the process of playing with the textures of experience to emerge as text—so the murders (if I can momentarily equate the mishandling of Pnin and of Lucette with murder) in these four novels all serve to point to the price each narrator must pay in the arranging of his rhetorical strategy. The narrator of *Pnin* loses Pnin's friendship. The narrators of *Lolita* and *Pale Fire* shall forever be hounded by the memories of their principal creations. The narrator of *Ada* can never forget the travesty of his failure with Lucette. In each situation, as part of establishing a relationship to his text, each narrator makes himself vulnerable to later recriminations. Texts in Nabokov are never cheap, but if the narrator recognizes and finally accepts the high cost, the opportunity for realizing a narrative loaded with incident and significance is rich.

Nabokov may have moved beyond the now classical stance of the modernists, but to the extent that all his verbal play, or his sometimes nearly incredible display of linguistic facility, is subsumed under the overriding consideration of narrative strategy, he continues to reflect a major concern of the modernists from Conrad to Faulkner. Perspective counts heavily in Nabokov, and in the sense that language achieves its depth by virtue of perspective, it must be recognized that in Nabokov's fiction, regardless of the verbal pyrotechnics, language is the servant of narrative structure. Nabokov always challenges his structures—as when Pnin challenges his narrator, or Humbert murders Quilty, or Gradus murders Shade (or is it a convict who mistakes Shade for Judge Goldsworth?), or Ada contradicts Van—and in the end such challenging, even though it results in a significant embellishment of the novel, must reinforce the primacy of the problem of perspective. Nabokov's genius, then, lies in his full and sensitive understanding not merely of language but of the profound relationship that exists between language and consciousness and that makes the matter of perspective so critical. By always referring himself to the interactions of memory and the imagination, he makes of himself a genuine scientist of perspective.

If Nabokov focuses his attention upon the intricate problems of perspective, Barthelme seems to accept those problems as insoluble and thus concentrates his energies upon the curious status of language within any given text. Perspective, to be sure, still matters to Barthelme—especially in such stories as "The Sandman" and "Alice," in both of which the narrator addresses himself to the limits that perspective places upon human experience. In "The Sandman," for example, the narrator is determined to confront Dr. Hodder with the "skewing" of perspective that has occurred as a result of Hodder's reference to "norms." Or in "Alice" the narrator, having become aware of his desire for a married woman (one of his patients), faces up to the complex character of his own perspective—especially its inherent contradictions as a result of its having been built up, over the years, out of a wide variety of experiences. Barthelme's narrators and characters are conscious of perspective, but instead of enjoying the security of a perspective that successfully packages all their experience together, most of his narrators and many of his characters are aware only of the fragile, even the fraudulent, status of their "vision." In "Views of My Father Weeping," for example, the son comes to the realization that he shall never gain a solid view of his father, either alive or dead. The test for him, consequently, will be whether he can suspend himself in human experience without despairing over the lack of a comprehensive, consistent overview of his life. In a story such as "City Life," the effect of this lack of perspective in Barthelme's fiction is even more apparent. In that story all the characters (with the possible exception of Moonbelly) lose the orientation toward human existence that they have fashioned for their early adulthood, and the consequence is that they—as well as the story—become repositories of language largely unleashed from context and thus a function merely of impulse. Ramona cannot verify who is the father of her child, but she can launch a vision of a virgin birth that in the confusions of the city achieves some currency. In the absence of strict context—the web that packages all experience—poetry alone can prevail. For the reader wedded to tradition, such poetry may seem desperate—a sign of culture and civilization having run amok—but in those of Barthelme's stories where perspective has disappeared, the poetry of language is all that is left.

The best illustrations of the retreat from perspective in Barthelme's fiction, however, are his novels, for in both of them the relationship between perspective and murder that is at the heart of Barthelme's fiction appears in full dress. *Snow White* is a brilliant excursion into the dreck of language, the trash of human experience, or the by-products of the decline of Western traditions. The dwarfs may still conceive of themselves as entrepreneurs, and Snow White herself may continue to await the arrival of the traditional prince-figure, but essentially their anticipation of success and fulfillment serves only to indicate how fully out of touch with their times they are. In this novel it is the wicked stepmother-figure, Jane, who best understands the dilemmas of contemporary existence. She is herself, when seeking her revenge, conscious of playing out the role assigned to her by tradition, but at the same time she is the character who is most aware of human experience as an unending series of confrontations among conflicting universes of discourse, none of which enjoys the sanctions of a tradition that fully unites the community. In the end, in fact, it is she who concludes that language represents an exercise in power: if she speaks her universe of discourse, she dilutes the other universes about her. In other words, by speaking herself, she imposes upon those about her and, perhaps, "murders" them: to speak or to use language is in this novel tantamount to murder. That this is the case is even more evident once Jane commits herself to her revenge. She prepares a poisoned vodka Gibson, and when Paul accidentally saves Snow White from its peril and thus—ironically—identifies himself as the prince-figure, it is he who dies. In this fairy tale, told in an age when the traditions supporting such a tale have collapsed, the wicked stepmother-figure reigns supreme. Jane may be the character of malice, but because she is also the character who (with Hogo) most fully comprehends the acts of language as acts of imposition and murder, it is she who finally must dominate the tale. Her understanding does not make of her a heroine, but it does enable her to act—when most of the other characters (and especially Snow White, Bill, and Paul) sit around waiting for a fulfillment that shall never come.

Jane's dominant stature in *Snow White* serves as an important springboard for appreciating Barthelme's achievement in *The Dead Father*. In this novel language as an act of murder again surfaces, particularly in the propensity of the Dead Father himself to kill whatever is in sight in moments of personal consternation. More than that, however, the juxtaposition of Thomas's answer to the Riddle of the Great Father Serpent ("like murderinging") with the injunction of the manualist that fatherhood be "turned down" reinforces the notion that in an age lacking strong community cohesion the acts of language must be played down. In light of the fact that the world of the twentieth century has become the scene of so many strident and conflicting voices, of course, the potentially catastrophic effect of speaking as an act of dominance is disturbingly clear. Men must speak, but in Barthelme's fiction the question has become whether they can speak with less insistence—with less murder on their minds. For him, in fact, the question is also whether man can, as does the Dead Father by the end of the funeral procession, separate himself from the heroic uses of language (such as the heroic catalogues) and indulge himself in the spectacular linguistic play, say, of the Dead Father's Papsday speech. Or, to use a better illustration, whether man can, in the fashion of those four lengthy yet confusing conversations between Julie and Emma (which seem to punctuate the novel), separate himself from the web of logic and coherence that has traditionally informed his speaking and thus, at least for a time, sensitize himself to the manner in which the very structures of language and communication victimize him from the moment he opens his mouth. The father who would be alive must at a minimum reconsider the whole character of his utterance.

In Barthelme, then, the matter of language involves not only the discovery of a new verbal key but also an appreciation of what lies at zero—where language can surface as a response to an open field. Barthelme may seem to concentrate upon the dreck, upon the trash and verbal litter of contemporary man, but such concentration is only a symptom of the process that lies much deeper in his fiction. He does parody, and he does satirize, and in both his parodies and his satires he captures, as so many critics have pointed out, the inane and absurd qualities of recent history. In the end, nevertheless, Barthelme's real genius as a writer is his ability to move beyond the trammels of perspective, upon which both parody and satire depend, and to play with the origin of language itself. By employing language himself, to be sure, Barthelme can never entirely separate his fiction from the prison-house of language, but through his unyielding examination of what the act of speaking consists in, i.e., varying intensities of murder, he is able to move his readers toward a shrewd appreciation of both the confusions of contemporary life and the dangers implicit in their own language acts. Whereas Nabokov's games with language drew their support from his sophisticated appreciation of the problems of perspective, Barthelme's games tend to spring from a more radical excursion into the processes of language itself. There is, perhaps, a sense in which perspective and language cannot be separated—to speak is to have a perspective—but here it is enough merely to have identified certain propensities or emphases that define the work of these two writers.

With Kosinski the problem of language—and of murder—takes a new turn. Unlike Barthelme, who resorts to a discontinuous narrative viewpoint in order to approach the mysteries of language, and unlike Nabokov, who employs incredibly intricate narrative structures in order to recover the complex interactions of memory and imagination, Kosinski returns to a surprisingly conventional use of first- and third-person points of view. There are certain disruptions, to be sure, as when the narrator of *Steps* arranges his material in blocks of fragments that show little chronological or transitional weaving—or when the narrator of *The Devil Tree* moves his narrative from first to third person. The principal disruption, however, is the tendency on the part of all his narrators to suppress that adjectival detail, that pattern of modification and qualification, which fleshes out the character of any given perspective. By removing the detail that identifies the attitudes and the values that underlie human perspective, Kosinski essentially turns his narrators and protagonists into explorers who can never escape their awareness of what lies at zero. All of Kosinski's protagonists are conscious of the fundamental arbitrariness of human experience, and as they play out their daily activities, that consciousness goads them into the pursuit of fresh and ever more complex means of observing themselves react and respond. Despite the use of what seems a conventional point of view, therefore, Kosinski's fiction may develop a more radical character than that of either Nabokov or Barthelme—at least on the ground that its deliberate disorientations leave the reader with little to build an interpretation upon. With its language almost stripped bare, especially when compared to the richness of Nabokov and the intricate playfulness of Barthelme, the Kosinskian text almost falters—to be dismissed by the cursory reader as a shocking, even outrageous, portrayal of the human condition. But stripped bare, a Kosinskian text does recover the dilemma of language that lies at zero—where all structures begin.

That this is the case is especially apparent in Kosinski's later novels. In *The Devil Tree*, for example, the matter of Jonathan Whelan's inheritance is not the receipt of his father's bequest but the adoption of a mature stance toward his uses of language. Whelan, having traveled widely in an effort to avoid the war, finds himself at the age of twenty-one without a convincing conception of his self. Because he recognizes himself as the victim of contradictory impulses, in fact, he knows that any conception he might establish for himself can only constitute an arbitrary gesture, one that is belied by a host of other attitudes and impulses within his being. For a time he seeks out the interaction of an encounter group in the hope of solving his dilemma, but rather quickly he discovers that the playacting of such a group provides no help at all. Indeed, as he plumbs the depth of his being in an effort to strike bedrock, he realizes that there is no formula, no conception, no stance, that can provide a common foundation for all human beings. The upshot is that he, in the face of the corporation's enormous power and the Howmets' unthinking support of it, must strike out for his own freedom by rejecting what he knows to be insidious and pernicious. When he murders the Howmets, he strikes a blow against a pervasive capitalist system that not only worships the achievement of success but also prevents those who fail from gaining significant stature within the community. In the context of a large society such a blow may not mean much. Even for Whelan, given the fact that in its immediate aftermath he succumbs to a particularly devastating bout of fever, the blow may not represent much more than an act of questionable validity. In the sense, nevertheless, that Whelan finds it necessary to strike his own stance—at least if he is to enjoy any sense of personal freedom—the act of murder does serve as a sign, to Whelan himself, that he can and has committed himself to a course of action, which thereafter he can modify at his discretion. For Whelan—and finally for Kosinski as well—the act of freedom is tantamount to the act of murder, and to the extent that he recognizes the equation implicit in this statement he shall enjoy the full inheritance of human existence.

The Devil Tree is an important novel for Kosinski because it illustrates, better than any of the others, that important moment when a Kosinskian protagonist accepts the burden of genuine humanity. In his other major novels, *Steps, Cockpit,* and *Blind Date,* Kosinski builds upon the shift in attitude that is inherent in Whelan's murder of the Howmets.

Steps may precede *The Devil Tree*, but like *Cockpit* and *Blind Date*, *Steps* recounts the games of a protagonist who has already gained the stature of murderer in the profound philosophic sense at the heart of Kosinski's fiction. The narrator of *Steps* and Tarden in *Cockpit*, in fact, because they are so bent upon educating others to appreciate the insights that they have culled from their experience, serve as especially good examples of how the character of murder clings to the activities of all active men. The narrator of *Steps*, in addition to a bewildering sequence of terrifying acts, repeatedly confronts his girl friend with the sentimental nature of her language usage. Eventually, having at least made her self-conscious and receptive to a perspective similar to his own, he separates her entirely from her accustomed contexts—and then, at the end of the novel, leaves her to flounder about as she will, perhaps even to become the victim of suicide. Not only has he imposed himself, his views, upon her, but in the process he has also "murdered" her—especially if it is true that she does succumb to suicide at the end. Even should she survive the end and gain the typical Kosinskian stance, the narrator's act of "murder" will continue to serve, thereafter, as the ground for her own mature acts of language. In *Cockpit* the act of murder is even more clear. There Tarden overwhelms Anthony Duncan by matching his superior wits against Duncan's publicity scheme. Or later in the novel, in an episode that parallels the narrator's handling of the girl in *Steps*, he introduces Veronika to a well-defined contractual scheme of relationships and then murders her when she fails to live up to its terms. Both the narrator of *Steps* and Tarden are fully conscious of their games as originating in their language acts, and to the extent that both of them are committed to their language, to its support, they cannot escape the necessity of imposition—and finally of murder. Tarden's inability to let Veronika develop her own games and language, however, seems to have forced Kosinski to reconsider his views. For in his next novel, *Blind Date*, the protagonist, George Levanter, finds himself surrounded by "survivors" whose perspectives are at least the equal of his own—and there, consequently, the acts of the heart begin to weigh as heavy as the acts of the mind. Instead of dominating all parties by imposing his will and language, Levanter seems to have discovered the additional necessity of surrendering to those impulses of the heart that cannot be reduced to declarative statements.

In Kosinski, then, language again serves as the key for approaching the character of the protagonists' dilemma. Unlike Nabokov's protagonists, however, who were able—once they suspended themselves in the texture of human experience—to develop a richness of language based upon the interplay of memory and imagination, Kosinski's protagonists possess a language that is fragmentary at best. Whereas Quilty and Shade and the elder Van Veen become aware of their experience as having spiraled out into ever-increasing degrees of subtlety and sophistication, a Kosinskian protagonist such as Tarden is generally frozen within the experience—and the language—of the present. Tarden, to be sure, recognizes the nurturing of his insight in childhood, and he knows the significance of his career as a spy. For the most part, however, each wheel game that he participates in during the present belongs only to the present. Instead of seeking correspondences between the past and the present, he is interested primarily in the playing out of the game that is immediately before him. His language, consequently, remains rather bare, i.e., stripped down, for with little need to compare and contrast one game with another he need not worry about providing the transitions, the web of logic and coherence, that might hold all of his experience together at least in his own mind. Stuck in the present, with a limited concern for the past, he is genuinely free to indulge himself in what amounts to an open-field gesture: the building of a game, a language act, based upon a whim or impulse. For Tarden the chance to come into contact with himself is above all a matter of playing out the whims and the impulses of the present. To seek the coherence that ties the present to the past is to limit the potential field of his activity.

If Kosinski's protagonists develop a stance that sharply contrasts with that of Nabokov's protagonists, it would appear that his—Kosinski's—protagonists might compare rather favorably with Barthelme's. After all, just as Kosinski's protagonists avoid the emphatic pursuit of perspective typical of Nabokov's characters, so Barthelme's protagonists seem, as in "City Life" or "Daumier," to have surrendered themselves to the processes of the present. Finally, nevertheless, as is especially evident in Snow White and The Dead Father, Barthelme's characters do remain conscious of the heroic trappings of the past, and they do measure their present experience (or lack of it) against those standards of the past. In fact, when Barthelme reaches his conclusion about what man might do in order to avoid the succession of atrocities in the present, he suggests that the perspective associated with fatherhood should merely be turned down. When compared with Kosinski's rather aggressive exploration of the murder, the cruelty and the atrocity, that he sees within all his characters (and in all men), consequently, Barthelme's suggestion that man merely turn down the intensity of the perspective from the past seems rather timid. Barthelme clearly avoids the heavy emphasis upon perspective that underlies Nabokov's fiction, but to the extent that his characters sometimes fail to lodge themselves fully in the present, there is a profound sense in which perspective lingers on in his fiction.

Kosinski's fiction represents a sweeping attempt to limit man to the present, to force him to manufacture language acts that are in touch with his impulses in the present, and thus to bring him into a profound contact with his deepest being. Kosinski's characters never achieve a full conception of that being, but at least they know—even more than Nabokov's and Barthelme's characters—a radical freedom to discover new nuances of existence in the present.

In the end, then, all this attention to language and murder in the fiction of Nabokov, Barthelme, and Kosinski is largely a matter of emphasis. There is a sense in which all three authors manipulate narrative perspective, fracture the text, and disorient their readers in an effort to implicate them in the text. In general terms, nevertheless, Nabokov's strong suit lies in the manipulation of narrative perspective; Barthelme's, in the fracturing of text; Kosinski's, in the disorientation of his readers. For whereas Nabokov's richness of language is rooted in the intricate games of narrative perspective underlying all of his major novels, and whereas Barthelme's complexity of style is rooted in his playing off the various texts of contemporary experience against each other, Kosinski's stripped-down language is rooted in his determination to separate his audience from their customary texts and perspectives and thus to bring them into closer contact with their inner selves. If I can be glib for a moment, it is almost as if Nabokov directs his act of murder against his narrator; Barthelme, against his text; and Kosinski, against his reader. From Nabokov to Kosinski, consequently, there emerges an increasing radicalization of the fiction. That fact does not diminish the achievement of Nabokov and Barthelme. It merely reflects Kosinski's determined—and aggressive—pursuit of his readers.

Notes

1 Introduction: The Artist as Victim

1. For further discussion of this point see Sam Hunter, *Modern French Painting* (New York: Dell, 1956), pp. 42–52.

2. Two of the best examples are the portraits of Uhde and Kahnweiler.

3. Robert Morris, "Notes on Sculpture," in *Minimal Art,* ed. Gregory Battcock (New York: E. P. Dutton, 1968), pp. 228, 233–35.

4. John Cage, *Silence* (Cambridge, Mass.: M.I.T. Press, 1961), p. 4.

5. Ben Johnston, "How to Cook an Albatross," *Source* 4, no. 1 (1970):65.

6. The concert was presented on April 28, 1974.

7. Barton McLean, as quoted by David Cope, *New Directions in Music* (Dubuque: William Brown, 1971), p. 124.

8. Cage, *Silence,* p. 8.

9. Cage, *A Year from Monday* (Middletown, Conn.: Wesleyan University Press, 1967), p. 50.

10. Gustave Flaubert, *Correspondance,* Septième Série, vol. 15 of *Oeuvres Complètes* (Paris: Louis Conard, 1930), p. 280.

11. Ford Madox Ford, *Joseph Conrad: A Personal Remembrance* (Boston: Little, Brown & Co., 1924), p. 31.

12. Ford, *Joseph Conrad,* p. 204.

13. For clarification of the distinction between *readerly* and *writerly,* see Roland Barthes, *S/Z,* trans. Richard Miller (New York: Hill and Wang, 1974), pp. 3–4.

Part I: Nabokov

2 Nabokov's Texts: Authors vs. Editors

1. Consider, for example, the marvelous achievement of John Shade and of the elder Van Veen in their respective novels.

2. E.g., Page Stegner, *Escape into Aesthetics* (New York: Dial Press, 1966), p. 96.

3. Fred Moody, "At *Pnin's* Center," *Russian Literature Triquarterly* 14 (1976):79. Andrew Field, *Nabokov: His Life in Art* (Boston: Little, Brown & Co., 1967), p. 132, was the first to see the problem.

4. Paul Grams, "*Pnin:* The Biographer as Meddler," in *A Book of Things about Nabokov,* ed. Carl Proffer (Ann Arbor: Ardis, 1974), p. 196.

5. William Carroll, "Nabokov's Signs and Symbols," in *A Book of Things about Nabokov,* ed. Carl Proffer, p. 205.

6. Grams, p. 197.

7. Carroll, p. 208.

8. Page Stegner, p. 98, cites the source of Pnin's vitality as his conscious adoption of a "method of existence that protects him from the excessive cruelty invading his life and redeems him from the tediousness of self-pity." Julia Bader, *Crystal Land: Artifice in Nabokov's English Novels* (Berkeley: University of California Press, 1972), pp. 89–90, suggests in similar fashion

that for Pnin the mere recognition of his being alive is sufficient or, should that not be enough, the recognition of his uniqueness of self is. Charles Nicol, "Pnin's History," *Novel* 4(1971):198, on the other hand, seems to base much of Pnin's vitality on his adoption of Victor as his son.

9. All parenthetical page references are to Vladimir Nabokov, *Pnin* (Garden City: Doubleday & Co., 1957).

10. The best discussion, by far, of this pattern is Nicol's.

11. Nicol, p. 202, has pointed out that Pnin's etymological hunch is actually accepted scholarship.

12. Pnin's success in passing the truck and thus escaping the "frame" of two trucks contrasts sharply with Humbert Humbert's inability to escape the roadblock at the end of *Lolita*. Humbert drives off the road. Whereas Humbert is defeated, even mad, Pnin retains his vitality. For further discussion of this contrast, see Charles Mitchell, "Mythic Seriousness in *Lolita*," *Texas Studies in Language and Literature* 5(1963):342–43.

13. All parenthetical page references are to Vladimir Nabokov, *Transparent Things* (New York: McGraw-Hill, 1972).

14. Jonathan Raban, "Transparent Likenesses," *Encounter* 41 (September 1973):74.

15. Richard Patteson, in "Nabokov's *Look at the Harlequins!:* Endless Re-Creation of the Self," *Russian Literature Triquarterly* 14(1976):84–98, has begun to establish some of the more significant parallels between the two careers.

16. All parenthetical page references are to Vladimir Nabokov, *Look at the Harlequins!* (New York: McGraw-Hill, 1974).

3 Lolita: *The Pursuit of Text*

1. On this point, see Paul Grams, *"Pnin:* The Biographer as Meddler," in *A Book of Things about Nabokov*, ed. Carl Proffer (Ann Arbor: Ardis, 1974), pp. 193–217.

2. All page references in parentheses refer to Vladimir Nabokov, *Lolita* (New York: G. P. Putnam's Sons, 1955).

3. Donald Morton, *Vladimir Nabokov* (New York: Frederick J. Ungar, 1974), p. 70, simply calls Humbert "a genius-artist in whom Nabokov's passion for words finds its fullest expression."

4. Page Stegner, *Escape into Aesthetics* (New York: Dial Press, 1966), pp. 111–12, has argued that Humbert's problem stems from his desire for the timeless, the immortal, the uncomplicated—a desire that can be realized only in the imagination. While I can agree with such a statement superficially, the crucial problem that Humbert faces is his failure to understand that the realizations of the imagination enjoy no ultimate authority. As Julia Bader, *Crystal Land: Artifice in Nabokov's English Novels* (Berkeley: University of California Press, 1972), p. 64, puts it, Humbert pursues the mysterious but ends up with the "commonplace."

5. Stegner, p. 114, has even suggested that Humbert with his powers of imagination and language converts vulgarity into beauty. Similarly, Alfred Appel, *"Lolita:* The Springboard of Parody," in *Nabokov: The Man and His Work*, ed. L. S. Dembo (Madison: University of Wisconsin Press, 1967), p. 111, has suggested that Humbert's vitality of imagination "transform[s] a 'crime' into a redeeming work of art."

6. See Bader, pp. 57–64, for further discussion of this point.

7. Nabokov's novels are not *Bildungsromane*. His genuine artists (Pnin, Quilty, Shade) are artists from the very beginning of their respective works. The only significant exception is Veen, who experiences a profound change of attitude in 1922. Lolita's failure to gain the artist's privileged ground is thus hardly surprising.

8. In a certain sense Humbert makes himself the victim of the old conventions in fiction—rather than extending the character of his own "literary styles," which (at least in Van Veen's eyes) "constitutes the only real honesty of a writer."

9. Most critics, of course, have been extremely critical of Quilty. Stegner, p. 105, has called him a personification of Humbert's evil self. Morton, p. 80, has regarded Quilty's perverseness as merely an uglier version of Humbert's own. Bader, p. 64, has called Quilty a pseudoartist who develops thoroughly conventional art in a cold, calculating way. Only Brent Harold, "*Lolita:* Nabokov's Critique of Aloofness," *Papers on Language and Literature* 11 (1975): 78–81, has begun to see the alternative view—that Quilty is a real genius. Even though Harold recognizes Quilty has "out-authored" Humbert at the end, however, he also believes that "Quilty is too professional to produce the kind of art that *Lolita* represents and advocates." In my view Quilty's professionalism actually requires that curious struggle between Humbert and Quilty for possession of the text—a struggle that generally appears in all of Nabokov's English novels.

10. Most critics have, of course, concluded that Humbert kills Quilty in order to avenge the loss of Lolita. See Morton, p. 79. The actual reason for the murder is more sophisticated and complex.

4 Pale Fire: *The Reader's Possession of the Text*

1. All references in parentheses refer to Vladimir Nabokov, *Pale Fire* (New York: G. P. Putnam's Sons, 1962).

2. Julia Bader, *Crystal Land: Artifice in Nabokov's English Novels* (Berkeley: University of California Press, 1972), p. 47, points out that "the fountain is related to the Romantic metaphor of the mind and the creative faculty." The comment helps explain Shade's interest.

3. Timothy Flower, "The Scientific Art of Nabokov's *Pale Fire*," *Criticism* 17 (1975): 232, has pointed out that Shade is "like Shade's Aunt Maud and like Nabokov, who discover art in life instead of trying to make life do what only art can do. Instead of substituting a fictional world for the real world they see and know, they perceive the artistic patterns in life." Page Stegner, *Escape into Aesthetics* (New York: Dial Press, 1966), p. 119, on the other hand, has suggested that Aunt Maud is an "example of the pathetic collapse of the sensibilities that inevitably accompanies a lingering life." I agree with Flower.

4. Bader, p. 46, has suggested that Shade's feeling "distributed through space and time" is "the equivalent of authorial omniscience, and foreshadows Shade's ability to transform and nearly obliterate his ordinary surroundings—an ability manifested in the commentary." The comment seems a bit strong because it turns Shade into as much an escapist as is Kinbote.

5. For more discussion on this point, see Bader, pp. 45–48.

6. Mary McCarthy, "Vladimir Nabokov's *Pale Fire*," *Encounter* 19 (October 1962): 72, has pointed out that Kinbote is really the V. Botkin mentioned in the Index.

7. Kinbote's incarceration within a solipsistic vision has a parallel, deliberate on Nabokov's part, in his homosexual tendencies.

8. L. L. Lee, *Vladimir Nabokov* (Boston: Twayne, 1977), p. 136, has argued that the novel "is a parody and a satire of pedantic and sometimes inaccurate editors and critics." Donald Morton, *Vladimir Nabokov* (New York: Frederick J. Ungar, 1974), p. 106, has likewise suggested that the novel is "a lively parody of scholarly editing, in which the reader is audience to a strange literary struggle between a simple and homely but rather beautiful poem with its own innate meaning and a mad editor who tries to 'read into it' a story of his own making." Superficially, both critics have a point. The problems of editing, however, as shall become more apparent later, are bound up with the problems of reading.

9. Obviously I disagree with Stegner, p. 128, who argues that "the *more* ironical joke . . . is that Kinbote, crazy as he may be, has actually *understood* Shade's poem."

10. Morton, p. 114, completely misses the point of the novel when he argues that "the positive aspect of Kinbote's activity must be insisted upon because the urge to create is so vividly present in the power of his style and in the erotic motif threaded closely throughout his part of the book." Kinbote may have verve and enthusiasm, but he completely destroys Shade's poem.

11. Flower, p. 227, points out that Nabokov's purpose in writing the novel is to teach the reader "to make careful distinctions and avoid the simple either/or labeling that separates *Pale Fire* and its Commentary as poetry and prose, or takes Shade and Kinbote to be either opposite or the same." Flower's emphasis upon the act of reading is, I think, crucial to the novel.

12. H. Grabes, *Fictitious Biographies: Vladimir Nabokov's English Novels* (The Hague: Mouton, 1977), pp. 55–59, also emphasizes the importance of the act of reading to the novel, but he comes up with little helpful analysis of the dilemmas inherent in reading.

13. Kinbote may fail, but as Flower, p. 231, points out, "The artificiality of Nabokov's 'scientifically poetic' prose . . . provides a running commentary on itself, calling attention to the sheer artistry of the art, preventing us from making our own fictions out of Nabokov's, making us *see*, and in general revealing Nabokov's hand and asserting his ultimate control over his fiction." In my view "ultimate control" may be impossible, but at least Flower recognizes the extent to which Nabokov addresses the problem of reading in *Pale Fire*.

14. Bader, p. 39, comments on the significance of Shade's death: "The artist momentarily perishes with each of his creations, in order to give life to a work of art."

15. For views that support Kinbote's magic, rather than Shade's, see Stegner, pp. 123, 130, and Andrew Field, *Nabokov: His Life in Art* (Boston: Little, Brown & Co., 1967), p. 308.

5   Ada: *The Texture of Incest*

1. Such emphasis upon the generation of the text obviously turns *Ada* into a novel that is primarily concerned with the artist in the act of writing. See Julia Bader, *Crystal Land: Artifice in Nabokov's English Novels* (Berkeley: University of California Press, 1972), pp. 155–57.

2. All page numbers in parentheses refer to Vladimir Nabokov, *Ada* (New York: McGraw-Hill, 1969).

3. While critics have widely explored the conflict between Shade and Kinbote, they have largely ignored that between Quilty and Humbert. Quilty appears to be a depraved soul, one who is "clearly guilty," but there is also the possibility that it is he, not Humbert, who is "clearly quilting" the texture of *Lolita*.

4. Nabokov himself, in a letter to the *New York Times* published July 10, 1969, has called Ada and Van "both rather horrible creatures." What must be recognized here, however, is that in Nabokov's world all human beings possess their own peculiar dimensions of horror. By itself, the peculiarity of incest is not enough to warrant a blanket condemnation of Ada.

5. For a full discussion of the problem of language in Nabokov and especially in *Ada*, see Bader, pp. 126–28.

6. In the end Ada's participation in an incestuous relationship parallels her rejection of the text of fidelity. Incest and infidelity—both challenge the boundaries normally associated with human relationships. By a process of logic that is curious yet rather typical for Nabokov, both situations involve the pursuit of freedom.

7. Much like the narrator of *Pnin*, Humbert and Kinbote try to fix a text of their experience—and almost turn mad in the process. In Nabokov's fiction the pursuit, not of precise texts, but of a rich—if illogical and thus bewildering—texture is crucial to the retention of vitality and youth.

8. Captain Tapper did, however, know Demon Veen.

9. Most critics regard the deliberate paralleling of these two journeys as merely another instance of Nabokov's interest in the processes of memory.

10. Here the incest theme takes on an altogether new character. The fact that Ada represents hell (Hades) and Lucette, light, also complicates the pattern.

11. In this novel the colors black and yellow are generally associated with Ada. Here Lucette seems to be setting herself up as a surrogate for Ada.

12. This passage reveals the extent of Van's change of attitude. For further discussion of this point, see Nancy Anne Zeller, "The Spiral of Time in *Ada*," in *A Book of Things about Nabokov*, ed. Carl Proffer (Ann Arbor: Ardis, 1974), pp. 288–89.

13. Here see Jeffrey Leonard, "In Place of Lost Time: *Ada*," in *Nabokov*, ed. Alfred Appel and Charles Newman (Evanston: Northwestern University Press, 1970), p. 144.

Part II: Barthelme

6 Barthelme: The Essential Contradiction

1. For another view of the relationship between Nabokov and Barthelme, see James Rother, "Parafiction: The Adjacent Universe of Barth, Barthelme, Pynchon, and Nabokov," *Boundary 2* 5(1976): 21–43.

2. For further discussion of this point, see Leo Bersani, *Balzac to Beckett: Center and Circumference in French Fiction* (New York: Oxford University Press, 1970), pp. 14–16.

3. R. E. Johnson, Jr., " 'Bees Barking in the Night': The End and Beginning of Donald Barthelme's Narrative," *Boundary 2* 5(1976): 79, has shown that the problem is that "consciousness is plural rather than singular." Plural texts frustrate the achievement of sufficiency.

4. The page numbers in parentheses in chapters 6 and 7 refer to the following texts: *Come Back, Dr. Caligari* (Boston: Little, Brown & Co., 1964); *Unspeakable Practices, Unnatural Acts* (New York: Farrar, Straus and Giroux, 1968); *City Life* (New York: Farrar, Straus and Giroux, 1970); *Sadness* (New York: Farrar, Straus and Giroux, 1972); and *Amateurs* (New York: Farrar, Straus and Giroux, 1976). The titles are abbreviated, respectively, as *DC*, *UP*, *CL*, *S*, and *A*.

5. William Stott, "Donald Barthelme and the Death of Fiction," *Prospects* 1(1976): 373–74, has commented upon "The Dolt" and, in doing so, has pointed out that in Barthelme's fiction "public actuality defeats private imagination." The artist's ground is very limited.

6. As Johnson, p. 79, has remarked, however, "fictional language . . . offers the only ground for the realization of consciousness."

7. One suspects that Barthelme is right when he comments in his interview with Jerome Klinkowitz, in *The New Fiction*, ed. Joe David Bellamy (Urbana: University of Illinois Press, 1974), p. 52, that "the difficulties the painters are now having—the problem of keeping *themselves* interested—are I think instructive. Earthworks, conceptual art, etc., seem to me last resorts. Now there is a certain virtue in finding the absolutely last resort—being the Columbus of the last resort—but I don't think I'd enjoy the role." Barthelme himself avoids the gratuitously grand gesture.

8. For other discussions of this story, see Stott, pp. 381–82, and Johnson, pp. 72 ff.

9. John Ditsky, "The Narrative Style of Donald Barthelme," *Style* 9(1975): 388–400, provides a brilliant discussion of "Daumier" as an introduction to Barthelme's style.

10. John Leland, "Remarks Re-marked: Barthelme, What Curios of Signs!" *Boundary 2* 5(1977): 797, has put it this way: "Barthelme uncovers for us the play of signification rather than offering us its products for consumption."

11. Claude Lévi-Strauss, "From Cyclical Structure in Myth to Serial Romance in Modern Fiction," trans. Petra Morrison, in *Sociology of Literature and Drama*, ed. Elizabeth and Tom Burns (Baltimore: Penguin, 1973), p. 212, has pointed out that the serial novel appears as the "final state of degeneration in the novel." Barthelme's open structures, wherein the tentative gesture is everything, display a seriality that surely reflects this sense of degeneration.

12. Leland, p. 808, has commented upon this act of surrender in Barthelme: "Upon the trash heap of the world, Barthelme's fiction plays at (or with or in) the play of signification: it divides, fragments, and shatters to expose the essential subversion of non-meaning within the calling forth of

meaning—the repression, so to speak, of non-meaning which constitutes the possibility of surrogation." *Surrogation* is, of course, a term from "Daumier."

13. Ditsky, p. 398, has put it this way: "The Barthelmean man is the prisoner of language, using that very fire against itself in the hope of a brief release from his cage, an even briefer flight."

14. Rother, p. 25, has also noted the inescapable character of this murder: writers of parafiction "demonstrate not, as do the fictions of the Flaubertians, how difficult it is to give rise to a single utterance, but rather how difficult it is to keep a torrent of sentences from giving rise to themselves." Sentences and their context dominate men, and in the process of speaking men extend that domination—in their own lives as well as in others'.

7   *Barthelme's Short Stories: Ironic Suspensions of Text*

1. The complex strategies underlying Nabokov's texts are his means of approaching the fringes of human experience in an effort to understand them; in Barthelme the characters are at the fringes, and because there is no perspective that binds the experience together, there is no understanding.

2. John Leland, "Remarks Re-marked: Barthelme, What Curios of Signs!" *Boundary 2* 5(1977): 807, has pointed out that right reason is "a function of cultural codes and conventions which prescribe our ways of doing, thinking, seeing, being." The codes and the conventions define what is acceptable logic.

3. For further discussion of the relationship between questions and answers, see R. E. Johnson, Jr., " 'Bees Barking in the Night': The End and Beginning of Donald Barthelme's Narrative," *Boundary 2* 5(1976): 84.

4. James Rother, "Parafiction: The Adjacent Universe of Barth, Barthelme, Pynchon, and Nabokov," *Boundary 2* 5(1976):26, makes the point that "the trouble with words is that they are at our disposal, . . . and we use one another, dispose of one another, again and again" by manipulating words. Bloomsbury uses his wife through words.

5. Rother, p. 34, suggests that "the one purpose writing can boast at this stage of the game [tradition of fiction] is that of isolating us from our fictions, not sinking us deeper into them. . . . Parafiction invariably takes up where ordinary fiction leaves off, where characters, situations, events no longer attune themselves to climax and dénouement." Because the son in "Views of My Father Weeping" cannot stabilize his "fictions" of his father, whether alive or dead, he has a chance for achieving that openness of attitude at the heart of Barthelme's stories.

6. Claude Lévi-Strauss, "From Cyclical Structure in Myth to Serial Romance in Modern Fiction," trans. Petra Morrison, in *Sociology of Literature and Drama*, ed. Elizabeth and Tom Burns (Baltimore: Penguin, 1973), pp. 212–13, has commented: "Life, dreams, the past carry dislocated images and forms which haunt the writer when chance or some necessity . . . preserves or rediscovers in them the shadowy outline of myth. Nevertheless, the novelist drifts among these floes which the heat of history detaches from the solid formation which it has broken up. He collects these scattered materials and reuses them as they present themselves to him, though not without dimly perceiving that they come from another structure, and will become rarer and rarer as a current different from the one which kept them together bears them away. The decline and fall of the plot was contained within the development of the novel from the beginning and has recently become external to it—since we are witnessing the decline and fall *of* plot after the decline and fall *in* the plot." The collapse of plot is especially evident in a story like "City Life."

7. Johnson, pp. 79, 81, has expanded upon the importance of this new style: "Fictional language . . . offers the only ground for the realization of consciousness. . . . Fictional language is given the task of animating an object or objects which will, in the process, acquire emotional value." Peterson's fictions are the very ground of his being.

8. Leland, p. 809, has pointed out that this eloquence is a function of one's understanding the

processes of perception: "Orders are built up, only to be decomposed in a continual probing of the ordering of orders, an ordering which plays itself out over an essential abyss of non-meaning."

9. Johnson, p. 87, has pointed out that "Barthelme's is no facile optimism; he sees the inescapably destructive character of language as clearly as anyone today using words." I obviously agree with Johnson.

10. For a larger discussion of Barthelme's irony, see Alan Wilde, "Barthelme Unfair to Kierkegaard: Some Thoughts on Modern and Postmodern Irony," *Boundary 2* 5(1976): 45–70.

8 Snow White: *The Suppression of Text*

1. The page references in parentheses refer to *Snow White* (New York: Atheneum, 1967).

2. William Stott, "Donald Barthelme and the Death of Fiction," *Prospects* 1(1976): 378, points out that people today learn too many facts without any accompanying emotional values that might give these facts, and their lives, meaning. Cocktail parties in such a culture, consequently, can only become desperate enterprises.

3. For further discussion of the shower curtain, see John Leland, "Remarks Re-marked: Barthelme, What Curios of Signs!" *Boundary 2* 5(1977): 809.

4. The dwarfs fall into the trap that James Rother, "Parafiction: The Adjacent Universe of Barth, Barthelme, Pynchon, and Nabokov," *Boundary 2* 5(1976): 38, has warned about: "language, though itself a falsifier of reality, prevents us from imposing on things as they are that singular totalitarianism: the world as we think we know it." The dwarfs are uneasy, but they have contented themselves with their easy materialism.

5. The phrase *Marivaudian being* is from Barthelme's short story "Robert Kennedy Saved from Drowning."

6. Leland, p. 799, has pointed out that "it is precisely the romantic view of the imagination [Schelling and Coleridge linked creation and the joining of opposites] which Barthelme frustrates, thematically and structurally, in his novel *Snow White*." Snow White, however, cannot separate herself from that romantic bias.

7. Stott, p. 379, argues that Snow White transcends the dwarfs. Clearly she does not.

8. Ironically, with the hanging, Bill does becomes a "sky-hero."

9. R. E. Johnson, Jr., " 'Bees Barking in the Night': The End and Beginning of Donald Barthelme's Narrative," *Boundary 2* 5(1976): 83, has pointed out the importance of "retraction": "When there is no 'retraction,' no decreation of the linguistic fiction spun not only by others but by the self as well, everything is closed, nothing is expected." Paul is on the right track with his retractions, but he does not retract enough.

10. Leland, p. 802, suggests that both Snow White and Paul "represent, ultimately, a failure of the imagination—imagination's failure to escape *its* texts, which is also its teleological compulsion, its desire for closure and completion." I would add that Bill, and perhaps the other dwarfs as well, belong to the same category.

11. Here Jane would compare favorably with some of Jerzy Kosinski's protagonists, such as the narrator of *Steps* or Tarden in *Cockpit*.

12. This passage on the "frame" foreshadows the discussion between Thomas and the Dead Father on the matter of the frame. See *The Dead Father* (New York: Farrar, Straus and Giroux, 1975), p. 32.

13. For a view of Jane and Hogo similar to my own, see Neil Schmitz, "Donald Barthelme and the Emergence of Modern Satire," *Minnesota Review* 1(1972): 117. Schmitz comments, "It is Jane and Hogo de Bergerac, villainess and villain, who are finally sympathetic, who cut through the tedious *angst* of the Dwarfs and Snow White's indulgent *ennui* with the acidic simplicity of their desires, the 'vileness' of their realism."

14. Leland, p. 806, suggests, in fact, that Barthelme's fiction provides his readers, as well as his characters, with a sense of new directions: Barthelme's writing is "profoundly liberating, as we are forced to encounter again and again our conventions of making sense." Perceiving the conventions is a start to a life of freedom and renewed vitality.

15. Claude Lévi-Strauss, "From Cyclical Structure in Myth to Serial Romance in Modern Fiction," trans. Petra Morrison, in *Sociology of Literature and Drama*, ed. Elizabeth and Tom Burns (Baltimore: Penguin, 1973), p. 212, has pointed out that the serial novel appears as the "final state of degeneration in the novel." Barthelme's fragments in *Snow White*, wherein the tentative gesture is everything, display a strong sense of seriality—and thus the sense of degeneration as well.

16. Leland, p. 801, has extended this idea of the suppression of the text by suggesting that *Snow White* refuses "to be read merely in terms of its signifieds" or in terms of "beginnings and endings" (which implies a linearity) or in terms of high art. Instead, the novel is an excursion into the dilemmas of discourse.

9 The Dead Father: *The Turning Down of Perspective*

1. The page references in parentheses refer to *The Dead Father* (New York: Farrar, Straus and Giroux, 1975).

2. While commenting about *Snow White*, John Leland, "Remarks Re-marked: Barthelme, What Curios of Signs!" *Boundary 2* 5(1977): 804, makes a statement that is especially applicable to the conversations between Julie and Emma: "Alienated from the mythic paradigm . . . , [the conversations] must exist instead within structures of reduplication. And in the end, this succession of episodes, this fragmented reduplication, takes the place—inadequately—of the closed structure of myth." If the conversations are a serious alternative to the old structures, then their speakers and their readers must inhabit Barthelme's world of language sophistication and artistry.

3. James Rother, "Parafiction: The Adjacent Universe of Barth, Barthelme, Pynchon, and Nabokov," *Boundary 2* 5(1976): 23, has suggested that the parafictionists have "with little fanfare . . . undertaken to dramatize the decay of communicative language, of speech as the void's most formidable antagonist." The Dead Father fills up the void, but because he fills it up so swiftly, without thinking about it, he contributes to the decay of communicative language. The conversation with the bartender is a good example.

4. Rother, p. 25, goes on to point out that the parafictionists "demonstrate not, as do the fictions of the Flaubertians, how difficult it is to give rise to a single utterance, but rather how difficult it is to keep a torrent of sentences from giving rise to themselves." The Dead Father cannot silence himself. Accustomed to heroism, and the language that supports heroism, he must speak.

5. This passage serves, perhaps, as the ground for this book. Here Barthelme, as clearly as any writer in the present, addresses the crucial dilemma of contemporary man—the problem of voicing. The implicit equation in the term "murderinging" between murder and the ringing of voice is very suggestive and finally points to the murders, of varying types, enacted in the fiction by all three writers discussed in this book—Nabokov, Barthelme, and Kosinski.

Part III: Kosinski

10 Kosinski's Early Fiction: The Problem of Language

1. Kosinski himself, in "The Secret Life of Our Times," *New York Times*, January 13, 1974, p. 28, has stated: "By making the reader supply the details and make his own connections between characters and events, [fragments] demand the reader's involvement, insisting on the highest level of imaginative response."

2. Robert Morris, "Notes on Sculpture," in *Minimal Art*, ed. Gregory Battcock (New York: E. P. Dutton, 1968), pp. 228, 233–35.

3. In an interview conducted by Daniel Cahill, *"The Devil Tree:* An Interview with Jerzy Kosinski," *The North American Review* 9 (Spring 1973): 65, Kosinski has suggested that the act of reading is "an attempt at self. . . . Hence any act of reading . . . is an act of activating the projecting ability of the self."

4. From an interview conducted by Jerome Klinkowitz, in *The New Fiction*, ed. Joe David Bellamy (Urbana: University of Illinois Press, 1974), p. 155.

5. For further discussion of this point, see the interview conducted by Bruce Glaser, "Questions to Stella and Judd," in *Minimal Art*, pp. 151–54.

6. Klinkowitz interview, p. 148.

7. Klinkowitz interview, p. 149.

8. For an interpretation that argues a significant transformation in the boy, see R. J. Spendal, "The Structure of *The Painted Bird*," *Journal of Narrative Technique* 6 (1976): 132–36. Samuel Coale, on the other hand, "The Quest for the Elusive Self," *Critique* 14, no. 3 (1973): 33, has argued that the boy is reduced merely "to a reactor of events." Similarly Daniel Cahill, "Jerzy Kosinski: The Retreat from Violence," *Twentieth Century Literature* 18 (1972): 125, has suggested that for this boy "perpetual flight becomes his only means to avoid the corrosive human contact."

9. All parenthetical references in this chapter are to *Steps* (New York: Random House, 1968); *Being There* (New York: Harcourt Brace Jovanovich, 1970); and *The Devil Tree* (New York: Harcourt Brace Jovanovich, 1973). The titles are abbreviated, respectively, as *S, BT,* and *DT.*

10. This privileged view is akin to Kosinski's own appreciation of the role of language in his art: "There is no art which is reality; rather, art is the using of symbols by which an otherwise unstateable subjective reality is made manifest." The comment appears in *Notes of the Author* (New York: Scientia-Factum, 1967), p. 11.

11. Coale, pp. 28, 36, has concluded that in *Being There* "external reality has won out completely" and thus that "the self only observes; it no longer acts." Most critics have taken Chance's passivity as a sign that he is a television zombie. In actuality, however, it is television that gives contemporary man his content and thus underlies his intentions and motives. EE displays the influence of television more than does Chance, who has largely escaped the world of intention and motive.

12. For a view on *Being There* similar to my own, see Ivan Sanders, "The Gifts of Strangeness," *Polish Review* 19, no. 3 (1976): 171–89.

13. In the Cahill interview, p. 65, Kosinski himself suggested that Whelan is an "offspring of a very tragic tree in which the imagination has never been allowed to emerge as a meaningful way of communicating."

14. It is interesting to note, here, that Nabokov and Barthelme also satirize the modern tendency to consult the psychiatrist.

15. Sanders, p. 186, has suggested that *The Devil Tree* is a study of "inauthentic behavior," with characters who "keep vanishing into formulas of language which substitute for identity."

16. In the Cahill interview, p. 58, Kosinski has commented that "there is no place beyond words where experience first occurs." He is probably right, but the real point here is the insufficiency of all human texts.

17. The term is from *The Dead Father* (New York: Farrar, Straus and Giroux, 1975), p. 46.

18. The aggression in Nabokov centers upon who shall own the text.

19. Coale, p. 30, has argued that Kosinski is above all interested in "extricat[ing] the self from the collectivist sensibilities of the modern world," whether capitalist or communist.

20. Gerald Weales, "Jerzy Kosinski," *Hollins Critic* 9, no. 3 (1972): 9, has argued that Kosinski's greatest weakness as a novelist is "his desire to explain things—his symbols, the significance of his scenes, the political and philosophical implications of the action." I obviously disagree with that assessment.

11 Steps: Acts of Demystification

1. Samuel Coale, "The Quest for the Elusive Self," *Critique* 14, no. 3 (1973): 29, has suggested that "each scene is graphically described as objectively and fully as possible." In actuality, however, Kosinski strips his fiction as much as he can.

2. Kosinski himself, in *The Art of the Self* (New York: Scientia-Factum, 1968), p. 16, has argued, "Each incident in *Steps* is morally ambiguous. The reader is guided to an area of experience by himself. His gain is the product of his own sifting through and refining much of the author's imagery."

3. While there is some question whether this narrator is merely one voice, surely he is more than what Coale, p. 28, has suggested—"a disembodied voice howling in some surrealistic wilderness." The narrator may have difficulty reaching terms for his experience, but he does achieve some insight into its character.

4. All page references in parentheses are to *Steps* (New York: Random House, 1968).

5. The meaninglessness of the badges reminds one of Hemingway's use of World War I medals in *The Sun Also Rises*.

6. The emphasis upon mirrors here has a strong parallel in Nabokov's use of incest as a condition of his art.

7. Kosinski, in *The Art of the Self*, p. 16, has commented that "the only thing the protagonist of *Steps* is aware of, is his self, and that is ephemeral. He knows himself by hints, by allusions; he approaches and steps away from himself; he looks for himself in others, hoping that every new situation would bring forth a new 'I.' "

8. In the interview from *Paris Review* 54 (1972): 196, Kosinski has commented: "I wanted to make the language of my fiction as unobtrusive as possible, almost transparent, so that the reader would be drawn right away into each dramatic incident. I suppress in my prose any language which calls attention to itself. What I've just said carries no value judgment. It is the opposite, for instance, of what Nabokov does. . . . I think in *Steps* I came closest to what I really wanted to do with English." This comment surely serves as a key to the kind of sophistication the narrator has developed.

9. The phrase is from Conrad's *Lord Jim* (Garden City: Doubleday, Page & Co., 1923), p. 214.

10. The passage in which the narrator sympathizes with the slum-dwellers reinforces Kosinski's own comment, in *The Art of the Self*, p. 17, that "the priority of reality over imagination is established throughout *Steps*."

11. The concept of pure being is also stressed in the novel's epigraph, taken from *The Bhagavad Gita*: "For the uncontrolled there is no wisdom, nor for the uncontrolled is there the power of concentration; and for him without concentration there is no peace. And for the unpeaceful, now can there be happiness?" Being in Kosinski is associated with a profound state of consciousness.

12. In a limited sense the deaf-mute charade parallels Chance's state of being in *Being There*.

13. The term *murderinging* is from *The Dead Father*, p. 46.

14. Such consternation should prevent the reader from reaching Gerald Weales's conclusion, in "Jerzy Kosinski," *Hollins Critic* 9, no. 3 (1972): 10, that "for the most part, the fragments [of *Steps*] have the coldness of exercises and a few of them strike me as simple-minded." The novel possesses a great deal of authority as an exploration of the problems of human consciousness.

15. The narrator does experience difficulty at the end. Coale, pp. 28, 31, however, goes too far when he suggests that the end "reveals the breakdown of the self when faced with an external reality so powerful"; or that, in the execution scene, the narrator's "agonized self-consciousness leads to disintegration and paralysis." The narrator's lot at the end is not easy, but at least he enjoys a shrewd insight into the problems of human existence—particularly consciousness.

12   Cockpit: *Games and the Expansion of Perception*

1. It is true that the narrator of *Steps* alludes to his past experience as a student, but generally he does not reveal a nexus between the past and the present.

2. Again, I use murder in the sense of necessary self-assertion or that aggression whereby one man imposes himself upon another.

3. All page references in parentheses are to *Cockpit* (Boston: Houghton Mifflin Co., 1975).

4. Descartes's statement, *Larvatus prodeo* (I make my appearance masked), is an apt motto for Kosinski.

5. See *The Dead Father*, p. 32.

6. The term is from *The Dead Father*, p. 46.

7. Paul's isolation is especially evident in part 3 of *Snow White*.

8. As Donald Anderson, "The End of Humanism," *Quadrant* 113 (1976): 75, has pointed out, "the discipline and definition of self entails, in Kosinski, dominance over others, the supremacy of the individual will."

9. In the interview in *Paris Review* 54 (1972): 189, Kosinski has commented about the significance of fiction in everyday life: "What we remember lacks the hard edge of fact. To help us along we create little fictions, highly subtle and individual scenarios which clarify and shape our experience. The remembered event becomes fiction, a structure made to accommodate certain feelings." Tarden's use of the wheel game is his playing upon a fictional principle that he has matured over the years.

10. Ivan Sanders, "The Gifts of Strangeness," *Polish Review* 9, no. 3 (1974): 177, has suggested that the narrator of *Steps* believes that "to know people is to have power over them. If he is successful in manipulating them, he has perfect peace of mind." Much the same can be said about Tarden.

13   Blind Date: *The Resurgence of Relationships*

1. For further discussion of this point, see Allen Leepa, "Minimal Art and Primary Meanings," in *Minimal Art*, ed. Gregory Battcock (New York: E. P. Dutton, 1968), pp. 200–208.

2. While their number is small, the "survivors" in Kosinski's fiction have faced up to the decline apparent in Western traditions and have, accordingly, assumed the direction of their lives for themselves.

3. The term *wheel games* derives, of course, from *Cockpit*.

4. All page references in parentheses refer to *Blind Date* (Boston: Houghton Mifflin Co., 1977).

5. In the interview from *Paris Review* 54 (1972): 194, Kosinski does speak about the decision not to write in Polish: "I would never have written in Polish. I never saw myself as a man expressing opinions in a totalitarian state. Make no mistake about it: all my generation was . . . aware of the dimensions of our existence. To be a spokesman in a field which used language would require one to be a spokesman for a particular political situation. My generation considered this a trap. . . . So what happened was that I slowly moved towards visual expression, and I became a photographer."

6. Again in the *Paris Review* interview, pp. 193–94, Kosinski comments about the importance of learning English: "English helped me sever myself from my childhood, from my adolescence. In English I don't make involuntary associations with my childhood. I think it is childhood that is often traumatic, not this or that war."

7. In the interview, "Authors and Editors—Jerzy Kosinski," *Publishers Weekly* 199 (April 26, 1971): 15, Kosinski talks about the liberating influence of an adopted language: "Once you begin to write in another language, you discover how much freer you are, because the new language

disconnects you and requires from you—because you do not know all the clichés yet—some of your own."

8. In a certain sense this passage contradicts Kosinski's assessment of photography in the Klinkowitz interview, in *The New Fiction*, p. 148: "As a photographer I knew that the basic purpose of the photographic process was to reproduce reality and that photography would actually accomplish it. If there was a tree in the field and I photographed and developed it in my darkroom, I actually could do this so it would match exactly the imaginary photograph in my mind. Well, I found this profoundly distressing. If my imagination was able to conceive of the images which could be so easily reproduced in the Soviet darkroom—in any darkroom—then clearly there was not much to my imagination. I found it very humiliating that in a photograph I actually could produce what I thought. . . . With writing I can only approximate the vision I have." Here it is fiction, rather than photography, which is the unstable medium.

9. The page references prefaced with *C* in the parentheses refer to *Cockpit* (Boston: Houghton Mifflin Co., 1975).

10. Here the dangers of creating a tight, well-defined fiction become apparent. In Kosinski, fiction-making at its best is an open-field gesture.

11. Kosinski has acknowledged a major influence in Jacques Monod's *Le Hasard et la Nécessité* (Paris: Le Seuil, 1970).

12. Brain cancer may serve in this novel as a metaphor for the death of the mind. Clearly this novel stresses the vitality of the heart.

Selected Bibliography

1. Primary Sources

Barthelme, Donald. *Amateurs*. New York: Farrar, Straus and Giroux, 1976.

———. *City Life*. New York: Farrar, Straus and Giroux, 1970.

———. *Come Back, Dr. Caligari*. Boston: Little, Brown & Co., 1964.

———. *The Dead Father*. New York: Farrar, Straus and Giroux, 1975.

———. *Great Days*. New York: Farrar, Straus and Giroux, 1979.

———. *Guilty Pleasures*. New York: Farrar, Straus and Giroux, 1974.

———. *Sadness*. New York: Farrar, Straus and Giroux, 1972.

———. *Snow White*. New York: Atheneum, 1967.

———. *Unspeakable Practices, Unnatural Acts*. New York: Farrar, Straus and Giroux, 1968.

Kosinski, Jerzy. *The Art of the Self*. New York: Scientia-Factum, 1968.

———. *Being There*. New York: Harcourt Brace Jovanovich, 1970.

———. *Blind Date*. Boston: Houghton Mifflin Co., 1977.

———. *Cockpit*. Boston: Houghton Mifflin Co., 1975.

———. *The Devil Tree*. New York: Harcourt Brace Jovanovich, 1973.

———. *Notes of the Author*. New York: Scientia-Factum, 1967.

———. *The Painted Bird*. Boston: Houghton Mifflin Co., 1976.

———. *Passion Play*. New York: St. Martin's, 1979.

———. *Steps*. New York: Random House, 1968.

Nabokov, Vladimir. *Ada*. New York: McGraw-Hill, 1969.

———. *Bend Sinister*. New York: McGraw-Hill, 1947.

———. *Lolita*. New York: G. P. Putnam's Sons, 1955.

———. *Look at the Harlequins!* New York: McGraw-Hill, 1974.

———. *Pale Fire*. New York: G. P. Putnam's Sons, 1962.

———. *Pnin*. Garden City: Doubleday & Co., 1957.

———. *The Real Life of Sebastian Knight*. Norfolk, Conn.: New Directions, 1959.

———. *Speak, Memory*. New York: G. P. Putnam's Sons, 1966.

———. *Transparent Things*. New York: McGraw-Hill, 1972.

2. Secondary Sources

Alter, Robert. *Partial Magic: The Novel as a Self-Conscious Genre.* Berkeley: University of California Press, 1975.

Anderson, Donald. "The End of Humanism." *Quadrant* 113 (1976): 73–77.

Appel, Alfred. "*Lolita:* The Springboard of Parody." In *Nabokov: The Man and His Work,* edited by L. S. Dembo, pp. 204–41. Madison: University of Wisconsin Press, 1967.

Bader, Julia. *Crystal Land: Artifice in Nabokov's English Novels.* Berkeley: University of California Press, 1972.

Barthes, Roland. *Image—Music—Text.* Translated by Stephen Heath. New York: Hill and Wang, 1977.

———. *S/Z.* Translated by Richard Miller. New York: Hill and Wang, 1974.

———. *Writing Degree Zero.* Translated by Annette Lavers and Colin Smith. New York: Hill and Wang, 1968.

Battcock, Gregory, ed. *Idea Art.* New York: E. P. Dutton, 1973.

———. *Minimal Art.* New York: E. P. Dutton, 1968.

———. *Super Realism.* New York: E. P. Dutton, 1975.

Bellamy, Joe David, ed. *The New Fiction.* Urbana: University of Illinois Press, 1974.

Bersani, Leo. *Balzac to Beckett: Center and Circumference in French Fiction.* New York: Oxford University Press, 1970.

Boretz, Benjamin, and Edward T. Cone, eds. *Perspectives on American Composers.* New York: W. W. Norton & Co., 1971.

———. *Perspectives on Contemporary Music Theory.* New York: W. W. Norton & Co., 1972.

Brown, Norman O. *Life against Death.* Middletown, Conn.: Wesleyan University Press, 1959.

———. *Love's Body.* New York: Random House, 1966.

Bruss, Elizabeth W. *Autobiographical Acts: The Changing Situation of a Literary Genre.* Baltimore: Johns Hopkins University Press, 1976.

Burnham, Jack. *Beyond Modern Sculpture.* New York: George Braziller, 1968.

———. *The Structure of Art.* New York: George Braziller, 1973.

Cage, John. *Silence.* Cambridge, Mass.: M.I.T. Press, 1961.

———. *A Year from Monday.* Middletown, Conn.: Wesleyan University Press, 1967.

Cahill, Daniel. "*The Devil Tree:* An Interview with Jerzy Kosinski." *The North American Review* 9 (Spring 1973): 56–66.

————. "Jerzy Kosinski: The Retreat from Violence." *Twentieth Century Literature* 18 (1972): 121–32.

Carroll, William. "Nabokov's Signs and Symbols." In *A Book of Things about Nabokov*, edited by Carl Proffer, pp. 203–17. Ann Arbor: Ardis, 1974.

Coale, Samuel. "The Quest for the Elusive Self." *Critique* 14, no. 3 (1973): 25–37.

Cope, David. *New Directions in Music*. Dubuque: William Brown, 1971.

Ditsky, John. "The Narrative Style of Donald Barthelme." *Style* 9 (1975): 388–400.

Federman, Raymond. *Surfiction*. Chicago: Swallow Press, 1975.

Field, Andrew. *Nabokov: His Life in Art*. Boston: Little, Brown & Co., 1967.

Flaubert, Gustave. *Correspondance*, Septième Série, vol. 15 of *Oeuvres Complètes*. Paris: Louis Conard, 1930.

Flower, Timothy. "The Scientific Art of Nabokov's *Pale Fire*." *Criticism* 17 (1975): 223–33.

Flowers, Betty. "*Snow White*: The Reader-Patient Relationship." *Critique* 16, no. 3 (1975): 33–43.

Ford, Ford Madox. *Joseph Conrad: A Personal Remembrance*. Boston: Little, Brown & Co., 1924.

Glaser, Bruce. "Questions to Stella and Judd." In *Minimal Art*, edited by Gregory Battcock. New York: E. P. Dutton, 1968.

Goldmann, Lucien. *Pour une sociologie du roman*. Paris: Gallimard, 1964.

Gottlieb, Carla. *Beyond Modern Art*. New York: E. P. Dutton, 1976.

Grabes, H. *Fictitious Biographies: Vladimir Nabokov's English Novels*. The Hague: Mouton, 1977.

Grams, Paul. "*Pnin*: The Biographer as Meddler." In *A Book of Things about Nabokov*, edited by Carl Proffer, pp. 193–203. Ann Arbor: Ardis, 1974.

Hansen, Peter. *An Introduction to Twentieth Century Music*. Boston: Allyn & Bacon, 1967.

Harold, Brent. "*Lolita*: Nabokov's Critique of Aloofness." *Papers on Language and Literature* 11 (1975): 71–82.

Hassan, Ihab. *The Dismemberment of Orpheus: Toward a Postmodern Literature*. New York: Oxford University Press, 1971.

————. *The Literature of Silence*. New York: Alfred A. Knopf, 1967.

————. *Paracriticisms: Seven Speculations of the Times*. Urbana: University of Illinois Press, 1975.

————. *Radical Innocence: The Contemporary American Novel*. Princeton: Princeton University Press, 1966.

Hassan, Ihab, ed. *Liberations*. Middletown, Conn.: Wesleyan University Press, 1971.

Hunter, Sam. *Modern French Painting*. New York: Dell, 1956.

Jameson, Fredric. *The Prison-House of Language*. Princeton: Princeton University Press, 1972.

Johnson, R. E., Jr. " 'Bees Barking in the Night': The End and Beginning of Donald Barthelme's Narrative." *Boundary 2* 5 (1976): 71–92.

Johnston, Ben. "How to Cook an Albatross." *Source* 4, no. 1 (1970): 63–65.

Josipovici, G. D. *"Lolita:* Parody and the Pursuit of Beauty." *Critical Quarterly* 6 (1964): 35–48.

Karlinsky, Simon, ed. *The Nabokov-Wilson Letters*. New York: Harper & Row, 1979.

Kenner, Hugh. "Art in a Closed Field." In *Learners and Discerners*, edited by Robert Scholes. Charlottesville: University of Virginia Press, 1964.

Klinkowitz, Jerome. *The Life of Fiction*. Urbana: University of Illinois Press, 1977.

Kosinski, Jerzy. "Interview." *Paris Review* 54 (1972): 183–207.

———. "Interview." *Publishers Weekly* 199 (April 26, 1971): 13–16.

Lee, L. L. *Vladimir Nabokov*. Boston: Twayne, 1977.

Leepa, Allen. "Minimal Art and Primary Meanings." In *Minimal Art*, edited by Gregory Battcock, pp. 200–208. New York: E. P. Dutton, 1968.

Leland, John. "Remarks Re-marked: Barthelme, What Curios of Signs!" *Boundary 2* 5 (1977): 795–811.

Leonard, Jeffrey. "In Place of Lost Time: *Ada*." In *Nabokov*, edited by Alfred Appel and Charles Newman, pp. 136–46. Evanston: Northwestern University Press, 1970.

Lévi-Strauss, Claude. "From Cyclical Structure in Myth to Serial Romance in Modern Fiction." Translated by Petra Morrison. In *Sociology of Literature and Drama*, edited by Elizabeth and Tom Burns. Baltimore: Penguin, 1973.

Lippard, Lucy R. *Pop Art*. New York: Frederick A. Praeger, 1966.

McCaffery, Larry. "Barthelme's *Snow White:* The Aesthetics of Trash." *Critique* 16, no. 3 (1975): 19–32.

McCarthy, Mary. "Vladimir Nabokov's *Pale Fire*." *Encounter* 19 (October 1962): 71–84.

Meyer, Ursula. *Conceptual Art*. New York: E. P. Dutton, 1972.

Mitchell, Charles. "Mythic Seriousness in *Lolita*." *Texas Studies in Language and Literature* 5 (1963): 329–43.

Monod, Jacques. *Le Hasard et la Nécessité*. Paris: Le Seuil, 1970.

Moody, Fred. "At *Pnin's* Center." *Russian Literature Triquarterly* 14 (1976): 71–83.

Morris, Robert. "Notes on Sculpture." In *Minimal Art*, edited by Gregory Battcock, pp. 222–35. New York: E. P. Dutton, 1968.

Morton, Donald. *Vladimir Nabokov*. New York: Frederick J. Ungar, 1974.

Nicol, Charles. "Pnin's History." *Novel* 4 (1971): 197–208.

Nin, Anais. *The Novel of the Future*. New York: Macmillan, 1968.

Olderman, Raymond M. *Beyond the Waste Land: The American Novel in the Nineteen-Sixties*. New Haven: Yale University Press, 1972.

Pattesan, Richard. "Nabokov's *Look at the Harlequins!*: Endless Re-Creation of the Self." *Russian Literature Triquarterly* 14 (1976): 84–98.

Poggioli, Renata. *The Theory of the Avant-Garde*. Translated by Gerald Fitzgerald. Cambridge, Mass.: Harvard University Press, 1968.

Prioleau, Elizabeth. "Humbert Humbert *Through the Looking Glass*." *Twentieth Century Literature* 21 (1975): 428–37.

Proffer, Carl, ed. *A Book of Things about Nabokov*. Ann Arbor: Ardis, 1974.

Raban, Jonathan. "Transparent Likenesses." *Encounter* 41 (September 1973): 74–76.

Richardson, Anthony, and Nikos Stangos, eds. *Concepts of Modern Art*. New York: Harper & Row, 1974.

Robbe-Grillet, Alain. *For a New Novel*. Translated by Richard Howard. New York: Grove Press, 1965.

Rosenberg, Harold. *The Anxious Object: Art Today and Its Audience*. New York: Horizon, 1964.

————. *Art on the Edge*. New York: Macmillan, 1975.

————. *Artworks and Packages*. New York: Horizon, 1969.

————. *The De-definition of Art: Action Art to Pop to Earthworks*. New York: Horizon, 1972.

Rosenblum, Michael. "Finding What the Sailor Has Hidden: Narrative as Patternmaking in *Transparent Things*." *Contemporary Literature* 19 (1978): 219–32.

Rossi, Nick. *Music of Our Time*. Boston: Crescendo, 1969.

Roth, Phyllis A. "In Search of Aesthetic Bliss: A Rereading of *Lolita*." *College Literature* 2 (1975): 28–49.

————. "The Psychology of the Double: *Pale Fire*." *Essays in Literature* 2 (1975): 209–29.

Rother, James. "Parafiction: The Adjacent Universe of Barth, Barthelme, Pynchon, and Nabokov." *Boundary 2* 5 (1976): 21–43.

Rowe, William W. *Nabokov's Deceptive World*. New York: New York University Press, 1971.

Salzman, Eric. *Twentieth-Century Music: An Introduction*. Englewood Cliffs, N.J.: Prentice-Hall, 1967.

Sanders, Ivan. "The Gifts of Strangeness." *Polish Review* 19, no. 3 (1976): 171–89.

Schmitz, Neil. "Donald Barthelme and the Emergence of Modern Satire." *Minnesota Review* 1 (1972): 109–18.

Schwartz, Barry. *The New Humanism: Art in a Time of Change.* New York: Frederick A. Praeger, 1974.

Schwartz, Elliott, and Barney Childs, eds. *Contemporary Composers on Contemporary Music.* New York: Holt, Rinehart and Winston, 1967.

Sontag, Susan. *Against Interpretation.* New York: Farrar, Straus and Giroux, 1966.

––––––. *Styles of Radical Will.* New York: Farrar, Straus and Giroux, 1969.

Spencer, Sharon. *Space, Time and Structure in the Modern Novel.* New York: New York University Press, 1971.

Spendel, R. J. "The Structure of *The Painted Bird.*" *Journal of Narrative Technique* 6 (1976): 132–36.

Stark, John O. *The Literature of Exhaustion: Borges, Nabokov, and Barth.* Durham: Duke University Press, 1974.

Stegner, Page. *Escape into Aesthetics.* New York: Dial Press, 1966.

Steiner, George. *Language and Silence.* New York: Atheneum, 1967.

Stott, William. "Donald Barthelme and the Death of Fiction." *Prospects* 1 (1976): 369–86.

Stuart, Dabney. *Nabokov: The Dimensions of Parody.* Baton Rouge: Louisiana State University Press, 1978.

Sukenick, Ronald. "Twelve Digressions toward a Study of Composition." *New Literary History* 6 (1975): 429–37.

Vinton, John, ed. *Dictionary of Contemporary Music.* New York: E. P. Dutton, 1974.

Weales, Gerald. "Jerzy Kosinski." *Hollins Critic* 9, no. 3 (1972): 1–12.

Wilde, Alan. "Barthelme Unfair to Kierkegaard: Some Thoughts on Modern and Postmodern Irony." *Boundary 2* 5 (1976): 45–70.

Williams, Carol T. " 'Web of Sense': *Pale Fire* in Nabokov's Canon." *Critique* 6, no. 3 (1963): 29–45.

Winston, Matthew. "*Lolita* and the Dangers of Fiction." *Twentieth Century Literature* 21 (1975): 421–27.

Wolfe, Tom. *The Painted Word.* New York: Farrar, Straus and Giroux, 1975.

Zeller, Nancy Anne. "The Spiral of Time in *Ada,*" in *A Book of Things about Nabokov,* edited by Carl Proffer, pp. 280–90. Ann Arbor: Ardis, 1974.

Index